A BRILLIANT CHAPTER IN THE ANNALS OF MILITARY HISTORY

While air power, given the political ramifications and limited nature of the Korean conflict, could not "win" the Korean War, it could—and did—prevent the forces of Communist aggression from winning. As a major component of the Allied air power in Korean skies, naval aviation played a huge (if largely unrecognized) role in ensuring that South Korea remained non-Communist.

This book, then, is an attempt to tell the story of the naval air war in Korea. It is a tale of a war fought by dedicated men from several nations, many of whom died or suffered in their nation's service. Their deeds and sacrifices are a proud history and a warning to all nations bent on aggression against their neighbors.

—From the author's preface

THE NAVAL AIR WAR IN KOREA

Richard P. Hallion

D1562349

THE NAVAL AIR WAR IN KOREA

BY RICHARD P. HALLION

ZEBRA BOOKS
KENSINGTON PUBLISHING CORP.

ZEBRA BOOKS

are published by

Kensington Publishing Corp.
475 Park Avenue South
New York, NY 10016

First printing: January, 1988

Printed in the United States of America

CONTENTS

PREFACE

More than thirty years have passed since the signing of a truce agreement at Panmunjom ended the United States' first experience with modern limited war. Since that time, an uneasy peace has prevailed, punctuated by violations that cost the lives of North and South Koreans, and Americans as well. These violations underscore an important point: despite the relief and optimistic predictions made at the time, the truce at Panmunjom has at best imposed an uneasy peace upon Korea. Today, and for the forseeable future, the potential for renewed conflict unfortunately looms as large as ever on this strategic peninsula, despite sporadic attempts to open a useful dialogue between the hard-liners of both the North and South. It is likely that Koreans, Chinese, Soviets, Americans, Japanese, and other closely interested nations will have to live with the possibility until the generations directly concerned with the war of 1950-1953 recede, and cooler heads prevail in North Korea.

Despite the continued volatility of the Korean situation, awareness of Korea and the Korean War has slipped from the American consciousness to a remarkable and even alarming degree. Perhaps this reflects a subtle psychological recognition that the war really settled little except for curbing the expansionist tendencies of Kim Il Sung, Mao Tse-tung, and Josef Stalin at that time. This is regrettable. The Korean War was thrust upon the United States and its Allies, who responded promptly to the attack on South Korea, and displayed loyalty towards the underdog, fierce determination, and courage. At the same time, the United States restored its vital strategic position in the Far East.

Nowhere were such virtues better exemplified than in the conduct of the naval air war. Overshadowed in the public mind by the more glamorous (and certainly important) struggle of Sabres versus MiGs over the sinuous Yalu, naval aviation came out of the Korean War with little public recognition save for James Michener's evocative novel, *The Bridges at Toko-ri*. Though useful for creating an awareness that there *had* been a naval air war in Korea, it did not attempt to convey the full range and impact of naval air combat over the North and the South. Several specialized books and studies published during the 1950s and 1960s—notably those of Walter Karig, Malcolm Cagle, and Frank Manson—enabled military professionals to study the broad outlines of the naval air war, but problems with security classification (many records remained classified well into the 1970s, and some few—primarily on intelligence matters—remain so still) and the proximity of the events (with consequent lack of perspective) limited both the audience and the authors. As a new war in Southeast Asia intensified, the focus of historical study shifted from Korea's icy hills and dusty valleys south to the morass of Indochina and examination of conflicts there and in Malaya, Algeria, and Kenya. The pressing problems of the 1960s and 1970s consigned the Korean War to the ever-darkening archives of history.

It is time to bring the Korean War once again into the forefront of our awareness. For even today it has much to teach us, some of which is neither pleasant nor easy to learn. The Korean conflict was a watershed in the evolution of carrier air doctrine and the employment of naval air power. Whereas the aircraft carrier—typified by the large fleet carriers of the American and Royal navies—had ended the Second World War as a destroyer of fleets, decisively and firmly supplanting the battleship as the true Titan of the seas, it served in Korea in quite a different role: that of a mobile airfield projecting military force ashore from stations close to hostile shores. During the climatic sea battles of the Pacific war, carriers had sortied forth on what were decisive but relatively short-lived strikes and operations. In Korea, by contrast, American and British Commonwealth carriers served on station for weeks and months, save for periods of replenishment, rest, and recreation at several Asian ports. In contrast to their presence in the Second World War, Korea's carrier operations had much less visible impact upon the war, though sortie and ordnance consumption quickly soared well beyond that of the earlier conflict. Unlike many

9

naval analysts who deprecated the Korean experience as "untypical" at the time, more perceptive students of naval warfare recognized that Korea marked the beginning of a new chapter in the carrier's role: that of a force-projector in limited war where land-based air power either could not be brought to bear at all, or where the combined strength of sea- and land-based air power was needed to fulfill military objectives, and in an environment involving prolonged operations off a hostile coast. The subsequent experience gained during the naval air war in Vietnam served to confirm the operational and doctrinal shift first encountered in Korea.

The United States Navy and Marine Corps came out of Korea stronger, more cohesive, and with a better appreciation of the strengths and challenges they faced as a result of their experiences. Both had entered the war as forces in transition, caught between the era of the piston-powered airplane and the jet, and the war had highlighted some of the problems both would have to come to grips with in the ensuing years. Carrier operations off Korea lent increasing emphasis to both airborne early warning (AEW) and to antisubmarine warfare (ASW), as evidenced by the development of newer and more capable AEW and ASW aircraft such as the Grumman WF-1 Tracer and S2F-1 Tracker. The inferiority of the first generation of naval jet fighters to the MiG-15 and the threat posed by such Soviet-built jet bombers as the Il-28 caused rapid development of advanced missile-armed fighter and air defense interceptors typified by the Vought F8U-1 Crusader and McDonnell F4H-1 Phantom II, which entered service in the mid-to-late 1950s. This legacy continued into the 1960s and onwards into the 1970s and 1980s with the Grumman E-2 Hawkeye for AEW, the Lockheed S-3 Viking for ASW, and the present-day Grumman F-14 Tomcat fighter, the latter a superlative response to the disastrous F-111B program of the 1960s. The often frustrating record of day and night all-weather attack and interdiction in Korea likewise influenced and accelerated the development of new and more capable jet-propelled attack aircraft, typified by the Douglas A4D-1 Skyhawk and the Grumman A-6 Intruder; this concern continues, as is evident today with the procurement of the McDonnell-Douglas F/A-18 Hornet, advanced models of the A-6 family, and a projected Advanced Tactical Aircraft (ATA) to replace the A-6 in the attack role starting in the late 1990s.

To a great and fortunate extent, the Korean experience ended the fruitless bickering over the roles and missions that had fractured the defense community in the late 1940s, a struggle symbolized by the B-36 controversy, the cancellation of CVB-58 (the projected super-carrier U.S.S. *United States*), and the resulting and highly publicized "Revolt of the Admirals." The woeful state of preparedness of the defense establishment for the conflict in Korea demonstrated the bankruptcy of Louis Johnson's tenure as Secretary of Defense. He gutted both Navy and Marine aviation forces on the pretext that they were increasingly irrelevant to the projected combat needs of the United States. But within the months of the war's outbreak, naval air power had proven of critical importance in preserving the Pusan pocket, launching Douglas MacArthur's masterful counter-thrust at Inch'on, and preventing the withdrawal of the Marines from the reservoirs from turning into a rout in the face of overwhelming Chinese Communist strength. (That strength itself was subsequently decimated by naval and Air Force air strikes, setting the stage for the war of stalemate that lasted from 1951 to the truce in 1953.) While air power, given the political ramifications and limited nature of the Korean conflict, could not "win" the Korean War, it could — and did — prevent the forces of Communist aggression from winning. As a major component of the Allied air power in Korean skies, naval aviation played a huge (if largely unrecognized) role in ensuring that South Korea remained non-Communist.

This book, then, is an attempt to tell the story of the naval air war in Korea. It is the tale of a war fought by dedicated men from several nations, many of whom died or suffered in their nation's service. Their deeds and sacrifices are a proud history and a warning to all nations bent on aggression against their neighbors.

ACKNOWLEDGMENTS

A number of people gave generously of their time and insight; this work benefited considerably from their counsel. I alone am responsible for the views presented in this book, and the judgments expressed herein should not be construed as representing official positions of the United States government; rather, they are strictly my own, based on my interpretation of the documentation I have examined and the interviews I have conducted. As a child growing up near Anacostia Naval Air Station, I well remember the throaty roar of Tigercats and Skyraiders, and the healthy whistle of Panthers and Banshees. Korea had already passed into history, though as time went by, it seemed a fascinating topic for research. The following are individuals to whom I wish to acknowledge my very grateful appreciation:

Roy A. Grossnick, Office of Naval Aviation History; Capt. Richard C. Knott, USN, *Naval Aviation News;* Dr. Dean C. Allard, Bernard

Cavalcante, and Wes Pryce, Naval Historical Center; Dr. William Armstrong, Judith Walters, and Hal Andrews, Naval Air Systems Command; Maj. Frank Batha, USMC, and Evie Englander, Marine Corps Historical Center; Dr. Dick Kohn, Dr. Pat Harahan, Dr. Benjamin Franklin Cooling, Col. Fred Shiner, Maj. John F. Kreis, Capt. M. Susan Cober, MSgt. Roger A. Jernigan, Jack Neufeld, Bernard Nalty, and Bill Heimdahl, Office of Air Force History; Walt Kraus, Air Force Systems Command History Office; Maj. Gen. Peter W. Odgers, Col. John Madia, Lt. Col. Bill "Flaps" Flanagan, Dr. Jim Young, Ken Baas, Don Haley, and Bill Casale, Air Force Flight Test Center; Fitz Fulton and Ralph Jackson, NASA Ames-Dryden Flight Research Facility; Lt. Michael S. Kearns, USAF, Headquarters, Air Force Intelligence Service; Col. Dick Uppstrom, USAF, Jack Hilliard, and Tom Brewer, Air Force Museum; Professor Tom Hone, U.S. Naval War College; Lt. Greg Johnson, USN, Naval Weapons Center, China Lake; Cmdr. Tom Jurkowsky, USN, Naval Air Force, U.S. Pacific Fleet; Paul Stillwell and Patty Maddocks, United States Naval Institute; Alice S. Creighton, Nimitz Library, U.S. Naval Academy; Pat Richter and Deborah Edge, U.S. National Archives; Vice Admiral Malcolm W. Cagle, USN (ret.), The Association of Naval Aviation; Bob Lawson, the Tailhook Association; Tom Britton, The American Aviation Historical Society; Don Stone, American Institute

14

of Aeronautics and Astronautics; Paul E. Garber (Honorary Naval Aviator #16), Tim Wooldridge, Bob Mikesh, Dom Pisano, and Von Hardesty, National Air and Space Museum, Smithsonian Institution; Mike Long and Helen Wadsworth, National Geographic Society; Barrett Tillman, Champlin Fighter Museum; Phil Oestricher, General Dynamics Corporation; Chuck Sewell and Lois Lovisolo, Grumman Aerospace Corporation; Harry Gann and G. C. "Buddy" Gilman, McDonnell-Douglas Corporation; Hank Chouteau, Northrop Corporation; Col. Joe Guthrie, USAF (ret.), Flight Systems, Inc.; John Fozard and Graham Weller, British Aerospace; Bill Bettis and Ed Rugg, *Nieuport 17;* Richard and Jeanne Blalock, and Jack Grant, *Mr. B's Twin Lakes Inn;*

and:

Vice Admiral Charles S. Minter, USN (ret.); Maj. Gen. Philip Conley, USAF (ret.); Brig Gen. Jay Hubbard, USMC (ret.); Capt. Gerald G. O'Rourke, USN (ret.); Col. Tighe Carvey, USAF; Col. Walter Flint, USAF (ret.); Col. Jim McFeeters, USAF (ret.); Col. John Taylor, USAF (ret.); Dave Anderton; Ed Forslund; Corwin "Corky" Meyer; Tom Miller; Art Neff; Al Taddeo; Tom Doll; Capt. Harry Ettinger, USN (ret.); Col. Jesse Jacobs, USAF (ret.); Maj. Gen. Pat Halloran, USAF (ret.); Capt. Steven Reinertson, USN (ret.).

Three very special salutes: To James Flynn, a naval architect and my late uncle, who helped lay out the *Essex* class as well as many of the other vessels that fought both in the Pacific and off Korea; a remarkable man with a keen appreciation of naval history, his last work updated the battleship U.S.S. *New Jersey* for service in the 1980s and beyond. To the late Cmdr. Terry A. "Ted" Damon, USN (ret.), director of the U.S. Navy Memorial Museum, good friend, fine curator, and attack pilot *par excellence*. Finally, to Dr. Eugene M. Emme, a naval aviator, professor at the Air University, founder of the NASA history program, and a pioneer in aviation historiography, who devoted his lifetime to studying the impact of aviation upon military affairs, technology, and society.

In closing, a special note of appreciation to Capt. Phillip Wood, USN, and the officers and men of the U.S.S. *Kitty Hawk* (CV-63), for the privilege of being able to witness naval aviation at its best: proud, professional, and pressing on.

1/NAVAL AVIATION AFTER THE GREAT PACIFIC WAR

On August 29, 1945, the battleship *Missouri*, accompanied by *Iowa* and *South Dakota*, entered Tokyo Bay and dropped anchor not far from where Commodore Perry had anchored on a very different mission in 1853. Already Americans were ashore, rescuing prisoners and preparing for the transfer of power from a defeated Emperor to an occupation government headed by General Douglas MacArthur, America's own five-star Mikado. Long, lean, and menacing in weathered grey and with its nine 16-inch rifles trained fore and aft, the *Missouri* was a fitting stage for the final drama of America's great Pacific war: the grandeur of Allied victory, the humiliation of Japan's defeat. On Sunday, September 2, a destroyer brought the surrender delegation out from Yokosuka; they boarded the *Missouri*. The atmosphere was cold, formal.

By 9:04 a.m., the preliminaries were over, the surrender document ready for signing. Mamoru Shigemitsu, Japan's Foreign Minister, signed first, fol-

17

lowed by the rest of the delegation and then the representatives of the Allied powers. At 9:25, Mac-Arthur concluded the ceremony with a prayer "that peace be now restored to the world and that God will preserve it always." As the Japanese delegation was led away, MacArthur put his arm around the shoulders of Admiral William F. Halsey. "Bill," he asked, "where the hell are those airplanes?" Just then, the morning sun broke through a cloud-studded sky, and a loud roar signaled a stately formation of B-29s. Offshore, the fleet fighter director called in a formation of 450 carrier airplanes, which "roared over the *Missouri* in tight formations and at low altitude in a show of Navy air power that was breathtaking and made the spine tingle." Onward they flew: the stately silver Superfortresses that had inflicted defeat on a scale unparalleled in Asian history, and the little blue airplanes that had destroyed Japan's fleet. Symbolically, as observers watched, the huge formation made a long graceful curve, and disappeared into the mists of Fujiyama, Japan's sacred mountain, as if the Allies were seizing possession of Nippon's mythic past as well as its devastated present.[1]

It took air power enthusiasts in the Army a long time to convince their leadership of the military airplane's promise, and naval aviation advocates, too, struggled long and hard to impress their own hierarchy with the revolutionary potential of air power at sea. In fact, diehards remained unconvinced until Britain's Fleet Air Arm savaged the Italian navy at Taranto and the Japanese navy furnished a tragic example of what carrier aviation could accomplish at Pearl Harbor. The victory fly-over at Tokyo Bay vindicated those who fought for American naval aviation. Present were many of the carrier admirals who had destroyed the Japanese fleet in a series of tenacious engagements from Coral Sea and Midway to the Philippine Sea, and the final marauding air strikes against the Home Islands. Though the surrender had been taken on the decks of a battleship, a representative of the Navy's *ancien regime,* the Pacific war was won in the skies over blue ocean and lush islands. In fact, air power had dictated the strategy of the Pacific war almost from the outset, the strategy of seizing territory to bring Japan ever closer to the striking power of Allied aviation. In this task, the carrier played a crucial role. Once battleships and battle cruisers had sallied forth to defeat enemy fleets; fast carriers now did battle with other carrier fleets. Once a column of battleships in Scapa Flow or the Jade by Wilhelmshaven typified sea power; now the flat-topped carriers, aptly dubbed "Murderers' Row," struck over ranges and with a precision undreamed of by advocates of the traditional big gun.

As clouds blanketed the *Missouri*, and the fly-over apparently disappeared into some uncertain future, a mantle of uncertainty cloaked naval aviation. What was its role in light of the development of the long-range strategic bomber armed with atomic weapons? Did the carrier have a viable role as a force-projector in an atomic age, or was the fly-over at once its triumph and swan song? It would be pleasant to record that such questions were answered without the tinge of partisanship; they were not.

Naval aviation after VJ Day was haunted by the spectre of obsolescence. The U.S. Army Air Forces had to adjust its strategy from the conventionally armed propeller-driven airplane to the possibility of an atomic-armed and jet-propelled force; so did the Navy. But in the Navy, the jet revolution was only just underway, and the poor takeoff and landing characteristics of early jet aircraft generated concern about whether jets could operate from a carrier. The challenge of flying from the limited space and pitching deck of a ship has always shaped naval aviation, and at no time did this challenge seem more formidable than at the dawn of the jet age. The jets, with their high landing approach speeds, added a new element of danger to what was already the riskiest form of military aviation. Clearly they could not be expected to operate safely or efficiently from the smaller classes of escort carriers, generally averaging 10,000-tons displacement; they would obviously pose problems for the 27,000-ton *Essex* class; and it was uncertain how effective they might be even with the gargantuan 45,000-ton *Midway* class just entering service.

There were other problems as well. America's mood after VJ Day demanded virtually instantaneous and total demobilization; retaining the coherence and organization of naval aviation was not easy under such circumstances. In mid-1945, the Navy had a total of 98 carriers on active status; one year later, there were just 23. Over the same time the total number of combat aircraft in naval service dipped from 29,125 in 1945 to 14,637 in 1946. (At the outbreak of the Korean War in mid-1950, the total number of carriers in service had fallen even further, to 15; likewise, 9,422 combat aircraft were on hand.) Personnel figures (unfortunately incomplete for 1946–1947) show a similar precipitous decline. In 1945, the Navy and Marine Corps had 60,095 officer and enlisted pilots; the figure fell to 12,578 in mid-1950.[2] Navy planners had to fight hard to justify development of new fighter and attack aircraft, new land and sea-based patrol planes, carrier-based bombers capable of carrying atomic weapons, and larger aircraft carriers, such as the projected CVB-58, the U.S.S. *United States*.

Traditionally, the Navy had relied for much of its research and development upon strong ties between its Bureau of Aeronautics (the forerunner of today's Naval Air Systems Command), the National Advisory Committee for Aeronautics (NACA, the predecessor of today's National Aeronautics and Space Administration), and private industry. There were several "Navy" firms; Grumman and Douglas for fighter and attack aircraft, and Martin for patrol planes, for example. Their designers, such as Douglas's legendary Ed Heinemann and Grumman's Bill Schwendler, understood the Navy's needs, and because of their equally strong grasp of the state of aviation technology, they drew up useful (and in some cases outstanding) aircraft to meet those needs. The Douglas SBD Dauntless, for example, was the Second World War's premier antishipping aircraft, and Grumman's stubby F6F Hellcat had produced more aces—300 in all—than any other American fighter serving in the war. Despite the technology, the critical factor remained the superbly trained naval aviator himself; as historian Clark Reynolds has written, "The average American naval aviator below the rank of admiral had so much training and experience that after Rabaul the Japanese could not have hoped to match him."[3] Designers such as Heinemann and Schwendler kept such men in mind as they practiced their craft. Leroy Grumman, himself a naval aviator in the First World War, often reminded his design teams that, "We design our planes so a tired 21-year-old pilot coming back from a tough mission can land safely aboard ship. We don't want the fastest, or the most maneuverable aircraft if it compromises the chance of that kid getting back on his carrier. Don't forget that."[4] Grumman's reputation for solid, workmanlike aircraft led Vice Admiral John McCain to remark during the war "the name Grumman on a plane or a part is like sterling on silver." The firm was affectionately known to generations of naval aviators as the "Grumman Iron Works."[5]

As VJ Day passed into history, the Navy's Bureau of Aeronautics was mapping out the technical requirements for the future of naval aviation. "BuAer" already had awarded Douglas a contract for development of a specialized high-speed aerodynamic research aircraft, the Douglas D-558, which would eventually spawn the near-sonic straight-wing jet-propelled D-558-1 Skystreak and the rocket-propelled Mach 2 swept-wing D-558-2 Skyrocket, a program equivalent to, and in some respects more challenging than, the concurrent Bell XS-1 effort. A number of guided missile projects were underway for air-to-surface and surface-to-air missile systems.

Confronting the new jet, rocket, and atomic technology, planners set their sights on expanding and modifying the capabilities of naval aviation. In June 1946, the Navy awarded a development contract to North American Aviation for the three-engine (two piston and one jet) AJ-1 Savage, the first carrier-based attack bomber intended to carry atomic weapons.

On July 21, Patuxent River test pilot Lieutenant Commander James Davidson made a series of take-offs and landings in the prototype McDonnell FD-1 Phantom, a twin-jet straight-wing design, from the deck of the *Franklin D. Roosevelt* off the Virginia coast; the success of the trials inspired an impromptu and exuberant victory roll following his last takeoff before heading back to "the River." Relieved at entering the jet age, the Navy pressed ahead with development of a small batch of production Phantoms primarily as jet familiarization aircraft, as well as three major jet fighter projects, the McDonnell F2D (later F2H) Banshee (a more powerful derivative of the Phantom), Grumman's F9F Panther, and Douglas's F3D Skyknight. A number of less satisfactory projects were dropped after limited production or abandoned completely, including the Ryan FR-1 Fireball and XF2R-1 Dark Shark (both mixed-propeller and pure-jet designs), the Chance Vought XF6U-1 Pirate, an undistinguished clunker noteworthy only for its experimental afterburner installation, and the North American FJ-1 Fury, a tubby straight-wing jet whose only claim to fame was helping inspire the design of North American's elegant sweptwing F-86 Sabre, perhaps the classic jet fighter of all time.[6]

As the years went on, there were numerous signs that the Navy was doing its best to adjust to the demands of global sea power projection in the jet and atomic age. In September 1946, the *Truculent Turtle,* a new twin-engine Lockheed P2V Neptune land-based patrol plane, set a world's record for the longest unrefueled flight, covering 11,235.6 miles from Perth, Australia, to Columbus, Ohio. At Christmas that year, Navy and Marine attack squadrons (which had replaced the outmoded scouting, torpedo, and bombing squadrons of the Second World War) received the first of the new Douglas AD Skyraiders, a beefy but trim propeller-driven aircraft having the performance of a Second World War fighter and an offensive payload that made it a worthy successor to the SBD. In February 1947, the *Cusk* launched a Republic Loon (a copy of the infamous Nazi V-1 "buzz-bomb") while surfaced off Point Mugu, California, the first test firing of a cruise missile from an American submarine. In August 1947, Navy and Marine test pilots set two new world's airspeed records in the D-558-1 Skystreak at Muroc Dry Lake, California, reaching level flight speeds averaging 650.796 mph during low altitude runs over the lake's baked clay. Early the following month, the carrier *Midway* launched a captured V-2, the first firing of a large surface-to-surface rocket from a ship at sea. In December 1947, the Marines commissioned their first helicopter squadron at Quantico, and the Navy followed suit the following April. In May 1948, VF-17A, the Navy's first jet fighter squadron, carrier-qualified aboard the

24

Saipan in their Phantoms.[7]

Though all this indicated the new directions in which naval aviation was headed, the large number of aging leftovers were far more typical of postwar naval aviation. Not all were obsolete, but most were obsolescent, and certainly over the next half decade, as the jet took firm hold in the United States and, more ominously, in the Soviet Union, they became anachronistic examples of outdated and surpassed technology. The bulk of Navy fighter squadrons operated large numbers of Chance Vought's versatile though piggish F4U Corsair, a tough and heavy fighter-bomber and night-fighter having distinctive inverted gull wings. Other squadrons flew Grumman's lightweight F8F Bearcat, a much-loved hot rod and a pleasure to fly. The Bearcat typified the last and logical extension of Grumman's heritage of stubby radial-engine fighters, stretching from the first FF biplane through the F2F and F3F, the monoplane F4F, the immortal F6F Hellcat, and on to the F8F. But in mock combat trials against the new jet-propelled Lockheed P-80 Shooting Star held at the Naval Air Test Center, the P-80 flew circles around the rasping Bearcat, which was unable to take the initiative from the jet, or to place itself in a position to attack the speedier aircraft: an ominous sign that the propeller-driven naval fighter was at the end of its long reign.

A few Marine squadrons operated the Grumman F7F Tigercat, a graceful twin-engine night-fighter and fighter-bomber that coupled 400 mph speed with heavy armament and good agility. As with the F8F, the F7F arrived just too late to see action in the

Pacific, where it undoubtedly would have served with distinction. And like the F8F and F4U, it had been outmoded by the newer jets, as evidenced by the Marine's great interest in the twin-jet Douglas F3D Skyknight for night air defense. Navy and Marine Reserve squadrons still operated the wartime F6F Hellcats, Grumman/General Motors TBF/TBM Avenger torpedo bombers, and Curtiss SB2C Helldivers. Patrol squadrons flew a mix of twin-engine Martin PBM Mariner seaplanes and Consolidated-Vultee PB4Y-2 Privateers, the latter a more powerful and heavily armed single-fin version of the Army Air Forces' wartime four-engine B-24 Liberator. Barely capable of fending off attacks by conventional propeller-driven fighters, these two were increasingly vulnerable to attack from the newer jets, typified by the Soviet Union's sweptwing MiG-15.

Naval aviation from 1945 until the early 1950s, therefore, was a force in transition, caught between eras. The challenge facing naval planners was not merely incorporating new technology, managing increasingly tighter budgets, and coping with reduced manpower. Rather, naval aviation confronted a serious threat to its very existence as the decade of the 1940s neared a close. As a result of bitter wrangling, the entire future of naval aviation lay in doubt through much of the late 1940s and, indeed, almost up to the Korean War itself.

These battles had long been brewing; in many ways, they echoed the interservice jockeying for position that had taken place in the 1920s. As is customary in "turf wars," compromise often appeared less attractive than zealotry, even if that zealotry courted martyrdom. At stake were a number of critically important issues, including uninfication of the military services under a Secretary of Defense, creation of a separate Air Force spawned from the wartime U.S. Army Air Forces, and questions concerning the roles and missions of Air Force, Navy, and Marine aviation. There was little consensus among service representatives on these matters, and little consensus even within the *same* service. So bitter were the feelings that reprimands were issued and people removed from office, or motivated by conviction or circumstances to resign. Argued amid sensationalistic journalism, uniformed and wildly speculative articles and books by alleged experts, and Congressional hearings, this senior defense debate took on a national drama unsurpassed until the subsequent McCarthy hearings of nearly a decade later.

There was, for example, the question of future aircraft carrier development in light of the atomic bomb. To some, the case was already closed. Admiral J. M. "Jocko" Clark, fresh from combat command in the Western Pacific, met with Admiral Marc Mitscher immediately after the Hiroshima and Nagasaki bombings to advocate a naval role in atomic weapons development. He was informed that the service already had studies underway for a "supercarrier" capable of carrying aircraft lugging the ponderous 10,000-pound atomic bomb. These eventually produced the proposed U.S.S. *United States,* subject of so much acrimony in the postwar years, as well as the Project 27A improvement program, which upgraded nine *Essex*-class carriers with strengthened decks, more powerful catapults, and nuclear weapon storage magazines.[8] In fact, however, there was considerable doubt (especially after the postwar Navy-organized Bikini Atoll atomic bomb tests devastated a fleet of target ships, including several aircraft carriers) whether the carrier had a viable role to play. Vannevar Bush, America's chief scientist during the Second World War, expressed the misgivings of many when he wrote that the advent of high-flying bombers with precision-guided bombs threatened the future of all large fighting ships. Of carriers, he said, "Their cost is large, and their impregnability questionable." But he stopped short of dismissing them as obsolete. Rather, he cautioned, "This is not a matter to be judged hurriedly; one must remember that it takes years to build a large carrier, and that the decision not to build is the irreversible decision if war comes suddenly after an interval."[9]

Not all the carrier's critics were as thoughtful or temperate. Alexander de Seversky was a Russian-born emigré engineer and aircraft designer whose gadfly advocacy of strategic air power, strident criticism of national defense policy, and vitriolic denunciation of all whom he perceived as his critics were often as offensive to his supporters as they were to his detractors. He had already predicted the "twilight of sea power" in his controversial wartime book *Victory Through Air Power*.[10] In his post-war writings, he went even further, alleging that "Sea power in the strategic sense is finished. It will remain in vestigial form as an auxiliary antisubmarine and transport force. But even these uses are temporary."[11] Of carriers, he wrote, "The great floating islands on which the American Navy has set its heart and its hopes are a military monstrosity."[12] His writings complemented such popular naval critics as William Bradford Huie (whose own works turned decidedly anti-military in the 1960s and 1970s), but Seversky did have more substantial credentials, and his views echoed those of the more outspoken air power advocates within the newly created Air Force.

In this war of words, the Navy could call on a number of popular writers, such as Hanson Baldwin and Marshall Andrews, the military editors, respectively, of the *New York Times* and the *Washington Post*. Andrews, in his *Disaster Through Air Power* (the title of which pointedly echoed Seversky's earlier work), criticized overoptimistic assumptions concerning the effectiveness of strategic bombing (even with atomic weapons), and cautioned against blithely dismissing the aircraft carrier. Both Baldwin and Andrews had impressive reputations as military critics, and senior-level military decision makers often consulted them; their writings carried great weight. For example, S. L. A. Marshall, one of America's foremost military historians, wrote the foreword to Andrews's book.[13]

Sniping over the question of unification and postwar roles and missions of the respective services ultimately led to a "Revolt of the Admirals" in late 1949, characterized by an open assault upon the wisdom of Truman-era defense policy. This jumbled story defies easy analysis, and like an earthquake began with the sudden shock and upheaval of the national defense structure, and continued in after-shocks as the various strata within the services sought to position themselves optimally within the new bedrock of the defense establishment.

The initial tremors began almost before the cheering of VJ Day had died away. In December 1945, President Harry S Truman had announced his desire for a unified military establishment to replace the War and Navy Departments. There was no great enthusiasm within either branch. The long-standing desire of Army Air Forces' leaders to separate themselves entirely compounded the problem. Many admirals, for example, rejected the idea of a separate Air Force. Rather, they believed, the air faction within the Army should come to dominate the rest of that service as naval aviation had the Navy. This unrealistic view—for the Army Air Forces had certainly earned the right to a separate existence, as evidenced by its wartime accomplishments—stemmed from the fact that a third service would disrupt the traditional Army-Navy balance on key issues. That, in the minds of most naval leaders, raised the spectre of 2-1 split votes between the Army, an Air Force sympathetic to Army interests, and the Navy. The Marine Corps was most fearful. Marines saw unification as disastrous; they believed their "organic" aviation would be stripped off by the Air Force, with the rest of the service rudely joined to the Army. Those fears had some ground in fact, and gained greater credence when Army Air Forces' Brigadier General Frank A. Armstrong called the Corps "a small bitched-up Army" and threatened to "put those Marines in the Regular Army and make efficient soldiers out of them."[14]

President Truman's pro-Army bias was no secret (he had once accused predecessor Franklin Roosevelt of running "a damned wardroom") and the Marines feared that in its desire to salvage naval aviation, the Navy might abandon the Corps as a trade-off.[15] Such fears proved groundless; the Navy remained steadfast to the Corps. Their loyalty was not lost on the Corps' own leadership who would soon have an opportunity to repay the favor. Through astute politicking and impassioned testimony, the Corps made itself such a thorn in the side of unification proponents that they realized that if the Marines did not get their way, the goal of unification might be sacrificed. Accordingly, when Congress passed the National Security Act of 1947, creating the Department of Defense, the President Truman signed it into law on July 26, 1947, the Marine Corps was safe. The focus now shifted from the Corps to relations between the Navy, the Army, and the newly created United States Air Force.[16]

The passage of the National Security Act of 1947 did not end the postwar debate over the roles and missions of naval and Air Force air power; rather, it served to clear the board of extraneous issues and bring into sharp relief the positions of both services. As most Navy officials feared, the Army served as a tie-breaker on disputes between the Air Force and Navy in the struggles that followed. When James V. Forrestal resigned as Secretary of Defense in a squabble with President Truman, the situation became critical. Forrestal, despite his background as an early naval aviator (number 154) and having

31

served previously as Secretary of the Navy, followed a generally even-handed policy on unification and interservice matters. (Critics always alleged he did more for the other services than he did for their own, a good sign that he was doing his job.) That could not be said of his successor, Louis A. Johnson, a former Army lieutenant colonel and political fund raiser who had supported Truman's bid for the Presidency in the dramatic election of 1948, and who made no secret of his animosity towards virtually all things naval. Unfortunately, Johnson, even in the eyes of Truman administration insiders, such as Secretary of State Dean Acheson and James Webb (the future NASA administrator), simply lacked the ability and vision to run the Department of Defense at a time when America was assuming global responsibilities in the postwar world.[17]

The term *air power* meant many different things to its advocates in each service. Emboldened by the dramatic success of the atomic bomb and the postwar Bikini tests, some enthusiasts argued that the atomic revolution had not merely rendered naval aviation superfluous, but that the blast of atomic weaponry would decide all future wars, rendering tactical aviation obsolete. The Navy's function would shift to transport and antisubmarine patrol, with armies serving as mere occupation forces. Navy partisans often and irrationally leapt to the opposite conclusion: the atomic bomb revolutionized warfare, and the Navy was ideal to employ it in a dominant strategic role. Accordingly, much of the postwar roles and missions debate, coming on the heels of the unification struggle, centered on control of *stra-*

tegic aviation. Tactical air power advocates within both the Navy and Air Force had difficulty being heard. (But appreciation would come soon enough, after June 25, 1950.) The debate, typically for issues that become the fodder of politics, soon degenerated into a Navy-Air Force slugfest simplistically symbolized by two items of technology: the Convair B-36, a giant six-engine propeller-driven bomber of prewar origin passionately supported by Secretary of Defense Johnson and Secretary of the Air Force Stuart Symington, and the planned CVB-58, the 65,000-ton carrier *United States,* designed to carry an as yet unbuilt, long-range strategic atomic bomber with the study designation ADR-42.

Two of the key players at the opening of this debate were the Secretary of the Navy and the Chief of Naval Operations (CNO), the Honorable John L. Sullivan and Admiral Louis E. Denfield. A former Assistant Secretary of the Navy for Air, Sullivan had witnessed the power of naval aviation in the Western Pacific in the summer of 1945. Though impressed, he was no blind adherent to the carrier concept, and had to be convinced that the planned supercarrier was indeed a worthwhile defense objective. Once persuaded, however, he became a staunch supporter. Denfield, who had spent his career in battleships, submarines, and destroyers, was a quiet conciliator who relied for advice on naval aviation upon the Deputy CNO for Air, Vice Admiral Arthur W. Radford, one of the prewar "thinkers" of naval aviation who had served brilliantly as a combat commander. Denfield, a marked contrast to the passionate Radford, likewise totally supported the construction of the *United States,* whose keel was laid at Norfolk, Virginia, on February 18, 1949. Events reached a crisis point soon thereafter.[18]

Sullivan and Forrestal had both endorsed plans to built atomic-armed bombers for operation from modified *Essex*-class and newer *Midway*-class carriers, as well as from the projected *United States*. Forrestal had done his best to moderate disagreements between Sullivan and other service chiefs over this and other issues, but following his resignation in March 1949, all calming influence was gone. Burdened with an invalid wife, increasingly fatigued and depressed, Forrestal fell to his death from the 16th floor of the Bethesda Naval Hospital on May 22, 1949; it was only after his death that representatives of all camps came to recognize the accomplishment and dedication of this remarkable figure. The war between the services and their chiefs broke out in full force with Forrestal's departure, though Sullivan, a loyal Truman follower, did his best to work with Johnson; personally committed to unification, Sullivan argued forcefully that the Navy retain an important role in national defense as part of a unified interservice team. The debate enunciated in the press and before Congress questioned whether the Navy was usurping a strategic air mission rightfully and exclusively belonging to the Air Force, and whether the B-36 was capable of fulfilling the strategic air mission entrusted to it.

There were elements of truth in both these challenges. The Navy certainly could not expect to fulfill the strategic air mission undertaken so well by the Army Air Forces in the Second World War, despite the pronouncements of naval enthusiasts such as Rear Admiral Daniel V. Gallery, the Assistant CNO for Guided Missiles, who had rashly stated in December 1947 that the Navy should start a campaign "aimed at proving that the Navy can deliver an Atom Bomb more effectively than the Air Forces can." Predictably, in a climate where anonymous sources leaked memos almost weekly, this internal document got to the press; Sullivan disavowed it and reprimanded its author. Nevertheless, it made little sense to deny naval access to atomic weapons, as some advocated. Already the Navy's AJ-1 Savage and P2V-3C Neptune could carry bombs such as the Los Alamos National Laboratory's 20-kiloton Mk-IV (a descendant of the "Fat Man" that had pulverized Nagasaki) then under development. Captain John T. Hayward, commanding officer of Composite Squadron 5 (VC-5), the first carrier-based atomic attack squadron, dramatically affirmed the Navy's ability to strike at long range on March 7, 1949. Hayward was a distinguished combat pilot and expert in atomic weapons technology who had worked at the Los Alamos laboratory. He and his crew lifted a 74,000-pound P2V-3C from the decks of the *Coral Sea* off the Virginia Capes, flying 2,000 miles cross-country and dropping a 10,000-pound dummy bomb load, as big as the atomic bombs of the era, before returning another 2,000 miles to land at the Naval Air Test Center, Patuxent River, Maryland. Unfortunately, what the Navy did not emphasize in its arguments for the *United States,* was its need for larger carriers capable of accommodating the newer generations of jet-propelled naval aircraft entering service or on the drawing boards, which could not be expected to operate efficiently or safely even from the wartime *Essex* class. Neither did the service stress the potential value of a supercarrier in limited or tactical air warfare situations.[19]

For their part, the proponents of the B-36 failed to take into consideration the rapidly changing state of aviation technology. The turbojet revolution had begun in the late 1930s, and the supersonic breakthrough was in the midst of the 1940s. The future belonged to the pure-jet bomber, such as the swept-wing Boeing B-47 then being tested or the projected Boeing B-52, not to a propeller-driven aeronautical behemoth like the B-36. Korea would reveal all too quickly how vulnerable the propeller-driven bomber was to attacking interceptors, even when it operated with a protective escort of jet fighters; yet in their eagerness to secure development of the B-36, some of its supporters overemphasized its supposed invulnerability to jet interception. (In fact, at one point during the subsequent B-36 hearings, a well-meaning but misguided officer asked famed Air Force test pilot Charles E. "Chuck" Yeager to distort test results revealing the ease with which it could be intercepted; he bluntly refused.) Then, there was the matter of cost. The first atomic bomber, the B-29, cost $640,000 per copy; the AJ-1 raised this to $1,105,599 apiece; the B-36 jumped this to $5,757,584 for each of the large aircraft. While certainly cheap compared to later bombers, the B-36 was nevertheless expensive in the budget-conscious era of 1945-1950. It dominated procurement funding, to the acute discomfort of tactical air power

36

advocates such as Major General Elwood R. Quesada who perceived, correctly, that the needs of tactical aviation were not being met. And on top of it all, murmurs questioned the B-36's design rationale. Today, it seems hard to escape the conclusion that the B-36 was not the airplane needed for the strategic requirements of the early 1950s. (Neither, of course, were the AJ-1 or P2V-3C, but they were intended—and well suited—for the limited employment of atomic weapons in the kind of naval war-fighting strategy that emerged after the Second World War.)

In contrast, the B-47 and B-52 were genuinely brilliant designs, and even Northrop's radical YB-49A Flying Wing, a smaller jet-propelled rival of the B-36, appears to have warranted cautious development rather than tempestuous cancellation. But if the desirability of the B-47, B-52, and Flying Wing (in terms of performance, efficiency, and potential for growth and modification) over the B-36 smacks too much of 20/20 hindsight, one need only keep in mind how briefly the B-36 served. It went fully operational in 1951 (coincident with the B-47), only a year before the prototype B-52 made its initial flight, and remained a force in readiness for only seven years. Quite simply, as historian Roger Bilstein has stated, it "represented the apotheosis of the prewar preoccupation with long-range strategic bombing." It belonged to another age, that of the "iron bomb" droppers, pre-atomic, propeller-driven, non-air refueled, ponderous, and intended to operate from an isolated "Fortress America." In May 1948 a committee directed by Ferdinand Eberstadt (former chairman of the Army and Navy Munitions Board) working for the Hoover Commission said as much; it criticized the B-36 as incapable of penetrating Soviet air defenses. (The same committee endorsed construction of carriers capable of launching atomic-armed aircraft.)[20]

In the interest of unification, Secretary of Defense Johnson had axed a number of interservice committees, and refused comment on whether he would endorse construction of the *United States,* which had earlier received grudging approval from the Joint Chiefs during Forrestal's tenure. Sullivan, sensing the worst, testified before Congress and at public and military gatherings on the importance of sea power to future American security. But the Secretary of Defense, despite Hayward's impressive demonstration the previous month, already had his mind made up. On April 23, 1949, he cancelled construction of the supercarrier, consulting neither Sullivan nor Denfield, and perpetrating, in the words of military historian Walter Millis, "a reckless destruction of the extremely delicate balances which his predecessor had been at such pains to establish."[21] Sullivan, already contemplating resignation, had reached the breaking point. He flew back to Washington, met with Denfield, and then resigned. Committed to unification, placing the good of the national defense above the good of the Navy alone or above any personal preference, he was unjustly vilified nevertheless by Johnson as a unification opponent. Denfield's own time of crisis would come, but for the moment the CNO did his best to work with Johnson and the incoming Secretary of the

Navy, Francis P. Matthews; Denfield, typically, said nothing, despite personal outrage over the decision.

The incoming Matthews, in contrast to Sullivan, had no experience of and little appreciation for the Navy, let alone naval aviation; morale dropped lower than it had in the previous quarter century, despite an announcement by Representative Carl Vinson, a Democrat from Georgia and chairman of the powerful House Armed Services Committee, that he would chair hearings into the cancellation of the *United States,* the procurement of the B-36, the roles and missions of military air power, and other questions. Vinson, a shrewd and even-handed politician, had agreed with the cancellation; he argued that "we cannot afford the luxury of two strategic air forces. We cannot afford an experimental vessel that, even without its aircraft, costs as much as sixty B-36[s]."[22] Goaded by Republican Representative James Van Zandt of Pennsylvania into holding the hearings, Vinson worked to ensure an impartial airing of views. Meanwhile, despite conciliatory statements by Johnson to the contrary, rumors of cuts in naval aviation funding abounded, including a planned reduction cutting Marine Corps aviation forces by half and slashing the Navy to just four carriers and six carrier air groups.[23] To serving naval aviators, it seemed to be the end of the road. Not surprisingly, many wondered why Denfield remained silent. The CNO still hoped his unruffled approach would work and delayed speaking out. Further, contingency planning for the newly created North Atlantic Treaty Organization (NATO) alliance so preoccupied him that he delegated preparation of key naval testimony to Radford and then-Captain Arleigh Burke, a non-aviator but a tenacious and canny officer who possessed a distinguished combat record as a destroyerman and who worked effectively with naval aviators. Word leaked out that Denfield would be appointed to a second term as CNO when his first term expired in December 1949. Many naval officers now assumed the worst: that Denfield had sacrificed principle for position. Nothing could have been further from the truth; that such a rumor found fertile ground is indicative in itself of the increasingly suspicious and emotional climate that surrounded defense issues in 1949.

A sequence of events sparked the dramatic climax of the postwar defense debate. A civilian Navy Department employee leaked a document he had hastily prepared that criticized the B-36 and the awarding of its development contract. It was a sensationalist and foolish act that added fuel to the fires raging in the Pentagon and the Congress. A well-known carrier commander, Captain John W. Crommelin, leapt to the civilian's defense, called a news conference, and launched a polemic against unification that included the inflammatory challenge, "The Navy cannot support an organization whose methods and principles violate the Navy concept of a Navy man's oath.[24] Crommelin had strong supporters, including the charismatic Admiral Willian F. Halsey, and, to prevent further outcry, Denfield persuaded Admiral J. J. "Jocko" Clark (a friend of Crommelin's) to intecede. Clark extracted a promise from Crommelin that he would decline further public statements. Meanwhile, in an effort to promote

40

understanding, the Navy arranged for Louis Johnson, Stuart Symington, and General Omar Bradley to take an orientation cruise on the carrier *Franklin D. Roosevelt*. "Our simulated heavy air attack on the flagship *Midway*," Clark recollected, "demonstrated the effectiveness of naval aviation much better than Crommelin's utterances had."[25] Perhaps, but the controversy raged on, and despite Captain Hayward's flying the three men back to Washington aboard a P2V-3C (a parting plug for naval aviation), no evidence suggests that Johnson or any of the others underwent a conversion.

In response to a personal request from Secretary of the Navy Matthews, Vice Admiral Gerald F. Bogan, commander of the Pacific Fleet's First Task Fleet, submitted a confidential letter that had Radford's and Denfield's endorsement. It assented to Crommelin's views and took issue with the secretary's criticism of Crommelin's opposition to unification. It was the kind of memo that passes among decision makers all the time; a frank appraisal of an issue, written with the understanding that it is simply between two people, or, at most, for a very limited audience. Unfortunately, Crommelin secured a copy and promptly leaked it to the press. "Momentarily," Clark subsequently wrote, "Crommelin became something of a hero in Navy circles until the full import of what he had done came to light."[26] The unfortunate Bogan now received the full wrath of Johnson's and Matthew's displeasure, and eventually left for an early retirement. Denfield, furious with Crommelin, suspended him from duty and tried to patch up relations with Matthews and Johnson. Matthews, for his part, concluded that enough was enough, and decided to replace Denfield with someone whom he hoped would work harder to enforce the Johnson line, in spite of having previously assured the CNO that he would be reappointed.

As fall approached, however, attention shifted from the Crommelin affair to the Vinson committee hearings. Johnson and Matthews did their best to mute potential outbursts before the Vinson committee. Already, the first set of hearings had cleared Johnson (a former director of the Convair company) and the defense department of any wrongdoing in connection with B-36 procurement. But the second set of hearings, which concentrated on the larger questions of roles and missions, promised some real fireworks. Matthews reportedly offered Admiral Richard L. Conolly the post of CNO succeeding Denfield if Conolly would tone down his testimony before the committee; Conolly gave the offer the refusal it deserved.[27]

Hearings resumed on October 6, 1949, releasing the frustrations of all the parties; it was not a time for compromise or cooperation. In his opening statement, Matthews attempted to minimize the controversy, but his criticism of the Navy's outspoken aviation community left observers with few doubts as to the depth of controversy afflicting that service.[28] The next day, Vice Admiral Arthur Radford took the stand. Radford, as partisan in his own way as his critics, was an impressive witness, and his testimony reflected a recent study on the future of carrier aviation undertaken by OP-55 (the Air Warfare Division) following cancellation of the *United States*. Speaking in the measured, slow, and modulated tones that were a "Raddy" hallmark, he announced his commitment to military air power: the combined might of both sea-based and land-based aviation. He agreed that the Air Force should have primary responsibility for strategic air power; he was concerned that the chosen instrument, the B-36, might not be equal to the task. Radford criticized the B-36's performance and intended mission, and said that the *United States* should have been developed in the interest of a balanced approach to national defense. He was, furthermore, one of the few witnesses who addressed tactical air power needs, again reflecting OP-55's study that had stressed the application of naval air power — including the possible use of atomic weapons — in tactical naval warfare. The B-36, he concluded, was draining resources that could be applied better to new and more capable tactical aircraft for the Air Force. It was a forceful and at times disconcerting talk; especially so since his comments emphasized the strange character of the hearings: men of one military service taking the stand and under oath testifying about what they believed best for other services. Air Force witnesses offered their views on the proper functions of navies; Navy witnesses professed concern over whether the Air Force could fulfill its mission; Army witnesses presumed to interpret the future role of the Marine Corps. Under questioning from Vinson, Radford, in contrast to Matthews, emphasized the congruency of his views with those of most naval officers. On this matter

43

there could be little doubt; during the previous day's testimony, many naval officers in the audience literally had jeered the Secretary of the Navy for his lame attempts at minimizing the Navy's increasingly poor morale. Radford was but the first of many naval witnesses, including a virtual galaxy of Pacific carrier commanders, who echoed his views and inspired the term *Revolt of the Admirals* to describe the resulting effect their testimony had upon public opinion. Denfield faced a choice between his personal loyalty to the Secretary of the Navy, and to what he thought was best for national defense. He opted for the latter, and in testimony before the committee on October 8, boldly announced that he "fully supported" the naval testimony that had preceded him. Matthews, embarrassed, stormed from the committee room. While the secretary planned for Denfield's successor, the hearings went on with unabated fury. Marine commandant General Clifton Cates echoed Denfield, repaying an old unification debt. Joint Chiefs chairman General Omar Bradley castigated the admirals as "fancy dans" unwilling to compromise, and, in a swipe at the Corps, predicted that the era of large-scale amphibious operations was over. (Within a year, MacArthur and the Marines invaded Inch'on.) Like other critics, Bradley professed failure to understand why the Navy refused to limit itself to antisubmarine and transport roles. Finally, on October 21, the committee adjourned.[29]

On November 1, 1949, Denfield left the Pentagon for the last time as Chief of Naval Operations, the most senior victim of Johnson's vendetta against the

Navy. The press and Vinson himself were quick to condemn the dismissal, which the committee judged a "reprisal" for "his frank and honest testimony."[30] Ironically, nothing became of Denfield's tenure as CNO more than his leaving of it; Denfield's stock within naval community shot upwards, many perceiving him as a martyr to the cause of the Navy, and, especially, naval aviation. In truth, of course, Denfield had vacillated far too long, preferring the role of conciliator to advocate; he was no Radford, but he was honest and principled, and did his duty as he saw fit. He paid the price for his convictions.

Naturally, many naval officers now transferred the skepticism they had held for Denfield to the incoming CNO, Admiral Forrest P. Sherman. They regarded anyone replacing Denfield as essentially hired to get along with Matthews and Johnson dubiously. Sherman had been one of the architects of unification. In fact, Sherman, a naval aviator with a well-deserved reputation as a loner with a glacial demeanor, was, like Denfield, a conciliator. But unlike his predecessor, Sherman had qualities of toughness and a sense of detachment from issues that made him more effective. An outstanding, if sometimes ruthless, worker, Sherman recognized the fear that he would dismantle the naval aviation community, and was determined to brook no interference with his plans to assert the Navy's vital and continuing interest in developing its aviation forces. He had championed, for example, development of the AJ-1. Cautious by nature, he had not sought the position of CNO, but now that it had fallen to him, he saw his immediate function as the promotion of

45

harmony. He recognized that since he was appointed by Johnson and Matthews, he was largely invulnerable to criticism from them. In the emotion-laden atmosphere of late 1949, they could not very well relieve him after having done so to Denfield. Accordingly, Sherman set to work tempering hotheads such as Crommelin (whom he retired) and saved officers that Johnson and Matthews now sought to cashier, such as Captain Arleigh Burke. The public outcry and the loss of much congressional support by the Johnson-Matthews faction as a result of the "Revolt of the Admirals" did not result in either Johnson or Matthews muting their criticism. In December 1949, for example, Johnson told Conolly that "the Navy is on its way out," adding that "amphibious operations are a thing of the past," and "the Air Force can do anything the Navy can nowadays."[31] Yet through it all Sherman worked steadily and decisively to strengthen the Navy's congressional ties, improve fleet morale, and restore aviation funding.

Over the winter and early spring of 1949-1950, Sherman supervised the salvaging of the postwar Navy. He reduced mothballing of ships, and, playing upon his generally good relations with Matthews, Johnson, and the Joint Chiefs, reversed the Secretary of Defense's planned cut of carriers, air groups, and Marine squadrons. In early 1950, emboldened by his success, Sherman ventured to the Congress, winning a $350 million increase in the Navy's budget for fleet modernization to support NATO needs. He pressed for funding an atomic-powered submarine, which became the revolutionary *Nautilus*. In April

1950, he scored a staggering *coup de theatre:* he secured congressional approval for a new supercarrier, reversing the debacle of the previous year. (It eventually emerged as CVA-59, the U.S.S. *Forrestal).* In six months, Sherman had accomplished more than his predecessors had since 1945, and he had done so with a tact and charm that few realized he possessed.[32]

So in the spring of 1950, the Navy was on the mend following the acute discord of the preceding three years. Ironically, the days of both Louis Johnson and Francis Matthews were numbered. Both fell victim to policy disagreements with President Truman in the months ahead. Johnson would plummet from office in September when the Korean war answered any remaining questions about the bankruptcy of his defense policies. With Johnson embroiled in an acrimonious feud with Secretary of State Dean Acheson, Truman decided he could no longer afford to have him at the helm of national defense, and replaced him with General George Marshall, a conciliator who worked well with Sherman. To both their credits, Matthews and Sherman also worked together, and the rancor of 1949 gradually abated. Matthews left graciously, in June 1951, to take up ambassadorial duties. Sherman died in office just a month later, on July 22, a victim of overwork. In the course of his tenure he had mapped out the path of naval development that the service followed in the years ahead. Matthews's and Sherman's successors were able men: Secretary of the Navy Dan Kimball, a former Assistant Secretary of the Navy for Air, and Admiral William Fechteler.

With the departure of the last holdovers from the days of the Admirals' revolt, the vestiges of ill feeling gradually disappeared.

But the struggle had taken its toll. Shortages of spares, lack of resources to permit extensive training, an increasingly obsolescent reserve air fleet, all troubled naval aviation as the spring of 1950 waned and summer approached. But naval aviation was alive and well, thanks to Radford and Sherman and the outcry that surrounded the Denfield dismissal. The first Mk-IV armed AJ-1 attack bombers were only months from being operational with the fleet; Ed Heinemann had a jet-powered successor (the future A3D) under study at Douglas. While many fleet fighter squadrons still operated propeller-driven fighters, more and more of the jet-propelled Panthers and Banshees were coming aboard. But it was still a force in transition. The switch from props to jets, from older carriers to newer ones, was incomplete. This was the greatest tragedy of the bitter Johnson years and the debate over roles and missions: the modernization of tactical air power at sea, and tactical air power on land as well, had been sacrificed.

At the time, all this seemed of academic interest. True, there were crisis points around the world. Soviet Russia dominated Eastern Europe and had recently bulldozed over any hopes Czechoslovakia might have had for an independent existence. The Berlin situation had led to a Soviet blockade and an international airlift (including Navy transports) to keep the city open. A nationalist insurgency movement with strong Communist overtones was growing in French Indochina. Communist North Korea was taking an increasingly strident tone towards its southern brother. On mainland Asia, China had at last fallen to the forces of Communist revolutionaries. And, of course, the Soviet Union had detonated its own atomic bomb and demonstrated several types of new jet fighters, as well as a strategic bomber copied directly from America's B-29. But while American military professionals had reservations about the national capacity to fight if called upon to do so, to the public at large as well as to most political commentators, 1950 seemed unremarkable as years go. That conventional wisdom was shattered at 4 a.m. local time on June 25 when North Korean forces invaded South Korea from across the 38th Parallel.

2/THE OPENING ROUND: PRESERVING THE PUSAN POCKET

The invasion of South Korea shocked the West. As military historian Walter Millis wrote, "To the American people it was a truly and completely unprovoked attack. The reaction was not (as it had been to Pearl Harbor) one of massive unity in defense and retaliation; it was one, rather, of bewilderment. Nothing quite like this had ever happened to us before . . ."[1]

In shape, Korea resembled an appendix of the Asian mainland, 600 miles long and 150 miles wide. Like Poland, for example, Korea has had a profoundly troubled history, serving as a strategic gateway for various neighbors who sought to annex it to their own spheres of influence to buttress their borders. At various times, China, Japan, and Russia all coveted Korea, deceptively and evocatively named *Chosun:* Land of the Morning Calm. Forced into "protectorate" status by Japan following the Russo-Japanese War, Korea again found itself torn apart after 1945, when, as in Europe, the Allied settlement divided it into a Soviet-controlled northern zone, and an American-influenced southern one. The declining stability of postwar relations took its toll, and what had been a convenient division pending the outcome of elections determining the fate of the entire nation, became a hard-and-fast border as the 1940s drew to a close. In the south, Dr. Syngman Rhee, a "nineteenth century liberal with autocratic tendencies," presided in the capital of Seoul.[2] In the north, premier Kim Il Sung wielded vastly more dictatorial power from the capital of P'yongyang. Forty years old in 1950, Kim had taken the name of a dead national hero, favoring it over his blander Kim Sung Chu. A dedicated Communist, he allegedly fought at Stalingrad with the Red Army, studied at China's Whampoa Military Academy, and returned to Korea as a major in the Soviet occupation forces. Portly but tough, with ruthlessness evident in his humorless visage, Kim was not without a strong streak of vanity. In post-Korean War years, he took the title of "the all-triumphant, resolute and incomparable commander and outstanding military strategist."[3]

At the end of the Second World War, the Allies divided the Korean peninsula along the 38th Parallel, a meaningless map reference devoid of a natural geographical frontier. Korea is really sectioned lengthwise: rocky high cliffs along its eastern coast by the Sea of Japan, spiny mountain ranges traversing the length of the country, and, in the west, gradual plains that drop down to the Yellow Sea. The coastline is tortuous and twisted, with many small islets and islands. The division granted the

North one major advantage: North Korea is the industrial heartland of the nation, and, after the Second World War, possessed the industrial plants, hydroelectric power stations, and rail system that Japan had built during its occupation of the country. Further south, the Republic of Korea (ROK) was, by contrast, primarily agricultural. The Yalu and Tumen rivers separated North Korea from Manchuria. In the northeast corner of the country, Korea touched the Soviet Union, not far from the port of Vladivostok.[4]

By the end of 1948, both North and South claimed sovereignty over the entire country; the war of words gradually evolved into attempts at outright subversion. Surprisingly, in view of President Truman's subsequent decision to intervene, most American diplomats and not a few military officials were willing to write off South Korea, they believed the United States lacked any strategic interest in its fate, and that mounting a reasonable defense or undertaking active intervention would be virtually impossible as well as undesirable. Such a notion ran counter, however, to the general outline of postwar American foreign policy. Three years before the Korean War erupted, Soviet expert George Kennan, chief of planning for the Department of State, had published an anonymous article in the prestigious journal, *Foreign Affairs,* in which he enunciated the notion of "containment" of Communist expansionism; the article was thought-provoking, and the State Department soon elevated it to doctrinal status. Simply stated, Kennan's article recommended that the United States work to contain the expansionist impulses of the Communist nations as they arose.[5] Strangely, several months later, in September 1947, the Joint Chiefs of Staff prepared a memorandum for the Secretary of State that essentially dismissed Korea from any serious consideration in postwar American defense policy.[6] In due course, both Soviet and American occupation forces left the troubled peninsula, though both the North and South relied heavily upon Soviet and American military advisors for training and instruction. North Korean infiltrators skirmished frequently with ill-equipped southern defense forces, sometimes inflicting heavy casualties, and gaining both combat experience and a detailed knowledge of the capabilities and limitations of the ROK army.[7] In mid-January 1950, Secretary of State Dean Acheson provided what may have been the final necessary encouragement to the adventuristic impulses of the Soviet Union and North Korea; speaking before the National Press Club, he stated that America's defensive perimeter excluded Korea and Formosa (Taiwan), which would have to rely instead upon their own resources for defense, and possibly upon the United Nations.[8]

These muddled signals from Washington were not matched by equivalent indecision in the other camp. The Soviet Union developed a strong partnership with North Korea that, in some respects, amounted to *de facto* control over the North Korean government. Senior governmental positions typically went to Koreans who had come from Korean communities within the USSR itself and who were then transplanted into North Korea following its "liberation" from the Japanese. The Soviets themselves designated Kim Il Sung as premier, and arranged for his introduction "to the North Korean public by the most respected non-Communist leader in North Korea, who subsequently disappeared."[9] By the end of 1948, the North Korean armed forces numbered 60,000, excluding para-military forces. Departing Soviet troops left them weapons, including T-34 tanks (the finest armored fighting vehicle in general service during the Second World War), and some propeller-driven aircraft, mostly Ilyushin Il-2 and Il-10 *Shturmovik* ground attack airplanes and Yakovlev fighters. In 1949, North Korea's military forces doubled, and "several thousand" personnel returned from the USSR where they had undergone up to three years of training for armored and aviation units. By early 1950, the North Korean armed forces numbered nearly 180,000 troops, and the Soviet Union delivered large numbers of tanks, aircraft, heavy artillery, and automatic weapons. Colonel General Terenti Shtykov, the Soviet Ambassador to North Korea and a veteran of both the monumental siege of Leningrad and the short Soviet blitz of Japan, supervised the activities of military advisors and representatives of five Soviet state ministries, including the Ministry for State Security. Soviet civilian technical personnel served in a number of key industries, most notably the Wonsan oil refinery built by the Japanese.[10]

Major General Wang Yong commanded the North Korean air force (for convenience, abbreviated NKAF, though this is not a precise translation of its actual name). Slight and deceptively mild, but with a reputation as a stern leader, he had fought with Mao

Tse-tung's revolutionaries. He journeyed to the USSR and graduated from the Soviet Air Academy. He then served as a bomber pilot and instructor before he returned from Manchuria to Korea in October 1946 and took charge of the P'yongyang Political Institute's Aviation Section. Wang's propeller-driven air force, though not impressive by either Western or Soviet standards, was formidable indeed when compared with that of South Korea. On the eve of the war, it possessed approximately 62 Ilyushin Il-2 and Il-10 single-engine *Shturmovik* ground attack aircraft. The heavily armed *Shturmovik* had seen extensive action in the Second World War (the more advanced Il-10 entering service shortly before the end of the conflict), and was, arguably, the first assault and antitank aircraft of its time. Though outmoded by 1950, it was nevertheless a formidable adversary if aggressively and imaginatively flown. The same held true for North Korea's single-engine Yakovlev Yak-3, -7, and -9 fighters. Of the same family — lightweight airplanes of mixed wood and metal construction, powered by liquid-cooled engines — they were 360-415 mph aircraft with good agility and the ability to wreak havoc with limited opposition. They were technologically reminiscent of the Supermarine Spitfire and North American Mustang, though not as advanced as either of these Anglo-American machines. Wang's force possessed 70 of them, and received smaller numbers of the Lavochkin La-5, -7, -9, and -11 family of radial engine-powered fighters roughly comparable to the wartime Nazi Focke-Wulf Fw 190. Rounding out the NKAF were a mixed bag of light transports, several hand-me down Japanese trainers and fighters, and Polikarpov Po-2 biplanes, which would soon prove annoyingly effective as "night-hecklers."[11]

In contrast, South Korea's armed forces were pitifully weak. Just before hostilities, the ROK armed forces included an army of 82,000 troops, more accurately classified as a security force. This force had nothing more potent than hand-held weapons, heavy machine guns, and 81-mm mortars. It lacked heavy artillery and any meaningful air power. The ROK Air Force numbered only 16 aircraft, 13 of which were fabric-covered observation planes; the remaining three were North American T-6 Texan two-place trainers. So concerned had Syngman Rhee become over the state of Korea's air defenses, that he sought assistance of Claire L. Chennault, the prewar leader of the American Volunteer Group (the legendary "Flying Tigers"). Chennault drew up a plan for a 99-plane air force built around 25 F-51 Mustang fighters. This plan fell apart amid fears it would escalate and destabilize relations between North and South Korea.[12] Cognizant of the increasing tensions in the Far East that followed Acheson's widely reported National Press Club address and the increasingly hostility between the two Koreas (as well as between the two Chinas), Chief of Naval Operations Forrest Sherman ordered the Seventh Fleet, early in 1950, to make a series of "show the flag" port visits. On April 5, the *Essex*-class carrier *Boxer* (CV-21) dropped anchor in Inch'on harbor outside Seoul while its Corsairs, Panthers, and Skyraiders flew overhead and showed their stuff. "You are our friends," Syngman Rhee told the visiting seamen, adding not a little plaintively, "Come again, come often, and stay longer."[13]

The news that North Korea had invaded the South took Washington and the rest of the Western world by surprise. Fortunately, President Truman, his cabinet, and the United Nations' Security Council acted decisively. On June 25, the UN condemned the aggression and recommended a cease-fire, which North Korea ignored. On the advice of the Joint Chiefs (reversing their prewar stand), Truman ordered the Seventh Fleet to patrol the Taiwan Straits in case the Korean invasion was but part of a larger operation also threatening the capture of Formosa. On June 27, the Security Council followed up its earlier resolution by authorizing formation of a United Nations Command under the overall unified command of the United States. (Ironically, these Security Council resolutions passed because the Soviet representative was boycotting the council on another matter. Today such concerted action would probably be impossible. Korea will likely go down, then, as the first and last war where the UN's members could agree on a single course of action.) Already, on June 27, Fifth Air Force North American F-82 Twin Mustang night-fighters and Lockheed F-80 Shooting Star jet fighters had tangled with North Korean Yak and Ilyushin raiders, in one-sided dogfights that witnessed the destruction of seven NKAF planes without loss for the United States. Over the next few days, F-51 Mustang pilots and even B-29 bomber crews added to the score of NKAF aircraft shot down. Now, as the end of the month approached and still the ROK forces fell back in disarray before the North Korean invader, naval aviation had its opportunity to get into the fight.[14]

The war's outbreak found the ships of the U.S. Seventh Fleet, under the command of Vice Admiral Arthur D. Struble, divided among several Asiatic ports. Only one light cruiser, four destroyers, six minesweepers, and a small amphibious force cruised Japanese waters. Carrier Division 3 (CarDiv 3, under the command of Rear Admiral J. M. Hoskins)—the *Essex*-class carrier *Valley Forge* (CV-45), a heavy cruiser, and eight destroyers—left Subic Bay in the Philippines for Buckner Bay, Okinawa. In the early days of the war there was uncertainty about whether it might spread beyond Korea, and the Okinawa deployment seemed prudent until the direction of the war became apparent. There a contingent of Royal Navy vessels—carrier H.M.S. *Triumph*, heavy cruiser H.M.S. *Belfast*, and two destroyers—joined up. Vice Admiral Struble assumed overall command of this Anglo-American squadron, designated Task Force 77 Striking Force (subsequently renamed TF 77 Fast Carrier Force), consisting of a Support Group, TG 77.1, composed of the cruisers H.M.S. *Belfast* and U.S.S. *Rochester*, a Screening Group, TG 77.2, made up of the eight American and two British destroyers, and, finally, a Carrier Group, TG 77.4, the striking arm of the TF 77, consisting of the *Valley Forge* and the *Triumph*. Struble had already met with Vice Admiral C. Turner Joy, the commander of Naval Forces Far East (COMNAVFE), General Douglas MacArthur, overall supreme commander of UN forces, and Air Force

Lieutenant General George Stratemeyer, commander of the Far East Air Forces (FEAF). Together the four men decided that TF 77 could go to war by striking targets around the North Korean capital of P'yongyang, including its airfield, railroad yard, and bridges. On July 1, TF 77 weighted anchor and left Buckner Bay for the Yellow Sea. Because of prewar training exercises, British and American ships worked well together, despite *Triumph's* being 10 knots slower than *Valley Forge*.[15]

Many questions needed answers in this early round of the Korean naval war. Airfields ringed the Yellow Sea, and posed the threat of intense attacks upon the carriers. Likewise, the force had to take stringent precautions against submarine attack. Differences in the types of aircraft posed operational challenges. *Valley Forge's* Carrier Air Group 5 (CAG 5) consisted of two fighter squadrons (VF-51 and -52) flying Grumman's F9F Panther jet fighter, two squadrons (VF-53 and -54) operating Vought's older and slower propeller-driven F4U Corsair, and one squadron (VA-55) equipped with the new Douglas AD Skyraider attack aircraft. *Triumph* operated squadrons of Fairey Fireflies and Supermarine Seafires. The Firefly, a big two-seater, operated primarily as a antishipping and antisubmarine strike aircraft. The Seafire, a "navalized" derivative of the legendary Supermarine Spitfire, flew primarily on combat air patrol (CAP) and fleet air defense duties, with a secondary strike function. Like the Air Force's F-51 Mustang, both the Firefly and Seafire had a serious flaw: hits that damaged their liquid-cooled engine's cooling system could convert them into gliders in a hurry. Largely for this reason, the Navy had never operated a liquid-cooled fighter from the late 1920s onwards, preferring the reliability offered by the rugged, dependable radial air-cooled engine. Eventually, the eminently more suitable Hawker Sea Fury, a Corsair-like radial engine-powered fighter possessing greater elegance of line than its American predecessor, entered service with the Royal Navy's Fleet Air Arm and Commonwealth fighter squadrons operating off Korea.

Before sunrise on July 3, *Triumph* launched 9 Seafires and 12 Fireflies on a strike against the North Korean airfield at Haeju, approximiately 60 miles south of P'yongyang. While these droned to their target (subsequently attacking it without loss), CAG 5 readied its own strike force against the capital. As dawn broke, 12 ADs and 16 Corsairs, armed with rockets and bombs, clattered noisily into the air and set course for P'yongyang, 135 miles distant. Fighting 51 launched eight Panthers—the first combat sortie by naval jets—after the Corsairs and Skyraiders were well on their way. The faster F9F's, engines whistling, timed their arrival so they could hit the airfield just ahead of the strike force, destroying any potential air opposition to the incoming F4Us and ADs. As the Panthers arrived over the field, their pilots saw numerous Yak fighters scrambling into the air from its single 4,080-foot north-south runway, some, in their haste, actually taking off toward each other. ("Too hairy to watch," one Panther jockey recalled.) Scant feet above the field, Lieutenant (j.g.) Leonard Plog pulled in behind one, rapidly overtaking the propeller-driven plane, but before he could fire, he saw another Yak boring in from the left. "He had a perfect run on me," Plog later recalled, "but evidently had never shot at anything moving that fast before." Ensign E. W. Brown slipped in behind the Yak and blew away its tail assembly with the concerted fire of his four 20-mm cannon. Plog, now safe, concentrated on his own Yak, hosed it with cannon fire, and watched as it broke up and dribbled to the ground. Screaming low across the field, the Panthers strafed anything that looked worthwhile, costing the North Koreans a further three aircraft. Meantime, the ADs and Corsairs, having traversed a stormfront over the coast, broke into clear weather as they let down towards P'yongyang, arrived over the field, and amid several Yaks that stooged about indecisively, rolled into their dives, leaving four hangars and a nearby railroad yard wreathed in smoke, flame, and debris. The strike force and Panther escort returned and trapped aboard ship, and in the afternoon, another strike against P'yongyang's railroad net destroyed no less than 15 locomotives. The following day, British and American airmen returned to polish off a railroad bridge damaged the previous day; Skyraiders placed a pattern of 500-pound bombs that dropped one of its spans. With this important piece of business out of the way, the strike force scooted about at low level looking for targets of opportunity before returning to their carriers.[16]

Unfortunately, a landing accident marred the otherwise perfect two-day raids, indicating that more problems were to come as older straight-deck carriers coped with newer post-Second World War aircraft technology. One AD received a 37-mm cannon shell through its belly that damaged the craft's hydraulics and necessitated a "hot" no-flap landing back aboard the "Happy Valley." The ailing Skyraider bounced over the crash barriers strung across deck, hurtled into aircraft spotted forward, and wrecked itself and two Corsairs, as well as damaging three other ADs, another Corsair, and two Panthers.[17] Carrier landing accidents quickly became one of the most annoying features of the Korean naval air war. Bad as propeller-driven accidents were, straight-deck carriers seemed especially susceptible to accidents from damaged jets, or pilots who misjudged their approach. One jet squadron, in the first month of the war, logged no less than 15 crashes in three weeks. The second month, it logged 20 crashes in 31 days. In contrast, that squadron's planes had received a grand total of only one bullet hole from enemy fire, leading one wag to inquire, "Just who *is* the enemy?"[18]

The early jets, underpowered and lacking the sophisticated lift-augmenting technology of their successors, were particularly unforgiving and intolerant. Given their performance limitations and accompanying high fuel consumption, the tricky weather off the Korean coast, and the pitching, heaving seas of Japanese and Korean waters, the edginess of pilots is understandable. Some accidents were incredible; one F9F came in too high while landing on the *Midway,* missed all the landing wires, plunged right through the crash barriers, and, before going over the side, wiped out two other Panthers, starting a fire that damaged several others. "It never pays,"

Naval Aviation News bitterly reported, "to land a plane long."[19] But it seldom paid to land short, either, as the penalty for a short misjudged approach was usually a fatal ramp strike. (One lucky pilot did survive a spectacular strike that transformed his jet into a fireball: the cockpit section tumbled out of the flaming inferno, the pilot injured but alive; he subsequently made a full recovery.) Gerald E. Miller, who served as a TF 77 staff officer and squadron commander and eventually rose to the rank of Vice Admiral, witnessed a classic jet pile-up. During a transfer of planes between carriers cruising off Japan, weather closed the "beach," prohibiting safe recovery ashore. Differing sea and wind conditions produced nasty swells which, coupled with jet idiosyncrasies and pilot anxiety, generated numerous deck accidents. "I can still remember the admiral walking over to the opposite side of the bridge," Miller subsequently recalled, "putting his head down on his hands, and shaking. It was so bad he couldn't even get mad. It was a horrible mess."[20] Eventually, adaptation of the British angled deck, whereby planes landed with an unobstructed area ahead of them, permitting them to actually take off again if they missed the landing wires, together with intensive training, helped reduce such accidents.

By mid-July, the rampaging North Korean army had advanced well over 100 miles into the south. Before it, the remnants of the ROK Army fled, and the courageous but ill-equipped and ill-trained American 24th Division, hastily thrown into the Korean cauldron, absorbed bitter coordinated infantry and armor assaults. The NKAF, on the other hand, showed little inclination to attack Allied air and ground forces, likely because its pilots (rumored to be Russian instructors) had not proven their ability to stay alive in the air. To preserve the Allied presence in Korea before launching an offensive counterstroke in mid-September at Inch'on, the Navy undertook an amphibious operation to land the Army's First Cavalry Division at the east coast port of P'ohang, 70 miles above the port city of Pusan on the southeastern tip of the Korean peninsula.

Following the P'yongyang strikes, TF 77 had returned to Buckner Bay. Now it again sallied forth, this time for the Sea of Japan, cruising 60 miles northeast of P'ohang to support the upcoming landing. The landing on July 18, surprisingly, came off without any enemy opposition, for (though P'ohang would eventually fall) at this time the actual front ran slightly north of the port. Thus, the First Cav came ashore without the bloody fire most had expected. With the First Cav in place, the North Korean drive slowed somewhat, easing for the moment the pressure on what was increasingly being referred to as the "Pusan Pocket." TF 77's aviators looked for other targets the day of the landing; there was little need for them above the tranquil unloading of the ships.

North Korea's Wonsan Oil Refining Factory was a particularly lucrative target. The refinery, a Korean-Russian joint-stock company originally built by the Japanese in 1935 at a cost of 50 million yen (about $10 million), produced approximately 500 tons of refined petroleum products daily, including 150 tons of automotive-grade gasoline. On the morning of July 18, as soon as it became apparent that the P'ohang landing would go unmolested, VF-51 launched seven Panthers from the *Valley Forge* on an armed reconnaissance up North Korea's eastern coast. Abreast the curving harbor of Wonsan, the pilots noticed the refinery, pristine against the earth, and so far totally unmarked. It was an attack pilot's dream target: vital, vulnerable, and untouched. Late in the afternoon, CAG 5 launched 10 Corsairs from VF-53, each armed with eight five-inch diameter high velocity aerial rockets (HVARs) and a full load of 20-mm ammunition, as well as 11 ADs from VA-55, each carrying two rockets, a 1,000-pound bomb, and a 500-pound bomb. The Corsairs and Sky-raiders roared over the refinery like a swarm of angry hornets; they rocketed the storage and crack-ing facilities, and followed with bombs. As they pulled off target, the refinery belched orange flame and black smoke. From 60 miles away, the returning crews, jubilant with the mission's results, could see a towering column of smoke; the refinery burned itself out over four days at the cost of 12,000 tons of refined petroleum. When Wonsan temporarily fell into Allied hands in the fall of 1950 following the collapse of North Korea's armed forces in the after-math of the Inch'on landing, a Navy damage assessor inspected the plant and interviewed surviving workers. He concluded that the attack had left the plant

. . . a mass of twisted steel and rubble. Not one single machine was capable of operating nor was one building fit for occupancy. The streets throughout the plant were covered with from six inches to two feet of oil and many areas were impassable because of mountains of rubble. The engineers who accompanied me on this tour stated that no part of this factory can be salvaged or repaired.[21]

In short, it had been a good day's work for the "Happy Valley's," airedales.

The Wonsan oil refinery strike became one of the highlights of the naval air war in Korea, along with the Battle of Carlson's Canyon, the Kapsan strike, and the torpedoing of the Hwachon Dam, among others. But as July edged towards August, the attention of TF 77 turned from glamorous strikes to operations that held the key to success or failure of the Allied effort in Korea: close air support of beleagured infantry under attack as the North Korean Army attempted to breach the Pusan perimeter and throw the South's defenders off the peninsula entirely.

During the opening weeks of the Korean war; the United States Air Force had worked heroically to blunt the North Korean drive. Piston-engine B-29 Superfortresses lumbered out of Japan and Okinawa to attack targets in North Korea and, occasionally, to bomb in support of Allied troops; flying from Japan, Douglas B-26 Invaders, a twin-engine attack bomber with no less than 14 forward-firing .50-caliber machine guns as well as an armament of bombs and rockets, attacked North Korean troop columns, wreaking havoc. Lockheed F-80 Shooting

Star jet fighters flew in support of ground troops from bases in Japan and South Korea. But still the flood of North Korean forces continued. It is ironic that the NKAF had so little luck against the USAF and the naval aviators to Task Force 77: ironic because it fell not to the NKAF to offset and neutralize Allied air power, but to the North Korean Army. And, to a remarkable degree, the North Korean Army succeeded. Eventually, as the noose tightened around the Pusan pocket, the Air Force withdrew its tactical aircraft entirely from Korea and repositioned them in Japan. This worked a tremendous hardship: crews faced long journeys to and from targets; ground forces desperately needing air support experienced frustrating and sometimes fatal delays; tactical aircraft had to sacrifice weapons for more fuel. Most Fifth Air Force fighter squadrons, having switched from propeller-driven aircraft to jets, now found the fuel-gobbling jets a distinct liability. The North Korean Army, then, had found the perfect way to cope with land-based Korean air power: seize the enemy's airfields.[22]

The jets' range problem posed a major challenge. In a desperate attempt to improve the F-80's endurance, Air Force maintenance personnel jury-rigged special long-range wing tanks (dubbed "Misawa tanks") supplying an extra 100 gallons of fuel. As Lieutenant General Earle E. "Pat" Partridge, Fifth Air Force's commander, recalled more than 30 years later, "Kelly Johnson [the F-80's designer] came over and watched them take off from Taegu with two wing tanks full and a 500 lb. bomb in addition. He turned away and said, 'I can't watch it.' "[23] As a more practical solution, Fifth Air Force decided to trade some of its jets for older propeller-driven North American F-51 Mustangs, then serving with Air Guard and Reserve units, planes previously scheduled for scrapping. On July 23, in response to an urgent request, the *Boxer* arrived at Yokosuka, Japan, with 145 Mustangs, having crossed the Pacific in the record time of 8 days and 16 hours. Unfortunately, though having better range and payload, the Mustang, with its vulnerable liquid coolant lines and radiator, already had demonstrated its susceptibility to antiaircraft and small arms fire. Many pilots disliked going back to the F-51; as one Air Force analyst wrote, "A lot of pilots had seen vivid demonstrations of why the F-51 was not a ground-support fighter in the last war, and weren't exactly intrigued by the thought of playing guinea pig to prove the same thing over again."[24] A better selection might have been the Corsair-like Republic F-47 (formerly P-47) Thunderbolt, a massive radial engine fighter-bomber also of Second World War vintage. But the quite survivable F-47 was in such limited supply—most had been scrapped or sold abroad—that the Air Force possessed too few to utilize in Korea.

Meanwhile, as the Air Force made do with bases in Japan, the Navy found itself in a position to help. Its carriers could operate offshore with older Corsair and newer Skyraider attack aircraft carrying generous amounts of ordnance, serving as mobile airfields supplanting those overrun by the North Koreans. Pending a general escalation, for example, a North Korean and Soviet air force or Soviet navy attack on the carrier, carrier aviation could function at close range off the Korean peninsula with impunity. While it could not substitute for massive Air Force support, it could furnish air power on demand in response to specific crises, and in amounts that could devastate any foe.

Supreme Commander General Douglas Mac-Arthur had directed that all air support requests from General Walton Walker's beleagured Eighth Army in the Pusan pocket should be coordinated through Fifth Air Force. Nevertheless, the situation grew so critical by July 23 that the Eighth Army directly requested close air support from TF 77, with endorsement of the planned Navy strikes from Lieutenant General George E. Stratemeyer (commander of Far East Air Forces), MacArthur himself, and COMNAVFE Admiral C. Turner Joy. Following up on the emergency request, Air Force Brigadier General Jarred Crabbe called Admiral Joy's chief of staff to reiterate the urgent need for the assistance of TF 77. This frantic plea was triggered by southwest Korea's rapid collapse; it caved in like a rotten tooth, crumbling away and exposing the vulnerable western flank of the Eighth Army. TF 77 flew its first mission in support of ground troops on July 22. July 23 found it refueling from the fleet oiler *Navasota:* the next day, it journeyed to Sasebo for hasty rearming, and then, at midnight, stood out to sea, assuming position 30 miles south east of P'ohang and launching its first emergency close support strikes on July 25.[25]

Those support strikes triggered a controversy that lasted virtually throughout the war: a debate that, in some respects, echoed the roles and missions bickering of the 1940s and led to frequently acerbic memos from all parties — Navy, Air Force, Army, and Marines — about who had the correct interpretation of close air support. From the perspective of the summer of 1950, it is easy to understand how professional differences, coupled with the grave Korean situation and the lingering resentments of the 1940s defense debate, could escalate into alarmist pronouncements that, unless this or that system were followed, Korea was doomed. It is fair to say that both the Navy and Air Force systems of close air support had their merits, as well as their weaknesses. It must never be forgotten that both were responsible for destroying the hopes of Kim Il Sung, Mao Tse-tung, and Josef Stalin amid a welter of shot, bombs, rockets, and napalm that left the Korean landscape littered with the bodies of those unfortunate enough to serve the Communist cause.

In part, the difficulty stemmed from the vague definition of "close air support" (CAS): "Air action against hostile surface targets which are so close to friendly forces as to require detailed integration of each air mission with the fire and movement of those forces."[26] As a concept, CAS actually dated to the First World War, when the Royal Flying Corps (later the Royal Air Force) and the German *Luftstreikräfte* developed sound and widely utilized tactics for using "bomb-loaded" aircraft in an assault role over the battlefield. The RFC distinguished between "trench strafing" (a concept remarkably similar to CAS as practiced by the Navy) and "ground strafing" (operations across the front extending much further behind the lines, similar to the Air Force concept of CAS, but with overtones of latter-day interdiction doctrine as well).[27]

During the 1920s and 1930s, the Navy, Marine Corps, and Army Air Corps (the predecessor of the wartime USAAF and the later USAF) had experimented with "attack" operations. The Marines flew CAS strikes during fighting in Haiti, the Dominican Republic, and, especially, against Nicaraguan Sandinista rebels. For its part, the Army Air Corps developed a family of light, heavily armed attack aircraft, exemplified by the Curtiss A-12 Shrike and the Northrop A-17, that culminated in the wartime Douglas A-20 Havoc and later A-26 Invader (which, redesignated B-26, soldiered on in Korea). The Second World War solidified the concept of battlefield air support for naval and Air Force advocates. During the Allied drive across northern Europe, Anglo-American fighter-bombers and troops had worked together very effectively; in Italy, liaison pilots flying light spotter aircraft had started directing air strikes of fighter-bombers, which added a new wrinkle to tactical air control and freed the controller from the limitations of a ground-level perspective. In the Pacific, the Navy and Marine Corps evolved a joint CAS system starting with the bloody invasion of Tarawa; liaison parties with ground forces assisted commanders in selecting suitable targets, and then directed the incoming strike force, using both ground and airborne controllers. By Okinawa, improved air-to-ground radio communication enabled ground commanders themselves to call in air strikes; so effective were Marine Corsair

71

CAS strikes that the plane earned the nickname "Okinawa Sweetheart" from grateful Marine and Army infantry. Both the Navy and Air Force, then, had a heritage of imaginative use of tactical strike aircraft over the battlefield. But the two systems also had fundamental differences.[28]

Dealing as it might have to with a broad front covering dozens if not hundreds of miles, the Air Force adapted a tightly structured approach to close air support. Such operations were the joint project of the Army and Air Force, and Air Force doctrine stipulated a Joint Operations Center (JOC) composed of Army and Air Force personnel, together with an Air Force Tactical Air Control Center (TACC) operating side-by-side with the JOC. Up front with the troops would be Tactical Air Control Parties (TACP), each consisting of an Air Force pilot-controller and, usually, two airmen with a radio-equipped Jeep. When a TACP spotted a likely target or the need for a CAS strike, the pilot-controller would radio the headquarters of the Army division they served; the division would then relay the request up to Army corps headquarters, and the corps would pass it along to the JOC. If approved, the TACC would then contact an appropriate air-field, scrambling strike aircraft. They would report to the TACP (and perhaps to an airborne controller as well), get final instructions, and then attack. Under expeditious circumstances, a typical strike request might take 40 minutes from the time the TACP requested a strike until the bombs hit the target. A critically important assumption underlay this carefully developed structure: CAS should function as an adjunct to, and not as a substitute for, an Army division's own artillery. For this reason, the Air Force thought of CAS in terms of operations seldom closer than 1,000 yards in front of the troops. Conventional artillery fire, in theory, would be available to engage any threat closer than that, unless emergency conditions dictated "last ditch" air strikes immediately in front of the troops.[29]

In contrast, the Navy-Marine CAS system reflected a commitment to support landing forces. Born out of the Pacific war and influenced by earlier Marine aviation experience in the brushfire conflicts of the inter-war years, the Navy-Marine system viewed CAS as an artillery substitute. The Marines, relatively lightly armed shock forces, did not have the heavy artillery support the Army could call upon, except in specialized cases such as amphibious landings, when operating within the range of naval shipboard artillery. Yet even in those circumstances (as throughout the Pacific campaign), the Marines had recognized a need for close cooperation by air and ground forces to break enemy resistance, particularly when geography or the fear of shelling friendly forces limited gunfire support. Instead, the Navy and Marines employed strike aircraft as flying artillery, operating 50-200 yards in front of troops. Corps planners, echoing the notion that Marine air has always existed primarily to assist the Marine "grunt" on the ground, stipulated in 1946 that prospective marine aviators must first serve two years as "mud Marines." The Navy, concerned with a variety of other missions such as fleet air defense, antisubmarine patrol, maritime reconnaissance, and antishipping strike, could not devote as much attention to CAS as the Marines wanted; nevertheless, the service's planners ensured that naval aviation was "trained to attack with accuracy, economy, and precision targets designated by the ground forces it supports."[30] To do so, the Navy and Marines relied upon specialized ANGLICO (Air-Naval Gunfire Liaison Company) units to control Navy-Marine CAS strikes via frontline TACP parties. Typically, under the Navy-Marine CAS system, a Marine TACP radioed strike requests to a Marine brigade's Tactical Air Direction Center (TADC), which, in turn, contacted offshore carriers.

The Fifth Air Force established an Air Force-Eighth Army Joint Operations Center at Taejon in early June. It soon moved southeast to Taegu, and then down to Pusan as the perimeter closed; eventually it was resettled in Seoul (where it remained until war's end) after the success at Inch'on. Very quickly, the attendant TACPs, using old AN/ARC-1 radio-equipped Jeeps, discovered that the rugged Korean terrain and their elderly equipment were incompatible. At about this same time, Army aviators supporting the 24th Division began using Ryan L-17s (similar to the civilian Ryan Navion) to direct Air Force fighters and bombers in attacks upon North Korean columns. The L-17, with its limited visibility, soon gave way to much more fragile World War II-vintage Piper L-4 "Grasshoppers," a military version of the famed Piper Cub. North Korean Yaks found these more to their taste than Allied fighter aircraft, and quickly shot one down. On another occasion, however, the resourceful Cub pilot adroitly suckered a Yak pilot into a low-speed low-altitude turn; the heavier fighter stalled out and tumbled into a hill.[31] By mid-July the efforts of Army and Air Force personnel who were convinced that airborne controllers could work more safely, expeditiously, and with better results than the Jeep-limited TACPs, caused the Air Force to undertake its first airborne controller missions in Korea. They used modified two-place North American T-6 Texan trainers equipped with eight-channel AN-ARC-3 radios. Known as Mosquitos, the T-6s proved so successful that they quickly became a common feature of the Korean sky. Reasonably fast and nimble, the T-6 features a rugged radial engine, light armament, and provisions for firing smoke rockets to mark targets.[32] This, then, was South Korea's tactical air control network as *Valley Forge* turned into the wind and launched its planes at 8:00 on July 25.

As with the pre-emergency strike of July 22, the July 25 mission was tremendously frustrated. When the heavily loaded Skyraiders and Corsairs arrived over the front and attempted to contact the JOC and the airborne Mosquitos, there was total confusion. Most Mosquito channels were saturated, Korean plane names defied pronunciation, and maps proved incompatible. The Navy used aeronautical charts delineated in latitude and longitude, while the Air Force employed more useful gridded charts where controllers could pinpoint targets by a combination of letters and numbers. Most Navy planes gave up, roaming the front on their own, looking for targets. Others aborted and wastefully jettisoned their bombs and rockets for safety reasons prior to landing back aboard the *Valley Forge*. The next day, the aviators had better results. They destroyed 10 trucks and damaged a bridge, but in general they met with little success and Admiral C. Turner Joy, in a message to CNO Forrest Sherman, pronounced the two-day effort "disappointing."[33]

That the missions resulted in attacks outside the standard Navy-Marine CAS system was particularly disturbing to the Navy. On the other hand, the Air Force perceived an equally disturbing "go it alone" attitude on the part of the TF 77 flyers. Doctrinal differences aside—for partisans in both services remained committed to their notions of CAS throughout the war—the critical problem was communication. All too often radio discipline was poor, and basic incompatibilities existed between the over-utilized radio channels available to Army and Mosquito controllers (usually four, more typically eight) and the Navy's 12- or even 20-channel (plus "guard" channel) VHF sets. As General Partridge recalled, ". . . our major problem was communications. . . . with [the Navy's] new type radio you could call up anybody and get an answer. . . . The Navy was there, way down in the south tip of Korea. They were anxious to do something useful. They called and called and called and they couldn't get the ground controller. There probably wasn't one there anyway at the moment." Between July and mid-November 1950, the Navy scratched 13% of its CAS sorties (151 in all) because its planes could not contact controllers; in August, the figure was nearer 30%.[34]

Communications remained a fundamental problem through the first months of the war. When the *Valley Forge* and the carrier *Philippine Sea* operated together on CAS strikes in mid-August, their preliminary action reports seethed with annoyance. *Valley Forge's* intelligence officer wrote "The control channels were jammed with trivial transmissions, and positive controlling was never to be had. In an area so close to friendly troops, it is absolutely essential."[35] Likewise, *Philippine Sea's* action report stated:

> For this vessel the subject of close support is a touchy one. The inability to establish good communications with any controllers has limited its effectiveness. There is apparently no such thing as radio discipline. If a pilot has something to say he just tries to cut out whoever is on the air. Too many tactical air controllers and different support flights are on the same channels. With the present ground situation as it is (that is, fluid) it is mandatory that the pilots be informed exactly as to their mission. In the past this has not been done and has resulted in inefficient use of aircraft from this vessel engaged in close support operations.[36]

When the light carrier *Sicily* (CVE 118) commenced Marine CAS strikes in early August, Captain John S. Thach, a noted fighter tactician who had developed the famed "Thach weave," "just couldn't believe" that communications "could be so bad. . . . and neither could Admiral Hoskins who had TF 77. He'd send these planes down and the pilots would come back and say 'We couldn't help. We wanted to. We were there and we couldn't get in communication with people.' "[37]

Most frustrating to the naval aviators was circling overhead in their heavily loaded Corsairs and Sky-raiders, unable to get in touch with airborne Mosquito controllers (or worse, being told to "stand by"), while fuel-critical lightly loaded F-80s at the limit of their endurance were given priority to hit targets. Sometimes the frustration of the Mosquito controllers also surfaced; Thach recalled how F-80s:

. . . call[ed] the controller and the controller would answer, and they'd say, 'Give me a target, give me a target. I've only got five minutes more. Got to go back.' And it was required that they list the ordnance that they were carrying, so they'd be asked 'What is your ordnance?'

'I've got two one hundred pound bombs. Hurry up.'

I heard that so many times, and finally I heard—I think it was an Air Force controller—say:

'Well, take your two little firecrackers and drop them up the road somewhere because I've got something coming in that has a load.'[38]

One F-80 squadron, in 17 days of constant operations, dropped only 7,500 pounds of bombs, an average of just 441 pounds per day for the entire squadron. In contrast, the Corsairs and Skyraiders, operating at closer ranges, could carry remarkable amounts of weaponry. A typical day of support

78

missions consisted of formations of eight F4Us and eight ADs launched at three-hour intervals. Ordnance loads varied, but standard loads were as follows:

F4U Corsair

Load Able: 800 rounds 20 mm; one 1,000-pound bomb; eight 5" HVAR; one 150-gallon fuel tank; 4-hour endurance.

Load Baker: 800 rounds 20 mm; two 150-gallon napalm bombs; eight 5" HVAR; 2½-hour endurance.

AD Skyraider

Load Able: 400 rounds 20mm; three 500-pound bombs, 12 5" HVAR; 4-hour endurance.

Load Baker: 400 rounds 20mm; three 150-gallon napalm bombs; 12 250-pound fragmentation bombs; 4-hour endurance.

Load Charlie: 400 rounds 20 mm; two 1,000-pound bombs; 12 250-pound fragmentation bombs; one 150-gallon fuel tank; 6-hour endurance.[39]

As an immediate short-term solution to some of the problems encountered in these first CAS attempts, Admiral Hoskins sent a representative of *Valley Forge*'s Air Group 5 to visit the JOC. As a result of his visit, the Navy opened a direct communication channel from the JOC to TF 77, took steps to procure maps, and arranged to employ long-duration ADs as airborne controllers to assist the hard-pressed and overworked Mosquitoes. Controversy continued over roles and missions; one meeting attempted to spell out the precise relationship between naval air and the Fifth Air Force, but resulted in little more than misunderstandings and further wrangling. But gradually the CAS situation improved to the point where Major General O. P. Weyland, FEAF's Vice Commander for Operations, wrote to Air Force Chief of Staff General Hoyt S. Vandenberg that "Korea has provided an ideal area for employment of carrier-based aircraft in tactical operations. The type aircraft used by the Navy and USMC—fighters and dive bombers—are well suited to this type work. In the absence of hostile air opposition, they have performed well and have been of great assistance."[40]

By early August, the need for Eighth Army air support had taken on an urgency greater than ever. The Navy had already planned to increase the number of American carriers off Korea, and H. M. S. *Triumph* left TF 77 at the end of July to join an all-British squadron that continued to serve the Allied cause well. On the first of August, the carrier *Philippine Sea* (CV 47) arrived for duty; two smaller "escort" carriers, the *Badoeng Strait* (CVE 116, known as the "Bing-Ding") and the *Sicily* (CVE 118) were on their way. On the morning of August 2, *Sicily* entered Kobe harbor's channel under the command of Captain Thach, proceeding cautiously so as not to stray into uncleared portions of the channel still littered with sea mines from the Second World War. After narrowly averting a collision with a freighter whose skipper had evidently forgotten port from starboard, Thach came alongside a pier and docked, receiving word that COMNAVFE wished to speak with him immediately. He went to a phone, and at the other end of the line, Admiral Joy asked, "How soon can you get underway?" Thach averred that he needed until the next morning. "You don't understand," Joy replied, "I mean how soon can you get underway right now? Because if you don't there won't be any use in getting underway. It'll be too late." Thach asked for 30 minutes, went to the *Sicily's* loud hailer, and, motioning towards two supply vessels moored nearby, announced to all within earshot, "I don't care what you are, unless you're on watch, go over to those two vessels, pick up something that's good for a Corsair, and bring it back over to the *Sicily*. Make one trip. I'm leaving right after that." Later he recalled, "It was amazing how much they got." *Sicily* left harbor on schedule and, on August 3, VMF-214, the famed "Blacksheep" squadron, flew aboard in their Corsairs; they launched their first combat mission, and the first Marine air strike of the Korean War, later that day.[41]

The weaponry and tactics of both naval and Air Force aircraft were critical in saving the Eighth Army from extinction. North Korea's heavily armored T-34 tanks posed a special problem for Allied infantrymen. This Soviet-built vehicle, which had played a major role in whipping Hitler's *Wehrmacht* in the Second World War, was all but impervious to conventional antitank cannon and bazookas. In response, the Army rushed a special 3.5-inch "super bazooka" with an antitank round to Korea, and it proved effective. But the new bazooka remained in short supply through the summer of 1950, and pending the introduction of newer Allied tanks such as the American M-26 or the British Centurion, it fell largely to air power to cope with the T-34 menace. The aerial rocket was a standard antitank weapon. The British had used them effectively against Nazi armor, as had the Russians. During the war, the U.S. Navy had developed the High Velocity Aerial Rocket (HVAR), a solid-fuel fin-guided projectile with a 5-inch diameter explosive warhead, as well as a much larger (if less precise) rocket called Tiny Tim. But in Korea, in addition to the ever-present sighting and aiming problems, the HVAR often proved unequal to its task, sometimes ricocheting off the sloping armor of the T-34, and other times apparently exploding without effect against it. In a rushed response, the Naval Ordnance Test Station at China Lake, California, had taken the HVAR and replaced its warhead with a new and more powerful 6.5-inch diameter shaped charge. The new weapon, called the ATAR (for Antitank Aerial Rocket) but popularly known as the "Ram rocket," first arrived in Korea at the end of July 1950.[42] ATAR worked considerably better than HVAR against tanks and armored targets; accuracy continued to be its major limitation. Napalm, a thickened mixture of jellied gasoline, proved far more effective against armor. Corsairs usually carried two 150-gallon napalm bombs (weighing nearly 1,400 pounds apiece), while ADs could lug up to three. Dropped from as low as 200 feet in modified drop tanks, this hellish weapon required nowhere near the accuracy

82

of an ATAR or HVAR firing, and generated a fireball incinerating anything within a pear-shaped area up to 275 feet long by nearly 100 feet wide. Nothing so typified the air-to-ground war in Korea as napalm, for the Air Force, Navy, and Marines used it extensively against virtually all targets: tanks, trains, trucks, troops, airfields, railroad tunnels and yards, and harbors.[43]

Aside from napalm, rockets and fragmentation bombs proved deadly against troops, light vehicles, and emplacements; many pilots undertook low-level strafing with their 20-mm cannon. While the Air Force still relied on the .50-caliber machine gun, the Navy had opted for the 20-mm cannon. Corsairs (aside from those still armed with "fifties") and Panthers carried four, and early ADs had two (which proved too few, leading to four-gun production models.) Some controversy existed, primarily among "old hands" from World War II, over whether four "twenties" were better than the six "fifties" standard on Second World War fighters. Some held that the jamming tendency of 20-mm cannon led to a greater loss of firepower in a four-gun aircraft than the loss of a single .50-caliber would in a six-gun fighter. Though partisans took strong positions on both sides, airborne cannon supporters appeared more numerous. The 20-mm was undoubtedly more effective for bagging North Korean aircraft when communist planes made their appearance. Another controversy ranged over whether jet or propeller-driven aircraft made better close support airplanes. Propeller-driven airplanes had better endurance and heavier payload capability. But interrogation of prisoners suggested that they feared jets more because the faster planes had a better chance of striking before they were aware they were under attack. Interestingly, they feared "the blue airplanes," presumably because of their greater ordnance load, more than other Allied aircraft.

Survivability posed other questions. Jets had lower loss rates than propeller aircraft when employed on CAS sorties, presumably because their speed made them less susceptible to attack; defenders faced more difficulty tracing and firing. But their corresponding lack of accuracy offset this somewhat, since they could not safely operate as close to the ground as earlier aircraft, especially in the rugged mountains and twisting ravines typical of the Korean countryside. Overall, then, slower propeller-driven aircraft appeared better suited for ground support duties. On the other hand, the slower propeller-driven aircraft, such as the F4U, AD, Marine F7F, and Air Force F-51 and F-82, could certainly destroy targets, but survivability was a key problem. As mentioned, radial-engined aircraft fared better than liquid-cooled ones, but the Corsair had a badly placed oil cooler installation that invited small arms and shrapnel damage, and even the tough AD received additional armor sheeting on its undersides as a result of lessons learned in combat. This inconclusive debate continued through the Korean War, into the era of Vietnam, and, indeed, its echoes are heard today.[44]

On August 7, the 1st Provisional Marine Brigade — a force in truth no stronger than a reinforced regiment — entered combat in defense of Pusan, joining with Army infantry and striking towards Chinju in a campaign that ultimately stemmed the North Korean advance. Here Navy-Marine CAS had an opportunity to work effectively, with Marine TACPs calling in Corsair strikes from the carriers *Badoeng Strait* and *Sicily*. During daylight hours, the Marines maintained formations of 4-10 planes continuously over the troops, with an airborne controller, and a two-plane combat air patrol in case the NKAF made an appearance. The two carriers, operating as Task Group 96.8 under the overall command of Rear Admiral R. W. Ruble, each supported a single Corsair squadron: VMF-323 flew from the "Bing-Ding," and VMF-214 from the *Sicily*. For most of the month, the two squadrons participated jointly on strikes but whenever one carrier needed replenishing, the second remained on station, giving the Marines ashore the continuous support they had come to expect. The Corsairs of TG 96.8 and TF 77 were workhorses during August, flying a total of 6,575 combat flight hours, as compared to 1,600 for the AD and 727 for the F9F. For their part, TF 77's fast carriers *Valley Forge* and *Philippine Sea* shuttled along the Korean coastline, ranging from the Sea of Japan through the Korea Strait and into the Yellow Sea. Navy airborne controllers from the two ships directed strikes by both Navy and Air Force aircraft on a north-south bombline from Hanyang to Chinju, blunting resistance to the joint Marine-Army advance along a 30-mile front. Wider-ranging armed reconnaissance and interdiction missions hit targets as far north as Sonch'on, on Korea's west coast just 30 miles below the Yalu river, which separates Korea from Manchuria. The fast carriers generally launched formations of 12-24 Corsairs and Skyraiders four times per day, as well as four daily launches of eight Panthers. The hot summer weather proved a problem for the jets. *Essex*-class carriers equipped with hydraulic catapults needed every bit of wind available over the deck to launch jet sorties. One jet squadron launched only 60% of its scheduled sorties because of low winds, and even when launched, the low winds generally precluded arming the Panthers with the six HVAR rockets they had been outfitted to carry. On several occasions, afternoon jet sweeps had to be cancelled because of low winds, a foretaste of the next two years. (Much as landing accidents encouraged adaptation of the British angled deck, this problem accelerated adaptation of the steam catapult, another British innovation.) Thus the jets, in contrast to the heavily loaded ADs and F4Us, usually carried only ammo loads for their cannon, acting as top cover over targets where enemy air opposition might be expected, or, if in the "attack" mode, as high-speed strafers. Panthers didn't drop bombs for another eight months.[45]

During those hectic days, many incidents added to the lore of naval aviation. A mixed group of 15 *Valley Forge* ADs and F4Us shot up targets near Sinanju, and returned to report the destruction of, among other transport, "a 1948 Chevrolet convertible with a black top." Blacksheep pilot Major Ken Reusser, a much-decorated Pacific veteran, force-landed so many times that his Corsair squadron mates dubbed him "Rice Paddy Reusser." A Panther pilot from *Philippine Sea*'s VF-111 became so entranced in following his HVARs that he literally did, overflying his target at the same time the rockets exploded; he staggered back to the ship, the jet peppered with shrapnel and a total maintenance write-off. Two Marine spotters aloft in a little Consolidated OY-1 liaison plane from observation squadron VMO-6 attacked a North Korean staff car with revolvers, and so unnerved its occupants that they drove off a cliff. Another Marine spotter, in an episode recalling the First World War, carried hand grenades in his OY-1, dropping them on North Koreans having the temerity to fire upon him.[46]

In TG 96.8's attacks that month, operating in close proximity to friendly forces became a hallmark. The effectiveness of Marine CAS astonished Army troops fighting alongside the Leathernecks; the apparent ease with which the Marines could call up strikes and the overwhelming response added fuel to the CAS fires then raging between the services. The Marine Corsairs left a favorable impression for many reasons; the chief ones were the short distance between the carriers and the battle front, the small size of the front itself, bad weather limiting Air Force strikes from Japan, the 48 Corsairs available from the two escort carriers, the superior endurance and load-carrying capability of the Corsairs, and the proficient relationship between controller and strike force. All combined to make an indelible impression on the young Army infantrymen confronting a seemingly invincible foe. They cared little about the details of CAS; they only knew it saved their lives.[47]

Sicily's Captain Thach recalled one strike where Blacksheep Corsairs were attempting to destroy gun emplacements harassing friendly forces. The Marine TACP directed the four F4Us orbiting the target area to send one down on a dummy run so he could point out a particularly bothersome emplacement. The Corsair flight leader made the pass, as the controller coached him on the terrain until, finally, the pilot spotted the emplacement. The controller directed him to dive-bomb it with a 500-pound bomb, "But," he cautioned, "be very careful." Down plunged the Corsair, in that peculiar whistling dive (caused by air rushing through oil coolers) so characteristic of the big fighter. The bomb hit exactly on target, and the controller cleared the flight to return to the *Sicily*. But the flight leader had seen another target, almost on the edge of the last one, and radioed "Just a minute. While I was on the way down, on the righthand side of my gunsight I saw a big tank. I couldn't see it all. It was under a bush, but how about the target?" "I told you I was close," the controller answered, "let it alone. That tank is me."[48]

By mid-August, CAS strikes had taken a terrible toll of the North Koreans. A "last stand" by a particularly aggressive Communist division on "No-Name Ridge" west of Yongsan by the Naktong river (the line of furthest North Korean advance) crumbled under the weight of Corsair attacks delivered by *Badoeng Strait*'s VMF-323 combined with infantry assaults. On August 18, hundreds (and perhaps thousands) fell before *Sicily*'s Corsairs as troops tried vainly to retreat across the Naktong. A tenacious ground defense, coupled with merciless air assault, at last brought the North Korean advance to a halt. Though bitter (if futile) Communist attacks continued until the end of the month, Kim Il Sung now had little choice but to think of defense in expectation of an Allied knockout blow, which was soon to come at Inch'on.[49]

All this was not without a price, however. The first Navy plane lost to enemy action went down on July 19, and by the end of the month, the Navy had lost a total of three Corsairs and one Skyraider. In August, eight fell in combat: five Corsairs and a F9F-3 Panther, a P2V-3 Neptune (which ditched after being hit by flak, the crew being rescued), and a Marine OY-1 spotter. Corsair losses reflected the intense pace of CAS operations, though analysts realized that this already venerable fighter-bomber was clearly nearing the end of its useful years. They recommended its replacement as quickly as possible by newer jets for air-fighting purposes, and by the more rugged and capable AD for the attack role. The Panther's loss involved the Navy's first combat use of an ejection seat. Hit while strafing a North Korean target at 400 knots and at 2,000 feet, Lieutenant Carl Dace of VF-111 zoomed to 6,000 feet, trading airspeed for altitude. He turned out to sea, jettisoned his canopy (after a brief struggle that included his actually shoving it off its tracks until the wind blast carried it away), pulled the seat's face curtain, and shot into the air as his wingman looked on. The seat worked as advertised, and Dace separated from it, opening his chute and descending to a water landing. He spent the next seven hours in a cold and wet raft, uncomfortable but alive. A convenient destroyer picked him up, none the worse for the experience.[50]

The helicopter quickly proved its own worth as an air-rescue craft. VMO-6, based a Chinhae, was particularly active. Flying a mix of OY-1 spotters and four-seat Sikorsky HO3S-1 helicopters, the squadron had soon found itself in the thick of the fighting around the Pusan pocket. On August 10, a VMF-323 Corsair piloted by Captain Vivian Moses took flak damage, lost its oil pressure, and sputtered downwards, forcing Moses to parachute into the ocean. Along came one of VMO-6's Sikorsky's piloted by Lieutenant Gustave Lueddeke, and plucked the Marine from the sea. They flew him to Chinhae, and VMO-6 ferried him to the "Bing-Ding" the following morning. The next day, Lueddeke was again in action, this time carrying Brigadier General Edward A. Craig, the commander of the 1st Provisional Marine Brigade, on an observation hop to check the brigade's progress as it attacked Haesong. Overhead, four VMF-323 Corsairs—one piloted by Moses, fresh from his ditching the day before—circled protectively over the troops. A large group of North Korean vehicles attempted to exit the battle area, and the Corsairs dove earthwards amid intense machine gun and small arms fire, bombing and rocketing the column. Two Corsairs went down, hit in their vulnerable oil coolers. One ditched at sea, and Lueddeke clattered to the rescue. General Craig himself hoisted the pilot aboard and was rewarded with a backslap and a "Thanks, Mac" from the shaken airman, unaware of his benefactor's identity. The second Corsair's pilot, too low to jump, crashed while attempting a forced landing in a rice paddy;

this time, Vivian Moses was not so lucky, and he perished. But Lueddeke soon rescued another pilot whose plane ditched 70 miles at sea. "Helo" pilots like Lueddeke and the Navy's John K. Koelsch and Duane W. Thorin soon established a tradition for persistence, skill, and courage that has become an integral part of the air-rescue tradition. Many experienced grueling captivity when shot down behind enemy lines. Some, like Medal of Honor recipient Koelsch, died; most, like Thorin, survived to return home. Helicopter operations, by all services in Korea, became one of the war's distinctive marks. Carriers relied on "plane guard" helicopters to supplement the traditional plane guard destroyer that accompanied a carrier during flight operations. Later in the war, helicopters flew deep into enemy territory on rescue and intelligence missions, transported troops and battlefield artillerly, spotted for naval gunfire, and undertook evacuation of wounded. If Vietnam was largely a helicopter war, Korea saw the "pinwheel" come of age. It is hard to believe that the primitive piston-powered helicopters of the time—comparable in their own way to the early aircraft of the First World War—could have made the contributions that they did, but, like the aircraft and airmen of the "Great War," the accomplishments of these early rotorcraft and their indomitable crews must not be minimized.[51]

There were other elements in the first months of Korea's air war that foreshadowed the operations of 1951-1953, such as night attack and early attempts at night close air support. The night war, as we shall see, took on a fascinating complexity all its own. As

August slipped into September, the North Korean army had met its Marne on the banks of the Naktong river. The war of movement — from the North Korean perspective — had come to an end. Their offensive campaign became defensive. Already Allied air power had bought time for Douglas MacArthur's counterstroke. Naval aviation, in the bitter Pusan fighting, was crucial in acquiring that time. Already one lesson of Korean air warfare was apparent: short of using atomic weapons, air power could not on its own defeat North Korea. But while it might not be able to produce a United Nations' victory, it could and did prevent the North from overrunning the South.

3/VICTORY—AND RETREAT

Korea's wartime history separates roughly into four phases: the North Korean invasion, the Allied counterassault beginning in mid-September 1950, the Chinese intervention from early November to the beginning of January 1951, and, finally, the seesaw war of stalemate that followed until the armistice of July 1953. Following General Walton Walker's defense of the Pusan pocket, the second phase of the Korean War opened at 12:53 on September 13, as ships of the Inch'on invasion force took Wolmi-do island under fire.

MacArthur's Inch'on invasion—"a Twentieth Century Cannae ever to be studied," in the words of British historian David Rees—was a bold and ultimately successful attempt to strike deep into the enemy's rear areas, destroying the North Korean army's line of communications and logistical network, and opening a second front that would ease Walker's task as he began the long drive north from the Pusan pocket. In many ways, the Inch'on landing was typical of MacArthur: flamboyant, fraught with risks, and with the touches of shrewd calculation and broad strategy that were a hallmark of his remarkable career. MacArthur had labored long and hard to sell the Joint Chiefs of Staff on the idea of Operation *Chromite*, as the Inch'on landing was known, including a moving speech in which he concluded "Inch'on will not fail. Inch'on will succeed. And it will save 100,000 lives." In the audience, CNO Admiral Forrest Sherman answered "Thank you. A great voice in a great cause." But he added later to COMNAVFE Admiral Turner Joy, "I wish I had that man's confidence."[1]

Aside from its strategic goals, Inch'on had four sequential objectives: the capture of Wolmi-do island, a small but critically important spit of land controlling the harbor approaches; a landing in the city itself; rapid seizure of Kimpo airfield; and the liberation of Seoul and restoration of the Rhee government to power. To accomplish this, MacArthur created X Corps, commanded by Major General Edward Almond, a joint Marine-Army-ROK force composed of the First Marine Division and the Army's 7th Infantry Division. Both were understrength; the 1st Marines could muster only two regiments for the landing, with others following soon thereafter, and the 7th Division made up its shortages by filling 40% of its ranks with ROK troops. Many difficulties compounded MacArthur's problem, not the least of which were Inch'on's peculiar topology and hydrographic conditions. A landing bucked tricky currents, fierce tides, a high seawall, and narrow channels susceptible to enemy mining. Inch'on required skill, thorough planning, and not a little measure of good fortune. But, as Niccolò Machiavelli had written over five centuries previously, fortune "lets herself be overcome by the bold," and MacArthur and his commanders did not lack for boldness and audacity.[2]

Quite naturally, since the landing was a joint effort of the Navy and Marines, its planners recognized the necessity of supporting the operation through naval air power. The Fifth Air Force, therefore, flew in a supporting role (though a very important one to neutralize any North Korean airfields that might act as staging bases for attacks upon the invasion fleet or beachhead), cutting railroads and bridges, furnishing reconnaissance, and taking over the bulk of tactical air operations supporting Walker's planned breakout from the Pusan pocket. The heavy naval presence previously supporting Pusan now had to shift to Korea's west coast in support of Inch'on. Though occasionally querulous disagreements flared between the Navy and the Air Force over who would control what, such exchanges did not, in fact, endanger the success of the operation itself, and, indeed, the services' air activities ensured the destruction of the North Korean army confronting Almond and Walker.

The greatest assembly of naval air power since the Second World War was available to MacArthur at Inch'on:

Task Force 77
Fast Carrier Force
Carrier Division 1

U.S.S. Philippine Sea
  Air Group 11

VF-112	Grumman F9F Panther
VF-113	Vought F4U Corsair
VF-114	Vought F4U Corsair
VA-115	Douglas AD Skyraider

Carrier Division 3
  U.S.S. *Valley Forge*
    Air Group 5

VF-51	Grumman F9F Panther
VF-52	Grumman F9F Panther
VF-53	Vought F4U Corsair
VF-54	Vought F4U Corsair
VA-55	Douglas AD Skyraider

Carrier Division 5
  U.S.S. *Boxer*
    Air Group 2

VF-21	Vought F4U Corsair
VF-22	Vought F4U Corsair
VF-63	Vought F4U Corsair
VF-64	Vought F4U Corsair
VF-65	Douglas AD Skyraider

Task Group 90.5
Air Support Group

TG 90.51 (CVE Element)
  U.S.S. *Badoeng Strait*

VMF-323	Vought F4U Corsair

  U.S.S. *Sicily*

VMF-214	Vought F4U Corsair

Task Force 91
Blockade and Covering Force

H.M.S. *Triumph*

800 Sqdn FAA	Supermarine Seafire

827 Sqdn FAA   Fairey Firefly

Task Force 99

Patrol and Reconnaissance Group)

TG 99.1 (Search and Reconnaissance Group)

VP6   Lockheed P2V Neptune

88 Sqdn RAF   Short Sunderland

209 Sqdn RAF   Short Sunderland

TG 99.2 (Patrol and Escort Group)

VP-42   Martin PBM Mariner

VP-47   Martin PBM Mariner

With Task Forces 91 and 99 watching the flanks and extremities, MacArthur could count on supporting X Corps with no less than 10 Corsair squadrons and three Skyraider squadrons, with four squadrons of Panthers to provide cover and undertake secondary strike duties. Thus, if X Corps could get ashore, little doubt existed whether Navy and Marine air could support them. To ensure that operations went smoothly, without the kind of communication and liaison problems that had plagued operations around Pusan, Tactical Air Squadron One established a floating Tactical Air Direction Center (TADC) aboard the invasion flagship U.S.S. *Mount McKinley* (AGC-7), with a backup aboard the U.S.S. *George Clymer* (APA-27). "TACRON ONE" and responsibility for coordinating air defense and controlling the movements of all aircraft.[3]

The 230-ship invasion force, under the command of Vice Admiral Arthur D. Struble and designated as Joint Task Force Seven, began assembling in late August. Planners worried about the Soviet Union's reaction to an invasion; the fleet would operate deep in the Yellow Sea, no more than 200 miles from the Soviet Union's major military facilites at Port Arthur. Would Stalin lash out? On September 4, as TF 77 ravaged Korea's west coast, an incident occurred that disquieted invasion planners. In the early afternoon, shipboard radar detected a blip 60 miles out moving at about 200 mph on a straight-line course from Port Arthur towards the task force. A four-ship formation of VF-53's Corsairs vectored towards the "bogie" (unidentified aircraft), which split into two radar images; one aircraft reversed course and retired, but the other continued towards the fleet. Thirty miles from the task force, the Corsairs intercepted the latter, which turned out to be a twin-engine airplane bearing Soviet markings — probably a Tupolev Tu-2 light bomber and reconnaissance aircraft. The Soviet pilot panicked, went to full power, and dove east, towards North Korea. The Corsairs followed, and suddenly a gunner aboard the Soviet plane took them under fire, transforming the bogie into a "hostile." The Corsairs' flight leader radioed *Valley Forge*, received permission to return fire, and, together with his wingman, sent the Soviet plane flaming into the Yellow Sea. It was not the first time that Soviet and Navy aircraft had come into conflict: not quite five months before, on April 8, Soviet fighters had shot down a Convair PB4Y Privateer of VP-26 over the Baltic, killing all 10 crewmen; this time the results had been quite different. Was this a foreshadowing? Inch'on's planners could not know, but precautions increased, particularly air defense planning and antisubmarine patrols.[4]

Air activity in support of the Inch'on landing started at the beginning of September. TF 77's mandate for the operation included devoting 40% of its sorties to targets in the Inch'on-Seoul area, with the remaining 60% equally split on targets north and south of Inch'on. In early September, *Valley Forge* and *Philippine Sea* attacked targets ranging from Seoul and P'yongyang to the west coast port of Chinnamp'o; *Phillipine Sea* alone launched 82 sorties on 1 September. Meanwhile, to confuse North Korea about the location of the planned assault, intelligence planted the rumor that an invasion would take place at the southwestern port of Kunsan. To give the rumor credence, Marine troops received briefings on Kunsan's defenses. The briefers made certain that local Koreans—possibly including North Korean agents—were within earshot. To further the deception, the carriers *Triumph* and *Badoeng Strait*, together with FEAF's bombers, raided the transportation links and electrical power network around Kunsan. TF 77 went into Sasebo harbor for four days of replenishment, leaving only the two CVEs and *Triumph* on station in the Yellow Sea; *Boxer* was still enroute from Pearl, and Typhoon *Kezia* swept across its path, forcing a delay in its arrival so that it did not actually dock at Sasebo until the 14th. It sailed almost immediately with a team from TACRON ONE so that it could join its sisters on the line off Inch'on. *Valley Forge* and *Philippine Sea*, meanwhile, left Sasebo on the 11th. They took up station on the 12th in the Yellow Sea, and began intensive flight operations against Wolmi-do, P'yongyang, Inch'on, and Seoul, and attempted

99

to destroy any potential resistance on Wolmi-do and disrupt the road and rail network around the invasion area. The two CVEs went into Sasebo for quick replenishment and returned to the line. Finally, everything was set for the combined carrier power of TF 77 and TG 90.5 to blitz the Inch'on area on the morning of the invasion, 15 September.[5]

Like everything else in the Inch'on operation, the timing worked perfectly; already the North Koreans had been planning to sow Inch'on's approaches with Russian sea mines (as they did on the east coast port of Wonsan, with great success), but logistical problems and the rapid pace of developments fortunately prevented them from planting any of the lethal devices before the invasion commenced. At 4:54 on the morning of the invasion, as the first fingers of rosy light probed across the eastern sky, the blue strike aircraft of TF 77 and TG 90.5 commenced their runs on Wolmi-do, smothering it with rockets, bombs, napalm, and 20-mm strafing. The naval bombardment commenced at 5:40, and MacArthur went to the bridge of the *Mount McKinley* to monitor the landing. "As I watched," he recalled, "blue Corsairs swooped down from the clouds and added their strafing to the destruction."[6]

Assessing the havoc they had caused before the landing, one VMF-232 pilot concluded that Wolmi-do was "one worthless piece of real estate," but the Marines did not wish to take any chances, remembering, perhaps, how American troops on Omaha Beach had suffered from lack of air support as they came ashore. As the Marine landing craft approached the beach, 38 Corsairs from VMF-214 and

VMF-323 covered their run. The first Leathernecks scrambled onto Wolmi-do's Green Beach at 6:33; the Corsairs furnished CAS as close as 50 yards in front of them. MacArthur received word that the Marines had cleared Wolmi-do's primary objectives by 8:00; he turned to Rear Admiral James H. Doyle, the amphibious wizard who had planned much of the assault, and said, "Say to the Fleet 'The Navy and Marines have never shone more brightly than this morning.' "

At 5:33 in the afternoon, the first Marines hit Inch'on's Red Beach, supported by friendly fire from their comrades on Wolmi-do (still smoking from the napalm treatment), and the ever-present ADs and F4Us of TF 77 and TG 90.5. Some ADs flew so low over the incoming landing craft that they pelted Marines in the boats with a hot cascade of 20-mm shell casings as they fired on Inch'on's defenders. Unlike the bloodbaths of Tarawa or Iwo Jima, the Inch'on landing went smoothly, though fierce fighting took place nevertheless. As night fell, 13,000 troops had landed and the beachhead was secure; the success of this "impossible" landing was attributable to thorough planning and preparation, the courage of its participants, and the overwhelming application of Navy and Marine CAS in support of the landing force.[7]

During the first day of the invasion, TF 77 and TG 90.5 flew a total of 302 sorties for a loss of two aircraft, the pilots of which were recovered safely. *Boxer*, newly arrived from her second urgent transit of the Pacific, contributed 42 sorties. Overall, during two weeks of Inch'on-related operations, from

September 6 through 21, the five carriers off Korea's west coast maintained impressive sortie rates, as indicated below:

Ship	Sorties
U.S.S. *Philippine Sea*	878
U.S.S. *Valley Forge*	826
U.S.S. *Boxer*	545
U.S.S. *Badoeng Strait*	474
U.S.S. *Sicily*	366

The records of *Badoeng Strait* and *Sicily*, operating one Corsair squadron apiece, are especially indicative of the intense pace of combat operations.[8]

Losses, however, were not inconsequential. Altogether, during this time, the carriers lost two Panthers, nine Corsairs, one Skyraider, and one HO3S helicopter. North Korean flak, dismissed as largely ineffectual during the summer of 1950, had intensified greatly by the time of Inch'on; even relatively small units were able to defend themselves with 12.7-mm machine gun fire or even 37-mm cannon. Larger 76-mm and 85-mm flak cannon abounded around Seoul and north to P'yongyang. The incessant demands of close air support, especially to stave off large numbers of T-34 tanks that threatened the Marines during their advance on Kimpo field, the suburb of Yongdungp'o, and Seoul, led to heavier losses than expected and numerous close calls. On September 16, for example, eight Blacksheep Corsairs napalmed and rocketed a T-34 column that threatened Marine infantry, but lost one Corsair and

102

its pilot to flak. Blacksheep squadron leader Lieutenant Colonel Walt Lischeid took a hit and crashed to his death trying to nurse his crippled Corsair back to Kimpo field, which was captured on September 17. Another highly respected VMF-214 pilot, Major Robert Floeck, subsequently fell to antiaircraft fire as well. Inch'on had been a costly operation for the Blacksheep.[9]

Once some stubborn North Korean counterattacks had been driven off, Marine air moved ashore to Kimpo. On the evening of September 19, VMF(N)-542 landed, a night-fighter squadron flying two-seat Grumman F7F-3N Tigercats. Corsair squadrons VMF-212 and VMF-312 arrived the next day. The Tigercats went into operation on the morning of September 20, and flew daylight CAS missions as well as night harassment and support sorties. But even these powerful aircraft were not immune to losses. On September 24, the squadron lost its intelligence officer and his radar operator to flak during a CAS strike northwest of Seoul. The next day, squadron commander Lieutenant Colonel Max J. Volcansek took hits, and while staggering back to Kimpo, jettisoned a wing fuel tank which came adrift and wedged crossways between the engine nacelle and the fuselage, throwing the plane out of control and forcing the pilot to parachute to safety. Another Tigercat, on a reconnaissance sortie, took a 37-mm hit that blew a two-foot by four-foot hole in the right wing ("Enough to give a man a case of the willies," the pilot observed), but managed to limp back to Kimpo. Flown at night or in the hours of dusk and predawn, the heavily armed Tigercat could be lethal; flown on CAS or reconnaissance during the day, it offered an unacceptably large target to the ever-present gunners of the North Korean army.[10]

Such losses, never easy to accept, nevertheless did not endanger the success of the operation. Inch'on finished the North Korean army as a fighting force, inflicting a profound defeat on the troops of the "all triumphant, resolute and incomparable commander and outstanding military strategist," Kim Il Sung. There are revisionists who argue that Inch'on was unnecessary, that air power alone broke the back of the North Korean army, and the the troops landed at Inch'on could have accomplished more if they had been inserted into the Pusan pocket instead. Such critics would do well to recall the dreadfully slow struggle up the Italian peninsula during the Second World War or, for that matter, the post-1950 ebb-and-flow along the 38th Parallel. Given the often-times fierce resistance at Inch'on and the slow start of Walker's breakout from Pusan, it is likely that Allied casualties would have been immense if the North Korean Army had remained intact and confronted the Allies on a single front. By 1952, even the most sanguine air power enthusiasts recognized that overwhelming Allied air power alone could not force a decision; as the Navy's third Korean War evaluation report perceptively concluded, "The rifle-man is the central figure in the Korean War; he has *not* been supplanted by air power."[11] Planned as a combined arms masterstroke, Inch'on lived up to its promise; after it, the North Korean army was on the skids. But its success did nothing to resolve another nagging question in the minds of the United Nations

Command: what would Mao Tse-tung's reaction be as North Korea faced defeat? To those at the front, such matters seemed remote; as Marguerite "Maggie" Higgins, a gutsy war correspondent for the New York *Herald Tribune* wrote later, "We were giddy with victory. None of us could know how temporary that victory was to be."[12]

Twelve days after the landing at Inch'on, on September 27, units of the X Corps and the Eighth Army linked up near Osan. Only 25,000 of the estimated 70,000 North Koreans who had advanced south staggered back across the 38th Parallel: one division commander could muster only 200 officers and men. That same day, the Joint Chiefs of Staff authorized MacArthur's forces to pursue the North Koreans above the parallel; on the first of October, ROK troops advanced across the demarcation line into the north.[13] MacArthur planned a second amphibious landing at Wonsan for October 20, but the crafty mining of the harbor and its approaches aborted this operation. X Corps' and Eighth Army's rapid advance did not suffer from the mining, and, in fact, Wonsan fell to a land-borne assault by ROK troops on October 10, well ahead of schedule. On October 13, the first land-based Marine air arrived at Wonsan's captured airfield, and by the end of the month, the Corps had Corsair squadrons VMF-312 and VMF(N)-513 flying combat from Wonsan, though the lack of local logistical support by sealift caused numerous operational problems because the two squadrons required replenishment overland, or by airlift from Kimpo and Japan.[14] P'yongyang fell with desultory resistance on October 19, and Kim Il

105

Sung withdrew the remnants of his shattered government to Sinuiju, a border city on the Yalu river.

In preparation for the projected Wonsan invasion, Far East command had agreed that the Fifth Air Force would support the advancing Eighth Army, that Marine air would continue to support X Corps, and that TF 77 would control all air activities within a 50-mile radius of the Wonsan beachhead. But with the invasion plan scrubbed by the mining and the unexpectedly rapid advance of X Corps through the area, this plan came under criticism from Air Force representatives, who feared the loss of coordination over Allied tactical air power in Korea. MacArthur eventually concurred, and the Fifth Air Force received coordination control over the First Marine Air Wing (1st MAW), though the FEAF commanding general, Stratemeyer, wisely directed the Fifth's commander, Lieutenant General Pat Patridge, to continue utilizing the 1st MAW in support of Almond's X Corps. MacArthur's decision did not sit well with Navy and Marine commanders, but remained the basic operational arrangement through the end of the war. As a result, Fifth Air Force required X Corps to furnish it with a daily listing of air support tasks, using the list to generate orders to the 1st MAW. As the official history of Air Force operations in Korea concludes, "this was a burdensome procedure and represented an unrealistic compliance with accepted air-ground doctrine."[15]

In fact, however, actual employment of the 1st MAW often worked much more smoothly, as was evidenced in the bitter fighting during the retreat from Chosin and, for that matter, in the last weeks of the war itself. Major General V. E. Megee, commander of the 1st MAW at the time of the armistice, alluded to the problems in his general order issued on the last day of the war, writing that, "the Wing's association with the Eighth Army, the Fifth Air Force and the Seventh U.S. Fleet in combined operations had been a professionally broadening experience—teaching tolerance, teamwork, and flexibility of operations."[16] The official Marine Corps history notes that doctrinal differences "were never fully reconciled," but "the command structure did work."[17]

With the ground situation shaping up nicely as the North Koreans fell back in disarray, the greatest problem confronting the Navy as October began was the mining of the ports of Wonsan, Hungnam, and Chinnamp'o. Intended to thwart Allied invasion plans, the mines now served to hinder the usefulness of these ports for logistical supply. When conventional sweeping proved tedious and dangerous—several boats (including a destroyer) were lost or damaged with heavy loss of life—COMNAVFE gave TF 77 and the patrol squadrons a crack at it. Formation attacks of Skyraiders and Corsairs armed with hydrostatically fused bombs proved virtually useless, as the bomb pattern lacked the density necessary to trigger the detonation of a mine field. Helicopters proved useful as mine spotters, though one nearly crashed when it blew up a mine with gunfire and several other mines exploded sympathetically (a rare occurrence). Patrol planes, with their .50-caliber turret and waist gun positions, proved useful, but the work was often frustrating and tedious. A terse excerpt from the October activity report of VP-47, a squadron flying Martin PBM Mariner patrol seaplanes, offers a good example of these difficult operations:

On 10 October BA-9 [one of the squadron's planes] spotted [a] field of about 50 moored mines close in to Wonsan. Efforts to destroy mines with 325 lb. depth charges proved unsuccessful. On 11 October BA-1 exploded one mine by gunfire of waist-gunner but another failed to explode after many direct hits, but sank. On 12 October BA-6 discovered [a] large moored mine field near Yo-do island which was depth charged without results. BA-4 spotted approximately 30 mines east of Wonsan on 15 October. BA-1 fired 1200 rounds at a floating mine on 18 October, scoring many hits before sinking it. On 26 October, a beached mine failed to explode after direct hits. On 28 October a floating mine was destroyed with 30 rounds of gunfire, but a second one, washed ashore, failed to explode after several hits were observed. On 29 October BA-3 sighted a mine field of 26 mines and destroyed 4 with gunfire.[18]

On October 12, the Navy lost the minesweeper U.S.S. *Pirate* (AM-275) and U.S.S. *Pledge* (AM-277) to mines; only the presence of gunfire support ships and a VP-47 Mariner prevented the heavy loss of life from being worse. As the gunfire support ships shelled Korean gun positions menacing rescue operations, Lieutenant Commander Randall Boyd and his PBM crew circled around the harbor, strafing enemy positions with the Mariner's turret and waist guns. The improbability of the large and ungainly patrol plane serving in an attack role might have thrown off the North Koreans' aim. Boyd's tail gunner reported many large black bursts, indicative of 76-mm and 85-mm flak, but the fact that the flak burst *behind* the slow plane instead of ahead of it suggests that the gunners were woefully inept. In short order, Corsairs and Skyraiders arrived to plaster the defenses while rescue crews picked up survivors.[19] In time, the partnership of airplane and helicopter spotting, coupled with surface sweeping, ended the menace, and Wonsa, Hungnam and Chinnamp'o were open for business. But sweeping operations remained an integral part of the Navy's Korean mission through 1953, and the experience offered a clear warning for the future.

October 1950 brought changes to the fleet. On October 8, the *Essex*-class carrier U.S.S. *Leyte* (CV-32) reported to TF 77 after steaming 18,500 miles from the Mediterranean, bringing TF 77's carriers to four. When her Air Group 3 (consisting of Panther squadrons VF-31 and -32, Corsair squadrons VF-33 and -34, and Skyraider-equipped VA-35) participated in Wonsan area strikes with the other three air groups on October 15, it was the first time that four *Essex*-class carriers had operated together since the Second World War. *Boxer*, having performed steadfastly over the previous month, had stripped a reduction gear; the "Busy Bee" left the task force on October 22 and did not return to the war until the following March. Changes affected the smaller carriers as well. Though *Badoeng Strait* and *Sicily* continued operations, H.M.S. *Theseus* replaced the veteran *Triumph* on October 8 and introduced the Hawker Sea Fury to Korean skies when the pilots of 807 Squadron began operations. Sister unit 810 Squadron flew Fireflies. But worthwhile targets for the carriers were becoming increasingly scarce. Following the cancellation of the Wonsan invasion, TF 77 had responsibility for destroying enemy forces, communications, and installations in the area east of 127° East Longitude and north of the bombline established by Fifth Air Force's Joint Operations Center. (The bombline was essentially a demarcation beyond which one could attack ground targets without fear of hitting friendly forces, and without having to coordinate such strikes with ground commanders.) But the ground advance moved ahead so swiftly that the bombline advanced further and further north until the task force noted that worthwhile targets were becoming fewer and fewer. COMCARDIV 1, Rear Admiral Edward C. Ewen aboard *Philippine Sea*, remarked on October 21 that:

No attacks were made on enemy installations because of the confusing situation in the target areas. At this time it became definitely apparent that the remaining Korean territory held by the enemy forces was so small that there was not enough physical space for all the effective aircraft available.[20]

Thus, TF 77 actually began curtailing its operations.

110

But all this changed dramatically in early November.

For weeks, disquieting reports of a Chinese buildup in Manchuria, the crossing into North Korea of Chinese "volunteers," and bellicose statements from Peking, had worried Allied planners. By the end of October, a few Chinese prisoners showed up among captured North Korean troops. Then, in early November, events unfolded with ominous swiftness. Chinese troops attacked Walker's overextended Eighth Army and, in cautious response, he ordered a regrouping along the Ch'ongch'on river. On November 5, MacArthur, alarmed, ordered the destruction of the international bridges between Manchuria (China) and North Korea, stipulating that only the spans nearest the Korean shoreline be dropped. The Joint Chiefs of Staff countermanded his order, reversed themselves within a day, and left its execution up to the Air Force and Navy.[21]

Most disturbing to airmen, however, was the appearance of a new factor in the Korean air war: the Soviet-built MiG-15 jet fighter. On November 1, six MiGs crossed the Yalu river and bounced a formation of Mustangs and a T-6 Mosquito; the American aircraft managed to evade the clumsy attack, and raced back to their fields with the unwelcome news. While the appearance of the MiG in Korea was a shock, the discovery of the plane itself came as no surprise. The design bureau of Artem Mikoyan and Mikhail Gurevich had started work on the MiG-15 in March 1946, after extracting information on the sweptwing concept from the rubble of Nazi Germany's aeronautical establishment. The purchase of Rolls Royce Nene turbojets from Great Britain's postwar government (at a time when the Nene was not yet in British service!) greatly accelerated its development, as the Soviets put a Nene derivative into production for the MiG as well as other Soviet jet aircraft. The first MiG-15s prototype flew on December 30, 1947, barely 2½ months after the first flight of its greatest rival — and ultimate master — the North American F-86 Sabre. The MiG had a deceptively chunky appearance, with a heavily braced canopy, sweptwing and tail surfaces, anhedral (drooped) wings, a horizontal tail placed high on the vertical fin, and a simple "pitot" nose air inlet. Cleared for service in October 1948, the first MiG-15 had an armament of two slow-firing 23-mm cannon and an equally slow 37-mm cannon: ideal for shooting down Boeing B-29s, the "threat" aircraft Mikoyan and Gurevich had designed it to confront. In September 1949, the Soviet Union flew the more advanced MiG-15SD, popularly known as the MiG-15bis. It had faster firing 23-mm cannon, redesigned speed brakes, and boosted ailerons for better high-speed control effectiveness. Eventually both the early MiG-15 and the MiG-15bis appeared in Korean skies.[22]

Western intelligence had known of the plane following the prototype's appearance at the 1948 Tushino Air Show outside Moscow. At the 1949 May Day parade, 45 flew over reviewers perched upon Lenin's Tomb, and at the 1950 May Day parade, 139 streaked overhead, together with 64 Tupolev Tu-4 strategic bombers, a Soviet copy of the B-29. Originally dubbed the "Type 14" by American technical intelligence, by 1950 its true identity was known. An excellent three-view drawing and accompanying sketch appeared in the *Naval Aviation Confidential Bulletin* for January 1950, and the Air Force's *Air Intelligence Digest* ran a good photograph of one in its July 1950 edition.[23] The appearance of the MiG immediately posed problems for bomber and attack crews operating near Manchuria, as most of them flew comparatively slow propeller-driven aircraft. But the sweptwing MiG clearly promised to outperform even the straight-wing F-80 and F9F jets; how much remained to be seen. Already the Navy recognized that the peculiar conditions of Korean fighting, especially the lack of enemy air opposition, had permitted naval air power to operate with a relatively free hand. The introduction of the MiG threatened to change that.

With a crisis building in North Korea, FEAF's Bomber Command attacked strategic cities and towns near the border and, in a campaign echoing the late stages of the air war against Japan, launched Superfortress firebomb raids to destroy them. At the same time, Stratemeyer realized that the bombers could not destroy all the bridges across the Yalu on their own, and he called upon COMNAVFE to provide assistance from TF 77. At the time, TF 77 was fully committed to providing close support and interdiction strikes (the pace of combat had quickened appreciably since late October), but Admiral Joy changed this on November 8 with an urgent dispatch to Seventh Fleet's commander, Vice Admiral Struble. It requested that TF 77 participate in MacArthur's bridge-bombing campaign. The message stressed that Manchurian airspace must not be violated. Admiral Joy followed this with a message directed to all naval aviators participating in the raids, again stressing the necessity of staying on the Korean side of the Yalu and Tumen rivers. This imposed severe operational constraints. Traditional tactical practice called for aircraft attacking bridges to follow the road or railbed across the bridge, releasing their bombs so that they would "walk" across the bridge and inflict maximum damage. Under the best of circumstances, bridges are difficult targets, for the flooring of the bridge can be easily replaced, and the vulnerable points — trusses, supports, and abutments — are difficult to damage.

With Manchuria inviolable, MacArthur's aircraft had to attack the bridges from the side, as torpedo planes would a ship, but with considerably less prospect for success. If this were not bad enough, these rules of engagement also prevented flak suppression flights from attacking antiaircraft installations on the Manchurian side of the rivers. Fighters flying "TARCAP" (Target Combat Air Patrol) were prohibited from engaging enemy fighters over Manchurian territory, or from exercising "hot pursuit" of those that slipped across the border, attacked American formations, and then dove back across the river. The frustrations of fighter, bomber, and attack aircrew can easily be imagined.[24]

On November 8, FEAF's Bomber Command set out to drop the railroad and highway bridges across the Yalu at Sinuiju. Directly opposite lay the Manchurian city of Antung (now the city of Dandong) and its major military airfield. Predictably, a formation of MiGs crossed the Yalu and attacked the escorting F-80s; the F-80s met the attack smartly and, despite the obvious inferiority of the Shooting Star to the MiG, managed to send one of the sweptwing jets down in flames. The bridges remained standing, however, and the next day TF 77 set out to try its luck.[25]

In addition to the problems of attacking the bridges without violating Manchurian airspace, the strikes posed special operational difficulties. TF 77, then in the Sea of Japan, had to launch strikes across Korea; a distance of 225 miles separated the bridges from the carriers. Planners directed that ADs take out the bridges with either a pair of 1,000-pound bombs, or a single 2,000-pound bomb; the Skyraiders also carried full ammunition (400 rounds) for their two 20-mm cannon. Escorting F4Us carried a single 500-pound bomb, six HVARs, and 880 rounds of 20-mm to deal with flak emplacements. F9Fs furnished TARCAP, and carried only full ammunition (760 rounds of 20-mm) to deal with fighters. A typical strike group consisted of 8 ADs, 16 flak-suppression F4Us, and 8–16 TARCAP F9Fs. Because of the difference in cruising speeds and fuel consumption, the strike group's jet escort launched 50 minutes after the props took off, so that they could rendezvous with the prop aircraft and furnish them with 8–10 minutes of cover on the run-in to the target, and an additional 30-minutes coverage in the target area. A second jet launch 15 minutes after the first Panthers catapulted aloft would pick up the strike force as it left the target area, escorting it back to the fleet. Everyone recognized that fuel reserves would be critical, particularly for the thirsty jets.[26]

On November 9, *Valley Forge* and *Philippine Sea* launched strikes against various Yalu bridges; the Sinuiju strikes were the most important, and sparked the first encounters between MiG-15s and escorting Navy Panthers. During the *Philippine Sea*'s morning strike on Sinuiju, two MiGs attacked the formation, the prop planes turning into them and evading their attack. The escort leader, Lieutenant Commander William T. "Tom" Amen, commanding officer of VF-111, spotted one of the MiGs trailing his formation, and, with his wingman and another two-ship of F9Fs, turned to meet the MiG head-on. The MiG pilot broke into a rapid climb from 4,000 to 15,000 feet, then leveled off and began a fishtail motion, as if trying to keep track of the Panthers behind him or perhaps throw off their aim. All this did, however, was enable the Panthers to stay in range, blasting away with their 20-mm and scoring some hits. The MiG next entered an ever-steepening dive, with Amen "boresighted" and scoring heavily. At low altitude, the Panther buffeted violently from trim changes as it reached its limiting Mach number (still well below the speed of sound). At 3,000 feet the MiG rolled over on its back, still diving; "He's either nuts or got a wonderful airplane," Amen thought to himself, and pulled hard to level out at 200 feet and climb away as his wingman exultantly called out that the MiG had exploded in the wooded Korean hills, starting a forest fire.[27] Later in the day, VF-52 skipper Lieutenant Commander William E. Lamb and Lieutenant R. E. Parker shared a MiG for the "Happy Valley's" air group, following it in a high-speed dive to low altitude and leaving it smoking heavily as it curved back into Manchuria. As other *Valley Forge* pilots watched, the MiG suddenly exploded, bits of wreckage fluttering down over the Manchurian side of the river. Slightly over a week later, Ensign F. C. Weber of *Leyte's* VF-31 destroyed another. Was the MiG overrated?[28]

In fact, the MiG-15, if properly flown, could have devastated the Yalu river strike forces, and the 3-0 kill record in favor of the Panthers reflected the superior ability of the Navy's airmen and the sloppy flying of the Communist fighters. *Valley Forge's* action report

. . . noted with grave concern the reported superior performance of the MiG-15 as opposed to the F9F-3. It is believed that if they had been manned by pilots as aggressive and well trained as ours that [our] own pilot and plane losses would have been great.[29]

COMCARDIV 3, in an endorsement of the report to the Chief of Naval Operations, stated "If our fast carriers expect to maintain an offensive, an improved carrier jet fighter must be obtained in the near future."[30] The Navy's first Korean War evaluation report recommended:

At high priority provide a carrier fighter capable of combating contemporary developments of the MiG-15. The F9F had inadequate performance for fully effective defense against MiG-15 type jet fighters.[31]

The MiG-15 and the Ilyushin Il-28 twin-jet bomber (which soon appeared on Manchurian airfields, though it never entered combat over Korea) posted serious challenges to fleet air defense planning. If either or both of these aircraft sortied against the fleet, proper interception of them would require prompt detection. Radar detection depended upon a multitude of variables, including the number of targets, their altitude, size, and speed. By and large, Second World War era shipboard radars were disappointing. The newer SPS-6B system, installed on some vessels, did perform much better; it was able, for example, to detect a single B-29 operating at an altitude of 20,000 feet as far as 180 miles from the fleet. A single jet could get as close as 35 miles from the fleet before it had a 75% chance of being detected. Accepted fleet air defense doctrine held that an incoming strike had to be intercepted no closer than 25 miles from the fleet to allow for inspection, communication by the combat air patrol with the Combat Information Center (CIC) aboard ship, and at least one firing pass; at a distance of 10 miles, this doctrine held that fighters would break off combat to allow escort destroyers and cruisers to throw up a curtain of proximity-fused antiaircraft fire. The closure speeds of newer aircraft severely taxed fleet defense planning. Whereas, for example, a single Soviet Tu-4 (the Soviet copy of the B-29) cruising at 350 mph had to be detected no less than 84 miles from the fleet in order for intercepting F4U-5 Corsairs to engage it (78 miles for the faster F9F Panthers), a faster MiG-15 or Il-28 moving at 500 mph demanded detection at no less than 150 miles so that Panthers could have a chance of intercepting it. (Radar problems were not unique to the Navy; in 1951, a pair of MiGs escaped detection and boldly overflew Seoul before leisurely turning north again.)

The unreliability of airborne IFF (Identification Friend or Foe) radar transponders further complicated the situation and led to false alarms when friendly aircraft showed the wrong IFF codes, as well as uneasiness even when the system worked. Most Allied aircraft used the World War Two vintage Mark III IFF, 500 sets of which had been supplied to the Soviet Union during the war. The more modern jets used more secure Mark X IFF. That explains the nervousness of carrier commanders— particularly the CVE skippers operating in the restricted waters off Korea's west coast, surrounded on three sides by hostile territory—when large formations of airplanes, whether showing IFF or not, appeared on their screens. FEAF eventually decreed in May 1951 that just because an aircraft showed a Mark III IFF code on radar, operators should not assume it was friendly, a disconcerting factor in play until the end of the war.[32]

In response to the sudden appearance of the MiG-15 and its obvious superiority to the Navy's straight-wing jet fighters, the Bureau of Aeronautics began a search for a successor to the straight-wing Panther and Banshee then in service. The service already had the sweptwing McDonnell F3H-1 Demon under development, but the propulsion problems that would eventually cripple this program were already evident. The Bureau's search eventually resulted in three good airplanes. Grumman quickly developed a sweptwing version of the Panther, the F9F-6, -7, and -8 Cougar family, which entered squadron service in November 1952, a remarkably short time, though it did not, in any case, arrive in Korean waters until after the armistice. North American "navalized" the F-86 as the FJ-2, -3, and -4 Fury which likewise entered fleet service after the war. In 1953, BuAer authorized development of the Vought F8U-1 Crusader, a supersonic fighter that entered service in 1957 and which handily mastered the MiG-17 and MiG-21 in North Vietnamese skies a decade later. But in the meantime, for the rest of the Korean War, the Navy had to rely upon the superior training of its pilots and slightly more powerful versions of the proven F9F Panther.

Between November 9 and November 21, TF 77's airmen made repeated raids on the Yalu river bridges, always in the face of intense antiaircraft fire and sometimes with MiG oppositions as well. Though they dropped some spans, notably three of the Sinuiju highway bridges and two bridges at Hyesanjin, both FEAF's bomber campaign and the Navy's raids proved disappointing. Despite intense attacks, for example, the Sinuiju railway bridge remained standing. The campaigns also smacked of locking the barn door after the horse had already bolted. By mid-November, UN estimates of the total number of enemy troops (Chinese as well as North Korean) in the north topped 145,000. In reality by that time 180,000 Chinese troops had crossed the Yalu, in four armies comprised of three divisions apiece, starting with General Lin Piao's Fourth Field

Army, which entered North Korea in mid-October. The Yalu river strikes, then, only promised to complicate logistical supply to an enemy already in place; it could not prevent what had, in fact, already occurred: the large-scale movement of hostile forces into North Korea to prevent its total collapse in the face of an Allied onslaught aimed at annexing the north to the south it had so savagely assaulted. The raids taxed TF 77, for they required complicated planning; under the best circumstances, aircraft returned with minimal fuel reserves and no margin for leaks. Skyraiders returned from Sinuiju with the most fuel, nearly 170 gallons. But Corsairs came back with just 70, and the Panthers with 133 gallons, not much given the fuel consumption characteristics of the early "blowtorches."[33]

On November 24, the Allied line in North Korea ran from a point just slightly north of Sinanju on the west coast to the Chosin and Fusen* reservoirs, curving up to the city of Hyesanjin on the Yalu river itself (thus cutting North Korea in two), and over to a point on the east coast just below Ch'ongjin. Since mid-October, the weather had grown steadily colder. Snow had fallen near the two reservoirs, 3,400 feet above sea level, and Marines with X Corps received

---

*Spelled variously Choshin, Choshen, Changjin, and Pujon. The latter two are their Korean names, the former are derivatives of Japanese names. I have used Chosin and Fusen since these were in the most widespread use among Allied forces at the time of the war. Likewise, the town of Hagaru (also called Hagaru-ri) is now known as Changjin.

cold weather gear, including insulated trousers, heavy parkas, mittens, gloves, heavy socks, and shoe packs. At sea, snow squalls and ice on decks hampered flight operations, and forced frequent sweeping and clearing; jet exhausts were used to melt particularly heavy ice encrustations.

At 10:30 on the morning of November 25, Baker Company of the 9th Infantry Regiment came under fire; China's offensive and the third phase of the Korean War began. By the 26th, Chinese forces and Eighth Army engaged in bitter fighting all along the Ch'ongch'on river. Heavy seas, high winds, and low clouds cancelled TF 77's flight operations on the 25th, and snow squalls on the 26th kept them on deck. On November 27 and 28, despite the weather, they took to the air to help relieve the pressure on Eighth Army in the west and X Corps in the east; some had to divert to Wonsan when weather prevented them from returning to their carriers. By November 28, MacArthur's forces were on the retreat. A Marine drive westwards from the reservoirs to help the embattled Eighth Army met stiff Chinese resistance. Everywhere the Chinese appeared in large numbers, lying low by day (usually by crowding into villages and under cover) and attacking by night. Overextended, the Eighth Army collapsed despite massive air support from Fifth Air Force and even trans-Korea strikes by TF 77 that took an appalling toll on the Chinese. In the east, the forces around the reservoirs—primarily Marine, with some Army and British units as well—drew back for a long breakout through countryside filled with Chinese troops and down long narrow defiles running from

Haguru to Kot'o-ri, Hamhung, and on to the coastal port of Hungnam.[34]

As a precaution, the Navy had already studied the requirements of an emergency evacuation of Allied forces from Hungnam if the Chinese intervention took place and proved too strong for Eighth Army and X Corps. Now these preliminary plans appeared attractive as the west coast advance crumbled and the Marines contemplated their own withdrawal to the east coast. Meanwhile, Allied airpower attempted to offset the large numbers of Chinese troops by supplying the beleaguered Marines and Army forces with air support, air resupply, and aerial evacuation of wounded. By this time, the carrier *Valley Forge* had left TF 77 for a much-needed refit in the United States. Now an emergency recall summoned it back to the Sea of Japan. Pending its return, TF 77 had to make do with just two fast carriers, *Leyte* and *Philippine Sea*; the U.S.S. *Princeton* (CV-37) was on its way across the Pacific after having been reactivated from the mothball fleet over the summer. *Badoeng Strait* remained on station, but *Sicily* having disembarked VMF-214 at Wonsan, was in port, cutting CVE support for X Corps in half. H.M.S. *Theseus*, then at Hong Kong, hurried back in response to an urgent recall. Until they arrived, however, it fell to TF 77's two CVs, the "Bing-Ding," and Marine air ashore to hold the line.

In response to the Eighth Army's rapid collapse, the Navy, at FEAF's urging and despite growing pressure on the Marines at the reservoirs, sent strike forces of ADs and F4Us across the Korean peninsula to support Eighth Army as it fell back towards

P'yongyang and, eventually, past Seoul. But splitting the Navy-Marine air effort between the east and west coasts proved unsatisfactory; so chaotic were western conditions, with Mosquito controllers withdrawn and some control equipment overrun or lost, that the western strikes accomplished little to help stabilize the front. For several days, TF 77 sent so-called "armed reconnaissance" flights to a point near the Taedong river, with instructions to stand by for directions from any controller available. By the beginning of December, with growing combat near the reservoirs and the Marines beginning their breakout, such a division could no longer be tolerated, and TF 77 devoted its full attention to supporting the struggle from Chosin to the sea. The last trans-peninsula western strike occurred on December 2; thereafter, through the evacuation of Hungnam, the Navy rightly concentrated its effort in the east.[35]

The Marines began their breakout from Chosin on December 1. First, all Allied forces from the reservoir area — a total of 14,000 troops — were consolidated in Hagaru, at the base of the Chosin reservoir. This involved a particularly bitter withdrawal of Marines from Yudam-ni, on the western shore of the reservoir, down to Hagaru. Second, this large force would make its way to Kot'o-ri. Finally, it would withdraw from Kot'o-ri across the Funchilin pass to a secure perimeter at Hamhung and be evacuated from Hungnam. At the outset, Chinese forces controlled the roads and flanks of the narrow defile that embodied the Marines' escape route. But unlike the west, where Army units fractured and fell back in disarray, the forces of X Corps remained largely intact despite fierce attacks.

The fallback from the reservoirs was less a retreat than "an attack in another direction," as Marine Major General Oliver P. Smith aptly characterized it. The winding columns of troops and vehicles making their way to the coast became a magnet for Chinese attacks; they drew together the Chinese forces in concentrations that air assault coupled with savage infantry action repeatedly smashed. Without air power, the fallback from Chosin would have degenerated into disaster. As it was, it resembled few actions in previous military history. Certainly it was not Napoleon's Grand Army reeling back in frozen defeat; nor was it the frantic escape of the British Expeditionary Force to the coastal port of Dunkirk. It was, instead, an orderly fighting withdrawal that routinely displayed the highest standards of leadership, courage, and tenacity. Above all, it was a withdrawal in which the highly refined and combat-honed excellence of Navy-Marine CAS had an opportunity to prove itself. Navy planners faced two critical challenges: covering the withdrawal of the Marines as they made their way to Hungnam, and evacuating the port itself. The Navy conceived the latter operation as an Inch'on in reverse: carefully disestablishing a beachhead, withdrawing equipment, supplies, and personnel, and systematically destroying anything of value left behind. Most of all, the Navy wished to avoid the spectre of Dunkirk; the hasty, costly embarkation of demoralized and weary troops who lacked weapons, equipment, and spirit. To meet this second challenge, the Navy would have to meet the first; they would make sure that the Marines withdrew in good order. And that, of course, was largely up to the airedales.

The Chinese assault had triggered immediate calls for naval air reinforcement. *Princeton* joined TF 77 in striking at the invaders on December 5; *Sicily* reembarked the Blacksheep and returned to the fray on December 7. The light carrier U.S.S. *Bataan* (CVL-29), having just delivered aircraft to Japan, reported for duty with TF 77 on December 16, though it left for TG 96.8, joining the two CVEs, four days later. And *Valley Forge* (with a replacement air group, CAG 2, that consisted of Corsair squadrons VF-24, -63, -64, and Skyraider squadron VA-65) returned from San Diego, where it had disembarked CAG-5, reentering combat on December 23.[36] The first two weeks were particularly dangerous as the Marines struggled down to the coast. On December 1, FEAF had wisely transferred control of X Corps air support back to the 1st Marine Air Wing, and 1st MAW subsequently performed brilliantly in support of the withdrawal. Between December 1, when the breakout began, and December 11, when the Corps reached the safety of Hamhung, Marine pilots had flown over 1,300 offensive sorties in support of their comrades on the ground. *Badoeng Strait* had contributed 254 of these, and even the late-arriving *Sicily* accounted for 122; the rest came from land-based Corsair and Tigercat squadrons, with a few sorties thrown in by newly arrived VMF-311, the first Marine jet squadron in Korea, operating F9Fs out of Yongp'o. Offshore, TF 77 contributed 860 offensive sorties, 352 by *Leyte*, 300 by *Philippine Sea*, and 208 from newly arrived

126

Princeton. Between December 1 and 11, then, TF 77 and 1st MAW pilots hammered the Chinese with a total of approximately 2,200 sorties by carrier-based and land-based fighter and attack aircraft.[37]

To Marines on the ground, the seemingly endless Corsairs orbiting on call overhead were lifesavers; one Marine controller referred to them as "ambush-busters." The cold affected the airplanes as well as the infantry on the ground, and many Corsair pilots found that their 20-mm cannon froze up, leaving them with rockets, bombs, and napalm. Marine Anthony Campino recalled that on the road from Haguru to Yudam-ni "the airedales [were] the best buddies we had . . . Like a shepherd dog watching over its herd of sheep, so the airedales were our shepherd dogs." Still later, as the column worked its way from Haguru down to Kit'o-ri, correspondent Maggie Higgins (who had flown into Kot'o-ri strapped in the back of an old Grumman TBM Avenger to see for herself what was going on) reported that "an aerial curtain of Marine Corsairs and Navy fighters protected the head and tail of the column as it wound over the road." In fact, on an average, 24 CAS aircraft orbited over the column, while other attack airplanes bombed, rocketed, na-palmed, and strafed adjacent ridges to guard the tender flanks of the column as it wended its way to the sea. Chinese roadblocks were dealt with sum-marily; controllers called in air strikes, with infantry-armor teams waiting while Corsairs and ADs rolled in with deadly cargoes of rockets, bombs, and napalm. The strike force would no sooner pull off target then an assault party would attack the roadblock, rout or kill any surviving ambushers, and then press on.

Air-to-ground communication posed a serious problem in the deep ravines bordering the defile. To ensure that orbiting strike aircraft heard calls for assistance from the tactical air control parties on the ground, Marine transport squadron VMR-152 outfitted a four-engine Douglas R5D Skymaster (the naval equivalent of the Air Force's C-54 transport and commercial DC-4 airliner) as a super Mosquito. It had stations for three controllers, extra fuel and oxygen, a chartboard and situation map, and an extra radio. As the Marine column fought its way from Hagaru to Hamhung, the R5D circled all day, every day, 12 hours at a time, controlling the merciless Corsairs and Skyraiders. Late on December 10, the column reached Chinhung-ni and linked with Marine forces from the coast. The next day, they had reached Hamhung with their weapons, morale, and reputation for unsurpassed valor intact.[38]

The Marine breakout cost the Corps 718 battle deaths and many more nonfatal casualties, half of the latter stemming from frostbite. In turn, the column and on-call Navy-Marine air power destroyed no less than seven Chinese divisions, somewhat offsetting the calamitous collapse of the Eighth Army in the west. As with earlier North Koreans, Chinese prisoner interviews confirmed the decisive impact that close air support and air power in general had on the battlefield.[39] On December 4, with the breakout at the height of its intensity, the commander of the 1st MAW sent a message to the Seventh Fleet: ". . . saw the 5th and 7th Marines

A mixed formation of Navy strike aircraft overly the battleship U.S.S. *Missouri* immediately following the Japanese surrender, signaling both the end to the Pacific War and the triumph of American naval air power. (U.S. National Archives)

Two Grumman F6F-5 Hellcats from the U.S.S. *Shangri-La* (CV-38) prowl the Pacific in August 1945. (U.S. Air Force)

A formation of Fourth Marine Air Wing Vought F4U-1A Corsairs on their way to raid Japanese strong points in the Marshall Islands, 1944. The Corsair became the postwar mainstay of Navy and Marine propeller-driven fighter squadrons. (U.S. Naval Institute)

Grumman's stubby F8F Bearcat represented the ultimate derivation of that firm's classic line of propeller-driven naval fighters, but the rapid development of the naval jet fighter rendered it obsolescent virtually immediately. (Grumman archives)

The prototype McDonnell FD-1 Phantom, the Navy's first pure jet fighter to trap and launch from a carrier at sea, July 21, 1946. (Hallion collection)

The attractive Ryan FR-1 Fireball, which had a jet engine in its aft fuselage as well as a conventional piston engine, represented an interim attempt to introduce jet-propelled aircraft into the fleet. (Hallion collection)

The calm before the storm. H.M.S. *Triumph* steaming off the Philippine coastline, March 4, 1950, during joint Anglo-American naval exercises. Supermarine Seafires are spotted on the forward deck, and Fairey Fireflies on the aft deck. (U.S. National Archives)

Convair's B-36 constituted a veritable case of aeronautical gigantism. This is the B-36D, which added four jet engines to boost maximum performance, giving this impressive bomber a "six turning, four burning" propulsion system. (U.S. Air Force)

A Lockheed P2V-3C Neptune of VC-5 accelerates down the flight deck of the U.S.S. *Midway* (CVB-41) on April 7, 1949. Launched off the Atlantic coast, the Neptune subsequently flew 4,000 miles nonstop, crossing the United States, turning north over the Pacific to Alaska, and then southeast to Moffett Field, California for landing. (U.S. National Archives)

The key players in the 1949 national defense controversy stand fighting the wind over the deck of the U.S.S. *Franklin D. Roosevelt* (CVB-42), September 26, 1949. *Left to right:* Vice Admiral Felix B. Stump, General Omar N. Bradley, Secretary of the Navy Francis P. Matthews, General Hoyt Vandenberg, Secretary of Defense Louis A. Johnson, Secretary of the Army Gordon Gray, Secretary of the Air Force Stuart Symington, Admiral Louis E. Denfield, General J. Lawton Collins, Major General Clifton B. Cates, and Admiral William H. P. Blandy. (U.S. National Archives)

Two hefty North American AJ-1 Savage nuclear attack bombers from VC-5 being "spotted" on the deck of the U.S.S. *Franklin D. Roosevelt*, August 10, 1952. (U.S. National Archives)

The prototype McDonnell F2H-1 Banshee cruises over the Missouri countryside on a test flight. A more advanced model, the F2H-2, would do yeoman service in Korea as a fighter-bomber and reconnaissance aircraft, earning the affectionate nickname of "Banjo." (Hallion collection)

Grumman test pilot Corwin "Corky" Meyer shows off the prototype F9F-2 Panther over Long Island; the Panther would become the major jet fighter type fielded by the Navy and Marine Corps in Korea. (Grumman archives)

A Fairey Firefly from *Triumph's* 827 Squadron begins its takeoff roll as three Grumman F6F-5N Hellcats from U.S.S. *Boxer* (CV-21) prepare to follow suit during the March 1950 prewar exercises off the Philippines. The Firefly served primarily in attack and antisubmarine warfare roles with the Royal Navy and Commonwealth services. (U.S. National Archives)

The *Essex*-class carrier U.S.S. *Valley Forge* (CV-45) during flight operations; a Douglas AD-4 Skyraider has just taken off from the ship. Note the plane guard Sikorsky HO3S-1 hovering off the port side. (U.S. National Archives)

Valley Forge's Air Group 5 in action: A Grumman F9F-2 Panther of VF-51 is spotted prior to being readied for launch. (Grumman archives)

Valley Forge's Air Group 5 in action: A rocket-armed Vought F4U-4B Corsair of VF-54 begins its takeoff roll. (U.S. National Archives)

The results of the first Anglo-American air strike in Korea: railway moving stock and facilities burn at the P'yongyang railyards, July 4, 1950. (U.S. National Archives)

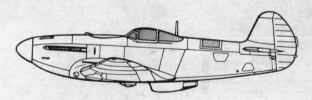

Yakovlev Yak-9P

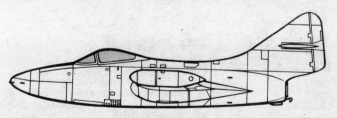

Grumman F9F-2 Panther

With sparks streaming from its collapsed nose landing gear, a Panther of VMF-115 screeches towards an inevitable collision as deck crewmen of the U.S.S. *Franklin D. Roosevelt* scurry to safety. Typical of deck-landing accidents in the era of the straight-deck carrier, this one fortunately resulted in no fatalities, though several Panthers were lost or damaged. (Grumman archives)

July 18, 1950: As Skyraiders and Corsairs from *Valley Forge's* VA-55 and VF-53 pull off target, the Wonsan Oil Refining Factory erupts in a succession of fireballs and secondary explosions, triggering a fire that burned for the next four days. (U.S. National Archives)

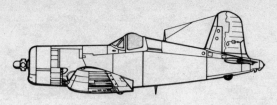

Vought F4U-4B Corsair

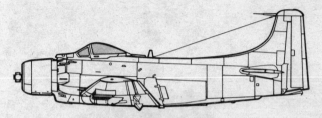

Douglas AD-4 Skyraider

The Douglas AD Skyraider, the Navy's beloved "Able-Dog," could carry a truly prodigious amount of ordnance. Here is an AD-4 shown at Naval Air Station Dallas in May 1953 after having lugged aloft a bombload of 10,500 pounds in a demonstration of what this powerful attack bomber could do. Early production ADs had only two 20-mm cannon in place of the four shown here. (McDonnell-Douglas archives)

A F4U-4B Corsair of *Philippine Sea's* VF-114 catapults off the bow on a strike against advancing North Korean forces, August 4, 1950. (U.S. Naval Institute)

A Navy Corsair pilot, wet but unhurt, is returned to the deck of the *Philippine Sea* scant minutes after his F4U-5N lost power and ditched; a watchful Sikorsky HO3S-1 from a detachment of HU-1 quickly plucked him from the frigid waters of the Sea of Japan. (U.S. National Archives)

During the grim defense of the Pusan perimeter, a strike is briefed in *Philippine Sea's* Flag Plot. Present, *from left to right,* are Lieutenant Commander E. T. Deacon, Lieutenant Commander G. M. Douglas, Lieutenant Commander L. W. Chick, Army Major K. R. Mitchell, Commander R. F. Jones, and Rear Admiral E. C. Ewen. (U.S. National Archives)

The payoff: North Korean vehicles blasted by air attack during the bitter Naktong River fighting, including a Soviet-built T-34 tank. (U.S. Naval Institute)

A *Philippine Sea* ordnance crew ready one of VF-111's Panthers for a Korean strike, loading belts of 20-mm ammunition for its four cannon. Note how the F9F's nose slides forward for ease of maintenance. (U.S. Naval Institute)

A F4U-4B of VMF-214, the famed "Black Sheep," is caught at the moment the catapult officer of the U.S.S. *Sicily* (CVE-118) gives the signal to launch, as Captain John Thach, *Sicily's* skipper, looks down from behind the glass on the bridge. The Corsair is carrying eight HVAR rockets, a 500-pound bomb, and an external fuel tank. (U.S. National Archives)

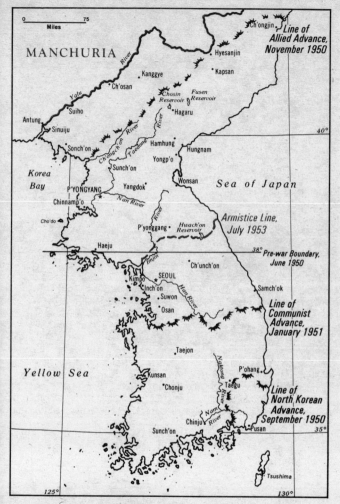

North and South Korea, showing prominent features and fighting fronts, 1950-1953.

A Corsair from *Philippine Sea's* VF-113 flies combat air patrol over Inch'on harbor, still filled with ships from the invasion fleet, October 2, 1950. (U.S. Naval Institute)

A Martin PBM-5S Mariner flying over the Florida Keys in 1949. Though vulnerable to fighter attack, the Mariner offered exceptional versatility in a variety of roles, and spawned the subsequent P5M Marlin, the Navy's last propeller-driven flying boat. (U.S. National Archives)

Mariner gunners explode a moored mine off Chinnamp'o with machine gun fire. (U.S. National Archives)

A Mikoyan and Gurevich MiG-15bis delivered into American hands by a North Korean defector after the armistice in 1953; the aircraft is shown several hours after its unexpected arrival, inside a guarded hanger at Kimpo. (U.S. Air Force)

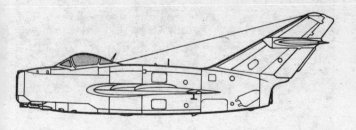

Mikoyan-Gurevich MiG-15bis

A MiG-15 goes down in a hail of 20-mm gunfire from the three aggressive Panther pilots of *Leyte's* VF-31 during a mid-November dogfight near the Yalu bridges. (U.S. National Archives)

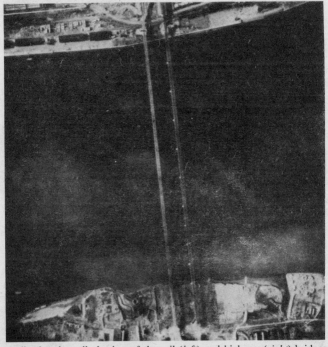

A dive-bomber pilot's view of the rail (*left*) and highway (*right*) bridges crossing from Antung, Manchuria (*at the top of the photograph*) to Sinuiju, North Korea (*at the bottom of the photograph*), November 10, 1950. Note that the Korean side is dotted with bomb craters from the attacks of the previous day. (McDonnell-Douglas archives)

Slightly over a week later, on November 18, a *Leyte* strike group leaves the highway bridge a shambles, as ripples radiate across the Yalu. The railway bridge, however, remains standing. Note the undamaged facilities on the Manchurian side of the river—a testimony to the United Nations' commitment not to involve Communist China in the war. By this time, however, 180,000 Chinese troops had already crossed over into Korea. (U.S. National Archives)

Deck crews turn to and clear the deck of the U.S.S. *Badoeng Straight* (CVE-116) of a November snowfall so that the Corsairs of VMF-323 can return to flight operations against the Chinese threatening X Corps. (U.S. Naval Institute)

With unexpended rockets, a F4U-4B Corsair of VMF-212 taxies in from a sortie for refueling and rearming before taking off again in support of the Marines fighting out of the reservoirs. (U.S. Marine Corps)

The Marine column wending its way over the mountains to Hamhung halts as a Corsair strike group drops napalm on Chinese ambushers. (U.S. Naval Institute)

Ensign E. D. Jackson of *Philippine Sea's* VF-112 traps safely aboard ship despite being injured and with his Panther badly damaged from flying into a North Korean cable trap. The cables mangled the starboard wingtip fuel tank, dented and punctured the wing leading edges, and fractured the canopy. With the assistance of his wingman, Jackson managed a safe return. (U.S. National Archives)

Not out of the woods yet: Admiral Arthur W. Radford (*center*) examines Communist troop dispositions with Rear Admiral Ralph A. Ofstie (*left*) and Vice Admiral Arthur D. Struble (*right*) aboard the U.S.S. *Princeton* (CV-37) during Radford's inspection trip to the Far East, January 26, 1951. (U.S. National Archives)

Striking at the source: A low-flying Corsair napalms North Korean minelayers, 1951. (U.S. Naval Institute)

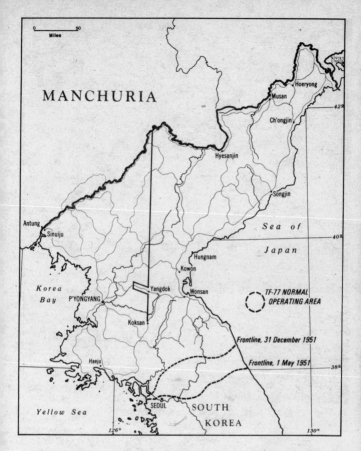

North Korean road network, showing zone of TF 77 responsibility east of 126°40′ east longitude, from Koksan north to the Manchurian and Soviet borders.

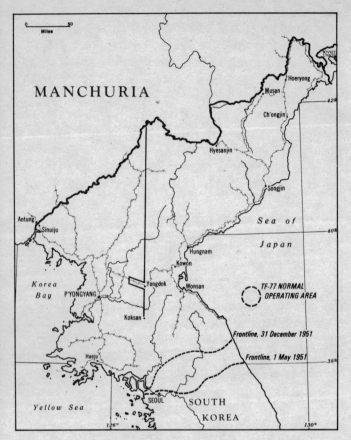

North Korean rail network, showing zone of TF 77 responsibility east of 126°40' east longitude, from Koksan north to the Manchurian and Soviet borders.

return. They thank God for air. I don't think they could have made it as units without air support. . . . Tell your pilots they are doing a magnificent job."[40] The Army recognized the contributions of Marine CAS by awarding the 1st MAW its Distinguished Unit Citation for the period November 22 through December 14, 1950, as well as by personal messages to the wing from various field commanders including Major General Almond.[41] But there was also loss, for the aviators faced numerous weather hazards as well as ubiquitous flak and small-arms fire.

On December 4, damage from small-arms fire forced down Ensign Jesse L. Brown near the Chosin reservoir. Brown, a Corsair pilot with *Leyte*'s VF-32, was the Navy's first black naval aviator. It had not been easy to move from childhood poverty in Mississippi to wings of gold, and he had endured his share of discrimination, both as a youth and as a naval aviation officer candidate at Pensacola. Such attitudes reflected the times; a 1941 book for naval officers' wives living in Pensacola suggested they hire black servants, but warned about theft, since black women, the authors cautioned, had to support "the usually lazy husbands and numerous off-spring."[42] Brown managed to overcome this climate of casual racism, and received his wings in the fall of 1948. When *Leyte* went to war, he proved an aggressive and able fighter pilot.

On December 4, piloting one of four Corsairs launched on an armed reconnaissance of the Chosin area, Brown, flying as section leader, received a damaging hit in the plane's oil system. Unable to climb or bail out, he elected to belly-in on the soft snow five miles behind Chinese lines. But the plane broke up on landing, and though Brown slid back the canopy and waved, he made no attempt to get out, even as smoke started pouring from the wreckage. While the flight leader radioed for a rescue helicopter, Brown's wingman, Lieutenant (j.g.) Thomas Hudner, decided to help his trapped section leader. Time was of the essence, and even if a helicopter arrived, it would do so after dusk. He jettisoned his drop tank and napalm bombs, fired his rockets, and executed a carrier-like approach, force-landing within 100 yards of Brown's wrecked plane. Hudner, at great personal risk, attempted to free Brown; he even scooped snow onto the wreckage to prevent the smoke from flaring into flame. A Marine rescue helicopter soon appeared over the hills and clattered to a landing, its pilot helping Hudner trying to free Brown, who now lapsed in and out of consciousness. Injured internally, the trapped pilot finally passed out, and died quietly as the two aviators worked frantically to free him. As night approached, the two men abandoned their task and wisely flew off under the protective watch of Corsairs, landing at Yonp'o. Several days later, with retrieval now out of the question as the wreckage lay deep within hostile territory, Brown's squadron mates flew low over the crash site; determined to prevent desecration of the downed pilot, they drenched the site with napalm, and created a surrealistic image of fire and ice that added a Wagnerian touch to this tragic story. On April 13, 1951, President Truman presented the Medal of Honor to Tom

Hudner at White House ceremonies. On February 17, 1973, the story came to an end with the commissioning of the U.S.S. *Jesse L. Brown* (DE-1089). Present was the barrier-breaking pilot's widow, and at her side stood Captain Thomas Hudner, USN.[43]

With the Marines safely down from Chosin and Fusen, the Navy turned to the evacuation of Hungnam. From December 11 to December 24, dock workers methodically loaded 105,000 American and Korean military personnel, 91,000 refugees, 350,000 tons of cargo, and 17,500 vehicles aboard ship, redeploying them safely and in good order to Pusan. Fearful that China's air force might attack, the Navy and Marines placed an air umbrella over Hungnam and stationed a radar picket destroyer off the coast to furnish advance warning of any possible assault. That assault did not occur, however, freeing the majority of the 22 shipboard squadrons available for support (4 of Panthers, 14 of Corsairs, and 4 of Skyraiders) to harass and slow the battered Chinese divisions (which already had sustained nearly 40,000 casualties, half inflicted by Navy-Marine air strikes) as they inched towards the Hungnam perimeter. On the night of December 15, the Chinese at last came within range of naval gunfire support, and thereafter ANGLICO parties supplemented air strikes with cannon fire from cruisers and destroyers and barrages of artillery rockets from vessels offshore. On Christmas Eve, a night-flying F4U-5N from VC-3's Detachment Fox aboard *Princeton* patrolled at 15,000 feet over Hungnam; its pilot watched fires consume anything of value in the port as the last ships filed out to sea. He radioed Christmas greetings to the faithful controllers on *Mount McKinley*, veteran of the glory days at Inch'on, then left for his carrier; the Navy's involvement with Hungnam was at an end.[44]

So United Nations Command had a bleak Christmas and New Year, though the orderly evacuation of Hungnam (and, on a smaller scale, Chinnamp'o, Inch'on, and Wonsan as well) furnished some brightness. In the west, the Eighth Army fell back so rapidly that it eventually lost contact with the invading Chinese, giving the Fifth Air Force a relatively free fire zone to ravage the advancing Chinese as they made their way down the Korean peninsula. The death of Walton Walker added to Allied woes; two days before Christmas, he perished in a Jeep accident near the front. His successor, Lieutenant General Matthew B. Ridgway (who was fond of posing in airborne uniform with a taped grenade perched jauntily and menacingly on his breast), eventually stopped the long retreat below Seoul, after that city had capitulated yet again. In early January, UN patrols resumed cautious probing northwards, though Seoul did not return to the Allied fold until March 14. MacArthur's own reputation suffered, tarnished (and to a degree unfairly) by the surprisingly successful Chinese intervention. Less on merit than for personal feelings and politics, Truman and his advisors arranged his recall on April 11. The old solder came home at last as Ridgway assumed his former chief's position. The tumultuous welcome MacArthur received on his return created a climate that helped topple the President's own party in the 1952 elections.

With the beginning of 1951, the Korean War entered its fourth and final phase: like the Western Front of 1914–1918, the war of movement had degenerated into stalemate. In part, this stemmed from politics; the war to preserve the South had evolved into a war to liberate the North, and now reverted back to its original goal. But there were clearly military reasons as well. The war increasingly was one between Chinese and American forces fighting on Korean soil. So large and well-equipped were Chinese forces that any compression of the front much further north than the 38th Parallel shortened their supply lines, reduced the effectiveness of Allied air strikes, and eased the Communists' logistical problems. It also increased the density of their deployed forces at the front, making subsequent advances more difficult and costly. Destroyed over the summer and fall of 1950, indigenous North Korean forces played little role in subsequent front-fighting; they were slowly rebuilt and then deployed at home or at selected points along the front, usually opposite South Korean forces, which resulted in combat marked by that peculiar ferocity so common in fratricidal warfare.

South Korea experienced widespread infiltration of North Korean guerrillas working with sympathizers in the south, forcing supply columns, road traffic, and even small troop formations to move with great caution. Ironically, North Korean forces proved more dangerous in this warfare than they had on the open field of battle, accomplishing results somewhat analogous to Fifth Air Force's and TF

77's disruptive air strikes against the Communists' logistical network. In a pattern that continued over the next two and one-half years, fighting largely hovered across a narrow band of land near the infamous 38th Parallel. The air war, however, ranged far beyond this, as planners turned toward interdiction of North Korea's logistical network. It was to that end that naval aviators increasingly applied themselves after the first six frantic months of the Korean War.

4/INTERDICTION AND ATTRITION

On January 15, 1951, United Nations forces established defensive lines in the south and began to consolidate their position. To hinder North Korea and Chinese resupply, the Navy blockaded Wonsan harbor, and eventually seized control of the harbor islands themselves. This bold move ultimately furnished Allied pilots with a small emergency airstrip on the tiny island of Yo'do. After nearly a month of consolidation, Allied troops again went on the offensive, liberating Seoul. In April, the Chinese launched a desperate counteroffensive; in seesaw fighting over the next two months, Allied air, ground, and naval forces handled the Communists roughly. The Communists eventually fell back, though slowly. By mid-June, the front once again curved above the 38th Parallel, northeast from Munsan above Seoul to Kosong on the east coast. On June 24, the Soviet Union suggested armistice negotiations, and the first of these occasionally tempestuous and constantly frustrating meetings took place in early July. From then until the end of the war, the front remained relatively stable, until fighting escalated sharply in the closing weeks of the war in last-ditch attempts to seize territory before a truce.

In the sharp fighting of early 1951, close air support missions predominated, though this soon changed. The fast carriers of TF 77, the escort carriers, and Great Britain's H.M.S. *Theseus,* pounded Communist forces on both the east and west coasts. An examination of sortie statistics and ordnance expenditures for Navy and Marine aircraft during the first five months of 1951 gives a clear indication of the intense pace of naval air operations by tactical aircraft[1]:

Tactical Aircraft Combat Sorties and Attack Runs on Enemy

Month	Combat Sorties	Attack Runs on Enemy
January	4,720	18,000
February	4,931	25,000
March	7,146	38,000
April	8,147	45,000
May	8,417	47,000

Ordnance Expenditures in Actual Combat

Month	Bombs	Rockets	Ammunition
January	12,000	7,500	1.2 million rounds
February	11,600	12,300	2.5 million rounds
March	21,996	15,918	2.8 million rounds
April	25,620	19,013	3.3 million rounds
May	32,929	15,669	3.3 million rounds

Unfortunately, as 1951 progressed, the number of

naval aircraft losses also increased. This stemmed in part from the bitter fighting in April and May, but also from the shift to static targets, such as bridges and railroads, and the consolidation by North Korea of large amounts of antiaircraft artillery of virtually all calibers around these sites. The older Corsairs, many of which lacked both oil cooler shut-off valves to prevent disastrous oil leaks if the coolers were damaged and engine cowling armor plate, proved particularly vulnerable.[2]

Tactical Aircraft Losses from Enemy Action

Month	F9F	F4U	F7F	AD
January	0	6	0	1
February	0	6	0	1
March	1	9	1	2
April	0	30	1	2
May	3	18	0	2

Most Corsair losses involved Marine squadrons, some of which took very heavy casualties in exchange for the dedicated service that they furnished ground troops. In April, for example, 21 of the 30 Corsairs lost came from Leatherneck units. On top of this, of course, there were operational losses; the Corsair was no piece of cake to bring aboard ship. For example, in February, the light carrier *Bataan* suffered three Corsair barrier crashes as its "U-birds" came aboard. Enemy fire damaged numerous airplanes, adding to the burdens of maintenance personnel on ship and ashore. But enemy fire was

137

not the only hazard facing Allied airmen; one's allies could occasionally be equally threatening. The faithful *Theseus* came close to tragedy when a Marine Corsair bounced two of its Sea Furies near Wonsan. The aggressive Leatherneck, apparently mistaking the two planes for Lavochkin fighters, peppered both with gunfire before he realized his mistake. Fortunately the tough Hawker-built fighters survived, and the two Fleet Air Arm pilots were not hurt. With characteristic aplomb, they made a safe return to ship.[3]

The emphasis of naval aviation in Korea from the winter of 1950 through the middle of 1952 gradually shifted from battlefield support to interdiction. Control of the Allied interdiction effort fell to the Fifth Air Force, in accordance with pre-Korean Department of Defense doctrine. In 1948, the Secretary of Defense had issued an Armed Forces Functions Paper that assigned the Air Force specific responsibility for "interdiction of enemy land power and communications," and gave the Navy and Marine Corps collateral responsibility for "enemy land, and air power and communications through operations at sea."[4] In mid-December 1950, Far East Air Forces had issued a directive for "FEAF Interdiction Campaign No. 4," which divided North Korea into 11 zones and targeted 172 railway and highway bridges, tunnels, marshaling yards, and supply centers for destruction.[5] General Stratemeyer envisioned drawing upon both Navy and Marine air resources as well as associated Allied air units and FEAF itself for this campaign, and approached Admiral Joy on January 15 about joining the effort. Joy responded that the Navy had its hands full with close air support requirements at the moment; he echoed reservations expressed in late December by Admiral Struble. At a major commanders' conference held at Taegu on January 18, 1951, Struble reiterated his views, offering to devote more attention to "armed reconnaissance" sorties, but stressing that strong close air support held the key to battlefield victory. He was overruled, and, as a result, the Navy reluctantly turned away from CAS and embraced interdiction, flying its first interdiction sorties since the great retreat on January 29. TF 77's planes struck at east coast bridges.[6]

To a limited extent, the Navy had been involved in interdiction operations since the outbreak of war. From July through October, these were "armed reconnaissance" sweeps by fighters and attack airplanes along roads and railroads to instill greater caution in North Korean forces that moved along roads by day. Interdiction took on greater urgency at the time of the Chinese intervention and the disappointing Yalu river bridge strikes of November. Now, at the request of General Ridgway, TF 77 flew interdiction sorties against east coast bridges. In theory, close air support still remained TF 77's first priority, but this quickly changed. On February 16, FEAF asked the Navy to assume interdiction responsibility for Korea's northeastern routes on a "temporary" basis. Less than two weeks later, however, this new responsibility was made a continuing one, largely because early Navy strikes appeared quite successful. Eventually, on September 20, 1951, FEAF released TF 77 from all CAS responsibilities;

except in emergencies, naval CAS in the future would come from Marines ashore or with the escort carrier support group. TF 77 left CAS for interdiction and did not return, except as special mission requirements or particular combat emergencies arose, until the last six months of the war.[7]

Eventually, TF 77 had responsibility for a large parcel of Korean territory that ranged 300 miles north from the bombline to the Manchurian border, and encompassed all territory east of 126°40' East Longitude; in mid-September 1951, FEAF granted TF 77 additional responsibility for a small but strategically important railway running west of this line, from Yangdok to Samdong-ni. North Korea's geography was both a help and a hindrance to TF 77's airmen as they went about their new task. Korea's east coast is ridged by steep and convoluted mountains and passes that dictate the path of roads and railroads. Thus, geographical considerations forced the Koreans—and the Japanese before them—to place road and rail lines as much as possible along the narrow eastern and broad western coastal plains. The eastern plain lay within easy range of naval gunfire as well as air strikes. But this terrain also imposed high risks for attacking aviators, especially during operations in marginal weather and heckling missions flown at night or before dawn.

At the time of the Korean War, Korea lacked any surfaced highways; all roads consisted of gravel or dirt roadbeds that usually paralleled existing rail lines. Most rail lines had but a single track. (By mid-1951, as a result of relentless air pressure from TF 77 strikes, North Korea had to shift the bulk of its rail operations to the west coast network, which gave the sinuous link from Samdong-ni through Yangdok and on to Kowon — a small railroad town just north of Wonsan — special significance.) Terrain dictated using many bridges and tunnels. Tunnels proved difficult to damage or destroy (despite early and misleading indications to the contrary), and the bridges (both road and rail) usually forded relatively shallow creeks and rivers which could be bridged quickly and easily by timbers or other means if a bridge was destroyed. Generally speaking, it took 60 rounds of 16-inch naval gunfire or between 12 and 16 AD sorties (dropping a total of 36–48 2,000-pound bombs) to destroy a bridge. But in the "low technology" environment of North Korea's road and rail network, repair crews, never in short supply, quickly restored road surfaces, removed rubble, replaced track, filled craters, or constructed bypasses that made both the Air Force's and Navy's interdiction prolonged and frustrating.

Communist logistical requirements played a key part in creating this frustration. An intelligence summary issued in late 1951 assumed that each Communist division (a force of approximately 10,000 men) required 50 short tons (units of 2,000 pounds) per day: 2,900 total tons per day delivered to the forward areas to support the 58 divisions then confronting the Allies in the field, or 10 pounds per soldier per day. This was half of the requirement for an equivalent ROK division, and less than 20% of that deemed necessary to support a single American soldier at the front. This meant that North Korea could make do with large numbers of peasants moving supplies south. The Communists did not require a complex logistical network as had, for example, Nazi Germany during the Second World War. North Korea used trains and trucks in a seemingly inexhaustible supply—Navy and Marine pilots consistently expressed amazement at the numbers that appeared at night; their destruction did not prove as decisive as FEAF's interdiction planners had hoped. Using the ubiquitous A-frame, peasants delivered mortar rounds, artillery shells, ammunition, food, small arms, and infantry weapons to the front in prodigious amounts; though they proved slower than transport by road or rail they were more reliable.[8]

The classic interdiction strike of the war—one that illustrated the tenacity of both sides and the difficulty of generating lasting successes—occurred in March and April of 1951. On March 2, Lieutenant Commander Clement Craig, squadron commander of VF-193, discovered two rail bridges, one under construction, on a line between Kilchu and Songjin, just inland from the Sea of Japan, while returning to the *Princeton* from another bridge strike further north. *Princeton's* Air Group 19 set out to drop them with enthusiasm. A hasty strike that same day damaged the approaches, but a strike the next day by eight of VA-195's Skyraiders (each armed with three 2,000-pound bombs) led by Lieutenant Commander Harold G. "Swede" Carlson, dropped one span, damaged a second, and knocked two others out of alignment. Rear Admiral Ralph Ofstie, then TF 77's commander, dubbed the cratered landscape "Carlson's Canyon."

A cat-and-mouse game began as the North Koreans tried to rebuild the bridges and repair the damage. Despite harassing night-heckler attacks by Corsairs and Skyraiders from *Princeton's* VC-3 and VC-35 detachments, bridge repair went smoothly until another strike in mid-March blasted it with napalm, destroying the wooden cribbing used to support the repair work. Air Force B-29s then stepped in, "seeding" the bridges with delayed action bombs to further discourage repair. But by the end of March they were *again* nearly ready for service, lacking only railroad tracks. Further strikes on April 2 left only the concrete piers standing, and brought the 30-day "Battle of Carlson's Canyon" to an end. But the North Koreans, while admitting defeat and not attempting again to rebuild the crossing, simply built a four-mile bypass consisting of eight shorter and lower bridges. "TF 77 knocked out several of these small bridges just before the tracks were laid then turned its attention southward in search of another key bridge," a summary photographic analysis report concluded.[9] Though this prolonged effort denied North Korea the use of a major rail complex for approximately two months, it was not the kind of effort that TF 77 could sustain with the continuing demand for strikes against many such targets. As General James A. Van Fleet (who ran the Eighth Army after General Ridgway replaced Douglas MacArthur) recalled after the war, "We won the battle to knock out the bridge, but we lost the objective, which was to knock out the traffic."[10] The frustrating sequence in which planes bombed a bridge, bombed efforts to repair the bridge, and, finally, confronted the problem of clever bypasses became a common one. Worse, bridges became great flak traps, as North Korean and Chinese gunners discovered their almost magnetic attraction for aircraft.

Bridges, from the time of the First World War, have held particular fascination as targets. When author James Michener, then working as a correspondent, heard the story of Carlson's Canyon, it seemed an ideal theme for a novel, and in time it appeared as *The Bridges at Toko-ri*. Always fascinated with aviation, Michener visited the *Essex*, whose Air Group 5, led by the colorful and aggressive Commander Marshal U. Beebe, flew McDonnell's F2H-2 Banshee. Michener built the novel around situations and characters inspired by the men and planes of the *Essex:* "Admiral George Tarrant"; "Beer Barrel" the LSO; the doomed "Harry Brubaker," "Mike Forney," and "Nestor Gamidge;" stocky and aggressive "CAG" (patterned on Beebe himself, to whom Michener dedicated the book); the mythical "bridges at Toko-ri"; and the fictional fast carrier *"Savo."* The book is among the finest novels of Americans at war, and certainly is the best novel of naval aviation ever written. It contains insights into the core of the naval experience in Korea, and in particular, a psychological insight into the interdiction campaign: the wistful notion of those conducting it that continued bridge, rail, and highway breaking *had* to force a settlement, *had* to have a decisive impact upon the war. At one point, Tarrant talks with Brubaker, who had just ditched in the Sea of Japan. Forney and Gamidge saved his life in their helicopter. Brubaker, a reservist and lawyer in civilian life, asks why TF 77 must knock out the bridges at Toko-ri. Tarrant, the professional soldier, replies:

> I believe without question that some morning a bunch of communist generals and commissars will be holding a meeting to discuss the future of the war. And a messenger will run in with news that the Americans have knocked out even the bridges at Toko-ri. And that little thing will convince the Reds that we'll never stop . . . never give in . . . never weaken in our purpose.[11]

Brubaker later flies against the bridges and is shot down. He dies in a muddy ditch along with Forney and Gamidge, in a firefight against Communist troops, separated from the ocean and safety by the towering blue hills of Korea's eastern coast. The next morning, *Savo* launches its Banshees, catapulting them two by two; they fly west, "seeking new bridges in Korea."[12] And the war goes on.

The interdiction campaign eventually moved from attacks on bridges and highways to attacks against the rail network that emphasized rail cuts to hinder Communist logistical supply. Selected quotes from the Navy's various *Interim Evaluation Reports* are a litany of disappointment:

> *April 1951:* The enemy has shown surprising capabilities of movement at night, concealment by day, repair of road and rail breaks, repair of bridges, and construction of bypasses. This is influenced by the apparently unlimited avail-

ability of human labor.[13]

December 1951: A lesson of Korea is that the less highly developed a transportation system is, the less susceptible it is to thorough interdiction, especially by air. It is probably impossible to achieve complete interdiction of a country only partially industrialized [and] processing mass manpower except by physical occupation. The interdiction campaign has compelled the enemy to devote a large body of manpower and military effort to counter-interdiction. But this cost to the enemy must be compared to the cost to the U.S. which in December [1951] was almost the entire offensive effort of TF 77, 60% of the offense effort of the First Marine Aircraft Wing, and over 95% of the offensive effort of the Fifth Air Force in Korea.[14]

June 1952: Most of the air interdiction effort from January to June 1952 was devoted to rail cutting with secondary missions of bridge destruction and armed reconnaissance. The task force accomplishments for rail cutting increased to a record of 211 cuts in one day, but the enemy's remarkable repair capability enabled him to repair the damage quickly. Bridges were repaired in a few days; rail cuts in a few hours. Rail traffic was often reduced to shuttling but the supplies went through. Armed reconnaissance prevented movement of vehicles by day, but was inadequate to prevent their movement by night. For any substantial increase in the efficiency of interdiction, night operations must be increased in magnitude and proficiency.[15]

January 1953: Despite the incessant efforts of the Navy and Air Force, interdiction of the enemy lines of communication by aircraft, although required by the stalemate accepted by both ground forces after the summer of 1951, was a costly and militarily unrewarding extension of the war. In January 1953, the enemy was better supplied, fed, and equipped than at any previous time. . . . There is no question that interdiction disrupted enemy daylight movements and reduced his daily supplies by a substantial margin. Yet the 'isolation of the battlefield' was never achieved.[16]

The most telling comments come from three key participants: General James A. Van Fleet, former Eighth Army commander; General Matthew B. Ridgway, former allied supreme commander; and Vice Admiral Ralph Ofstie, former commander of TF 77.

Van Fleet, writing in 1956 after his retirement, recalled that:

Repeatedly I was assured by my own staff, and by the Air Force and Naval Air, often supported by photographs, that 'a mile or more of rails at critical points' or 'the bridges at Sinanju' or 'the East Coast Line' were 'out for good.' But always, a few days later, locomotives pulling trains were operating at these very loca-

147

tions! In short, we were witnessing, this time to our own military disadvantage and frustration, another demonstration of the capacity, the durability, and the flexibility of railroads under war conditions.[17]

Ridgway, in his memoirs (published even as the morass of Southeast Asia mocked his optimism about limited warfare), recalled that:

Despite our constant and consistently successful effort to knock out railroads and bridges, to demolish marshaling yards and deny the highways to enemy traffic, supplies continued to flow down from Manchuria . . . Whatever may be said for the value of air power — and there is no question that without it many of our advances would not have been possible — it simply could not keep the enemy from bringing in the armament he needed. It could slow him down and keep him working nights; but it could not isolate the battleground.[18]

In May 1953, two months before the end of the war, Vice Admiral Ofstie, then serving as Deputy Chief of Naval Operations (Air), addressed a meeting of the Aircraft Industries Association at Williamsburg, Virginia. The AIA members had visited the impressive Langley Memorial Aeronautical Laboratory, run by the National Advisory Committee for Aeronautics, and had seen that revolutionary advances in aircraft design, particularly in supersonics, were already in hand. Ofstie's talk offered a dash of cold-water realism; his topic was the influence of cost on military air operations. One rail cut cost the Navy $18,000; knocking out a bridge cost $55,000. The explosives bill alone for displacing 30 cubic yards of dirt with a 250-pound bomb came to approximately $100 per cubic yard: "a pretty expensive dirt moving operation," in Ofstie's words. The North Koreans easily repaired such cuts and increasing antiaircraft protection took a high toll of attacking aircraft. "From my experience in Korea," Ofstie stated,

> I am beginning to wonder about the value returned for the present sustained attacks in carrying on the interdiction program in Korea. It may well be that we are being hurt more as a consequence of the cost of this operation and the losses sustained, than is the enemy with a somewhat reduced effectiveness of his supply routes. In other words, it may be advisable that we reduce the scale of our aircraft efforts of the air forces present, and restrict our air operations to those which can be assured of highly profitable targets, until or unless one side or the other becomes offensively inclined on the ground.[19]

Like artillery, aircraft, Ofstie concluded perceptively, "are a commodity which you need in large numbers. A few simply can't do the job."

Task Force 77 generally consisted of three fast carriers on station; two conducted flight operations and the third replenished at sea. A fourth carrier remained in port in Japan, on 12-hour recall should an emergency arise. A battleship or heavy cruiser accompanied the carriers for support, as did the ASW and radar picket screen between 9 and 16 destroyers. On average, the fast carriers could launch 100 sorties per carrier per day in the summer, and about 85 sorties per carrier per day in the winter. Ships replenished underway every fourth day, or during bad weather. A typical carrier air group left port with 81 aircraft:

One jet squadron	18 F9F-2 or F2H-2
Two Corsair squadrons	32 F4U-4 or F4U-4B
One Skyraider squadron	16 Ad-2, AD-3, or AD-4
Night-fighter detachment	3 F4U-5N or F4U-5NL
Night attack detachment	3 AD-4N, AD-4NL, or AD-4NA
Elint/ECM detachment	2 AD-3Q or AD-4Q
Photo recon detachment	3 F9F-2P or F2H-2P
Airborne early warning	3 AD-3W or AD-4W
Search and rescue helo	1 HO3S-1

It is apparent that the Corsair and Skyraider bore the brunt of the naval air war in Korea. Various versions of the F4U family flew day and night strike missions, and undertook day and night fleet air defense as well. The AD family already demonstrated the versatility for which this superlative aircraft would become famous. Specialized Skyraiders flew day and night attack, electronic intelligence and countermeasures sorties, and airborne early warning. "Q" and "N" models had two- or three-man crews

150

and specialized radar and electronic gear. The "NL" was a special winterized night attack model with expanding rubber de-icing "boots" on the wing and tail surfaces; the "NA" was a modified N carrying just the pilot. The "W" featured a belly radome, which had negligible adverse impact on its flying qualities. It functioned much as the Grumman E-2C Hawkeye airborne early warning aircraft does today, but with less efficiency or sophistication. As for the Corsair family, the F4U-4B differed from the F4U-4 in having four 20-mm cannon in place of the F4U'4's six .50 caliber machine guns. The F4U-5N was a radar-equipped night-fighter also used for night attack heckling missions, and its NL model, like the NL Skyraider, made use of de-icer boots. Early in the war a few carriers operated detachments of F4U-5P photo recon aircraft, but these quickly gave way to the faster (and hence more survivable) F9F-2P which itself gave way to the outstanding McDonnell F2H-2P photo Banshee.

As the war went on, the proportion of jet aircraft to propeller-driven aircraft changed dramatically, from roughly 25% of a total air group to 40%. This reflected the replacement of Corsair squadrons by Panthers and Banshees, so that by the end of the war, fast carriers generally operated two jet squadrons, one propeller-driven fighter squadron, and an attack squadron, as well as the remaining special mission aircraft. By the Korean war, the Corsair was neither fish nor fowl; it was not fast enough to provide meaningful air defense, and it lacked the payload and protection to adequately complement the Skyraider. Even the AD required additional armor sheeting bolted to its undersides with a concomitant reduction in payload, but the Corsair would have required virtual redesign to eliminate its weaknesses. Even so, Vought produced a small batch of specialized low-altitude heavily armored attack versions of the Corsair with thankfully relocated oil coolers, and these aircraft, designated AU-1, joined Marine squadrons in Korea in 1952, subsequently serving with distinction, though not without loss.

Safety aside, the AD was unquestionably the better of the two aircraft for ground attack. Although it required 50% more deck space than a Corsair, the AD could carry three to four times the load of the older fighter. At sea, ADs (prior to the introduction of the more heavily armored models) carried as much as a 7,500-pound bombload. Ashore, Marine units sometimes operated their ADs with bombloads of up to 10,000 pounds. As time went by and the interdiction campaign continued, the need to operate ADs with heavy 2,000-pound bombs decreased, since virtually all the major bridges were destroyed. ADs instead hit replacement bridges and bypasses with a mix of smaller weapons. By mid-1952, an AD on a typical interdiction mission carried 3 1,000-pound bombs and 8 or 12 250-pound bombs, the former ideal for bridge breaking, and the latter quite adequate for rail cutting. Two ADs could do the job of three Corsairs on interdiction sorties, and do it with greater precision and safety.[20]

At the end of May 1951, FEAF began "Operation *Strangle*," an attempt to paralyze North Korea's road network through interdiction of all main supply routes lying within a band across the peninsula between 38°15′ and 39°15′ North Latitude. Intelligence and targeting staffs designated *"Strangle areas,"* concentrating on roads in defiles and constricted passes where detours would be difficult, even impossible, to construct. Within the narrow band, Fifth Air Force designated three parallel north-south sectors. The Fifth Air Force itself would go after the westernmost sector; the First Marine Aircraft Wing would hit the east. Tactics included dawn and dusk heckling attacks, night strikes under flares, daytime interdiction and armed reconnaissance sorties, and "seeding" roads with delayed-action bombs fused for 6-, 12-, 24-, 36-, 72-, or even 144-hour delayed detonation. FEAF's B-26s and Navy and Marine aircraft sowed antipersonnel "butterfly" bombs to discourage repair. But the Communists' reaction disappointed the Allies. The North Koreans and Chinese stoically accepted casualties as the price of keeping supply lines open. Repair crews and troops exploded the smaller butterfly bombs with rifle fire. Cratered roadbeds generated impressive "moonscape" photographs, but the strategy proved virtually useless as the ever-present repair crews quickly filled them in and tamped down the earth, reopening the roads.

Strangle's optimistic name was an increasing source of embarrassment. Over the winter of 1951–1952, for example, the Communists called on 6,000-7,000 trucks, approximately 275 locomotives, and about 7,700 flatbeds, boxcars, and other associated rolling stock. FEAF eventually admitted that North Korea's inherently flexible logistical system had confounded *Strangle,* though the name lingered on, eventually becoming attached to a Fifth Air Force rail interdiction effort in 1951–1952. By then *Strangle* had too many pejorative connotations; as the official Air Force history of the Korean War stated, "By the spring of 1952 FEAF officers would have gladly expunged the tricky code name *'Strangle'* from the record." *Strangle* mercifully disappeared, and FEAF's ongoing rail interdiction program received the appelation "Operation *Saturate*" in late February 1952. *Saturate* continued with greater success, so that Air Force intelligence analysts eventually concluded that all but 4–5% of North Korea's prewar rail traffic had been halted. However, coupled with mass use of human transport and the large numbers of trucks operating at night, this small amount of rail traffic was enough to maintain Communist capabilities, and even allow expansion.[21]

Recognizing that many lucrative targets lay within both air and gunfire range of TF 77, the Navy established a two-part program, *Package* and *Derail,* in January 1952. *Package* involved targets first hit by strike aircraft, then marked by radar reflectors so that surface vessels could, in turn, attact them regardless of visibility conditions or time of day. *Derail* attacked targets left exclusively to surface forces; it consisted primarily of naval bombardment but sometimes involved commando or raiding parties. *Package* and *Derail* had some notable successes; intense pressure against Kowon, for example, resulted in suspension of traffic from the east-west and north-south rail lines into Wonsan for over a month in February and March of 1952. But the inability of surface vessels to remain on station long enough to ensure a full-time all-weather interdiction effort eventually limited the usefulness of both programs.

At the same time that *Package* and *Derail* began, TF 77 launched *Moonlight Sonata* which, though it lacked the grace of its namesake, nevertheless incorporated enough high explosive to have caught perhaps even the deafened Beethoven's attention. *Moonlight Sonata* consisted of strikes launched to take advantage of the improved visibility and reflectivity of the Korean landscape during moonlit winter conditions, when rail lines and surrounding terrain stood out in sharp relief in the bright sky. Strikes consisted of five sections of Corsairs and ADs, a total of 10 aircraft, launched in the predawn at 3:00 with each section patrolling a 50-mile stretch of rail line. *Moonlight Sonata,* however, depended too much on the right combination of visibility, weather, and target.

As the snows cleared, it gave way to *Insomnia,* a much more successful operation that utilized two strike groups of six aircraft, one at midnight and the other at 2:00. Subsequently, planners added a third group, launched it at midnight, and landed it at bases in Korea, so it could take off later as the two other *Insomnia* groups neared the end of their missions and continued the harassment effort. *Insomnia* began in May 1952 and concentrated on trapping locomotives by cutting rail lines ahead and behind them, so that daylight strike groups could attack the engines and rolling stock. *Insomnia* aircrews set up nine locomotives for destruction (strike teams damaged two others). *Moonlight Sonata* resulted in the destruction or damage of only two locomotives. Night attack crews generally favored 20-mm strafing coupled with napalm attacks. Late in the war, however, Skyraiders made use of the Navy-developed 2.75-inch folding fin aerial rocket (FFAR), a "podded" weapon originally designed as an unguided air-to-air rocket for inteceptors. High command from the Commander of the Seventh Fleet upwards believed that night attacks such as *Insomnia* had limited value as long as TF 77 did not station a designated night carrier (like the U.S.S. *Enterprise* with Commander William I. Martin's Night Air Group 90 in the Pacific war) off Korea. At the end of the war a plan existed, dubbed "Operation *No-Doze,*" for *Princeton* to serve as a night carrier off Korea, but a variety of factors, including the CAS requirements of the war's last days, prevented this plan from being implemented. TF 77's interdiction program, aside from sporadic attacks and continuing night-heckler strikes, remained primarily a daylight effort.[22]

Despite the disappointments of interdiction, TF 77 compiled impressive sortie rates and statistics of destruction and damage, reflecting the courage and professionalism of aircrews and the skill and dedication of the maintenance and support personnel who worked, often under difficult conditions, to keep their aircraft in the air. For example, between the first of May, 1951, and the end of the year, TF 77's airedales inflicted the following destruction and damage on the North Korean war machine[23]:

Target	Destroyed	Damaged
Railroad bridges	535	735
Railroad tracks (cut)	4,493	-*
Locomotives	84	132
Railroad cars/rolling stock	2,028	5,155
Highway bridges	179	234
Highways cratered or seeded	-*	490
Transport and other vehicles	2,028†	2,074
Armored vehicles/tanks	48	117
Supply, fuel, and ammo dumps	308	222
Villages housing troops	55	444
Warehouses and factories	411	650
Buildings	5,457	3,183
Gun and gun positions	615	482
Small boats	234	296

Costly losses and damage accompanied such accomplishments. Bridges and rail lines became flak concentration points, and, by mid-1952, over half of North Korea's antiaircraft artillery lay emplaced along bridge and rail lines, a threat estimated at 132 heavy guns (such as 85-mm and 76-mm artillery) and upwards of 700 automatic weapons (ranging from 37-mm cannon down to 12.7 mm and 7.62-mm machine guns). North Korean and Chinese Communist troops also employed barrage fire: shooting at aircraft on command with rifles and assorted small arms. One Corsair pilot had a clear picture of a

*Not applicable or meaningful.
†Coincidental statistic reproduced as in source document.

North Korean officer in full dress uniform, including white gloves and shoulders boards, blazing away with his sidearm. Damage and casualties from such "golden BBs" were high. Surprisingly effective, particularly as psychological intimidators, were North Korea's nontraditional defenses, such as lights strung across a cliff face above a highway to simulate a road convoy at night, or cables suspended across ravines and valleys; one Tigercat pilot returned with one engine out and 200 feet of cable draped around his mangled airplane. Navy pilots dubbed the vital trans-Korea rail link west from Wonsan "Death Valley," and Commander Marshall U. Beebe, Air Group 5's CAG, recollected that "one of my toughest jobs was the constant battle to keep pilots' morale up . . . the war in Korea demanded more competence, courage, and skill from the naval aviator than did World War II. The flying hours were longer, the days on the firing line more, the antiaircraft hazards greater, the weather worse."[24]

The following is a breakdown by carrier air group of TF 77's losses during the opening phase of the interdiction campaign, from May 1 through December 31, 1951[25]:

Ship	Aircraft	Aircrew
Philippine Sea	1	1
Princeton	14	8
Boxer	10	3
Bon Homme Richard	20	5
Essex	17	7
Antietam	8	1
Valley Forge	4	5
Total:	74	30 KIA/MIA/POW

Such losses in a seven-month period caused misgivings among strike planners and evaluators alike. The Navy's *Interim Evaluation Report* for May 1-December 31, 1951 bluntly concluded:

It is doubtful whether the interdiction campaign in Korea has been as costly to the enemy as to the U.S. The enemy has lost many vehicles, much rolling stock and supplies and has suffered heavy physical destruction of property, but it is doubtful whether this has placed a greater strain on the economies of North Korea, China, and the U.S.S.R. than upon the economy of the U.S. The cost of maintaining interdiction forces in and near Korea, the cost of the hundreds of aircraft lost and thousands of tons of munitions and supplies consumed, and the expenditure of national resources have been keenly felt. Certainly the value of the UN aircraft lost alone is greater than that of all the enemy's vehicles, rolling stock, and supplies destroyed. While the cost of the war assumes fantastic proportions to the U.S., the enemy largely offsets our efforts by the use of his cheapest and most useful asset, mass manpower.[26]

In August 1950, a classified intelligence summary credited North Korean antiaircraft artillery (AAA) units with "a fairly high state of training and an aggressive attitude," but concluded nonetheless that "North Korean AAA cannot be considered as having a high deterrent value."[27] All this changed by mid-1951, especially once North Korea began using early warning and gun laying radars. Of particular concern to B-29 crews, especially on night raids later in the war, was ground control interception (GCI) radars. North Korea's deadliest antiaircraft weapons were the Soviet-built M1939 85-mm and M1938 76-mm cannon (both of which had an effective ceiling of 25,000 feet and a rate of fire of between 15 and 20 rounds per minute), the M1939 37-mm cannon (with an effective ceiling of 4,500 feet and a rate of fire of 160-180 rounds per minute), and the single or dual-mount M1941 25-mm cannon (a copy of a Bofors design with an effective ceiling of 4,000 feet and a rate of fire of 240-250 rounds per minute).[28] Although such weapons incorporated time or contact fuses initially, later in the war Navy and Air Force strike crews increasingly encountered proximity-fused antiaircraft fire, a rude but not totally unexpected awakening. North Korea's increasing reliance upon and skilled use of radar generated greater concern, however.

North Korea used radars from the Soviet Union, Japan, Great Britain, the United States, and, perhaps, from the spoils of Nazi Germany as well. Many had been captured, then put to use against their former owners; others, however, came from wartime assistance to the Soviet Union now gone awry. North Korea's rapidly expanding radar capabilities posed particular problems for Strategic Air Command's B-29 fleet operating by night, and it created problems for daytime and night tactical aircraft strikes over the North. The Soviet Union had first employed radar near Leningrad in 1941, and had the opportunity to examine a number of Allied radar systems (including the excellent American SCR-584) as well as captured German radars such as *Wurzburg* and *Freya*. By mid-1951, North Korea had Soviet-designed and some Allied radars entering service. Typically, a new Soviet radar would first make its appearance in the Siberian and Sakhalin areas of the U.S.S.R., work its way down to Manchuria and North Korea, and, finally, move south along the China coastline. The basic radars appearing in wartime North Korea were the following:

RUS-2: Soviet-developed mobile truck-mounted 65-85 megacycle early warning radar

P2M Pegmatit: fixed-based version of RUS-2

Dumbo: 65-85 megacycle Soviet-built early warning and limited-use GCI fixed-based radar

Kniferest: improved *Dumbo* derivative

Token: Soviet-developed mobile early warning and GCI radar operating in the 10-cm band; initially detected at Antung

Whiff: Soviet copy of the American SCR-584 fire control radar

AA No. 2 and *AA No. 3:* British-developed searchlight control radars

AA No. 4: British-developed early warning radar

GL Mk. II: British-developed fire control radar

SCR-270: American-developed mobile pre-World War II early warning radar; SCR-271 was a fixed-base derivative

Tachi 18: Japanese-developed early warning radar

On August 12, 1951, the Strategic Air Command (SAC) began "ferret" electronic reconnaissance and signal intelligence operations over Korea using a Boeing RB-50G Superfortress on assignment from the 55th Strategic Reconnaissance Wing. SAC was soon locked in an increasingly intensive ECM war with North Korea's radar network. The capabilities of these radars ranged from mediocre, in the case of RUS-2 and the old SCR-270, to excellent, in the case of *Whiff, Token,* or any of the British equipment. Signal analysis also offered tantalizing hints of transferred Nazi *Freyas* that were never confirmed. By the end of 1951, North Korea had between 60 and 70 radars in service; it employed British searchlight control radars as early as September 1951, following these into service with so-called "S band" (approximately 10 cm) fire control radars a month later.[29]

TF 77's ECM detachments, composed of special purpose AD Skyraiders, noted North Korea's increasing radar order of battle with great interest. Navy patrol squadrons maintained their own electronic ferrets along the Soviet, Korean, and Chinese coasts, and kept track of new radar threats appearing in the Far East. By the summer of 1952, the various detachments, patrol squadrons, and the Air Force's own electronic intelligence effort located a total of 109 Communist radars in North Korea, some as close to the generally stable front as four miles. At that stage of the war, virtually all the North Korean radars were mobile, permitting the Communists to shift sites and thus frustrate UN strikes. Navy ECM crews concluded that North Korea's radar equipment was generally "of good quality and intelligently used."[30] The Communists constantly practiced cautionary and deceptive tactics. For example, a radar might make three sweeps an hour and then be turned off. Always alert to the presence of ferrets, the North Koreans noted if an ECM Skyraider or other "collection" airplane turned toward the station to take bearings, and, if it did, immediately ceased transmissions. In the hope that two might do better than one, ECM detachments learned to launch two Skyraiders, so that the pair might better fix the location of a North Korean radar. As in the Second World War (and in Vietnam), Korean ECM operations became an art; by the armistice, the Seventh Fleet had augmented its shipboard detachments and modified patrol bombers with four sophisticated long-range Martin P4M-1Q Mercator ferrets. The hefty Mercator, which had two turbojet engines in addition to its twin radial engines giving it extra power and a 400 mph high-speed dash flew a number of sorties off the Korean coast in the closing weeks of the war. Subsequently, the Mercator furnished the basis for the navy's first electronic reconnaissance and countermeasures squadron, VQ-1, formed at Iwakuni, Japan, on June 1, 1955.

On June 16, 1952, TF 77's airmen took action to thwart North Korea's radar defenses. During a strike against Kowon, two ECM Skyraiders preceded the strike group, detected two radars, and dropped rope chaff: radar confusion reflectors designed to fill an enemy radar screen with clutter and multiple images. Immediately, the radar-directed anti-aircraft fire went berserk; aircrews reported the flak burst as much as a mile off in deflection and several thousand feet off in altitude, in the midst of the slowly descending chaff. But there was little repetition of that success. The Kowon strike, for example, had exhausted TF 77's entire chaff supply! For security reasons, SAC did not clear its B-29s to employ chaff until the following September. Thereafter, however, chaff drops became a regular and highly successful feature of SAC's night war against North Korean radar-directed searchlights and flak.[31]

The following chart shows the 384 Navy and Marine tactical aircraft lost from the summer of 1951 through the armistice to antiaircraft fire. It offers testimony to the effectiveness of North Korea's defenses during the war[32]:

Quarters	F9F	F2H	F4U	F7F	AD	AU	Quarterly Total
July-Sept. 1951	6	0	34	1	12	–*	53
Oct.-Dec.	2	1	44	2	16	–*	65
Jan.-Mar. 1952	8	1	25	0	12	–*	46
April-June	5	0	35	4	14	–*	58
July-Sept.	3	0	17	3	13	4	40
Oct.-Dec.	8	1	14	0	15	5	43
Jan.-Mar. 1953	11	1	7	0	11	4	34
April-June	10	0	12	0	7	3	32
July	4	2	5	–†	2	0	13
Total: by Type:	57	6	193	10	102	16	(384)

As in previous wars, the Navy and Marine aviators serving in Korea flew with elan and dedication, especially in the face of adversity, as a few anecdotes quickly reveal:

• Commander Paul Gray, C.O. of VF-55 on the *Essex*, persisted in flying combat missions despite being shot down five times. He ditched so often in Wonsan harbor that the carrier's ready room posted a sign reading "Use caution when ditching damaged airplanes in Wonsan harbor. Don't hit CDR. Gray."[33]

*Not yet introduced to Korean service.
†Retired from Korean service before end of war.

• As an *Essex* Panther strafed a column of trucks near Wonsan, flak knocked the jet into a spinning dive. In its cockpit, the young fighter pilot instinctively regained control over the hurtling plane, recovering into level flight a mere 20 feet off the ground. The Panther immediately collided with a telephone pole, clipping 3 feet from its right wing. Again the pilot managed to regain control, and he staggered back up to 14,000 feet, reaching friendly territory before ejecting safely. Two days later, Ensign Neil Armstrong returned to VF-51. He had displayed the qualities of courage and skill that would lead to his selection as commander of the first lunar landing mission in 1969.[34]

• Another *Essex* airman, VF-55's Ensign Peter Moriarity, fell victim to flak while on a search mission for a downed airplane. He bailed out. Just after he landed, a North Korean soldier emptied his revolver at him from less than five feet, missing with all six shots. Moriarity, undaunted, bolted from his would-be executioner, sprinted to a rescue helicopter amid rifle fire from other Communist troops, and returned safely to the *Essex*.[35]

• VF-64's Ensign Ed Hofstra pressed a strafing attack against North Korean troops a little too zealously during a coastal armed reconnaissance sweep near Wonsan. He delayed his dive pull-out, and his Corsair hit the ground, scraping off all its external armament (including a napalm bomb, a fuel tank, and eight 100-pound bombs), and bending the propeller blades around the nose of the airplane like a closed flower. As the ordnance went off with a

166

roar, the Corsair bounced back into the air, burst into flame, and ricocheted 500 yards offshore before ditching in the sea. Hofstra spent the next three hours paddling frantically away from shore in his raft before a Royal Air Force Sunderland flying boat rescued him.[36]

• Lieutenant (j.g.) Howard Thayer masterminded two remarkable rescues. In 1952, while flying with VF-194 aboard *Valley Forge,* Thayer talked a fellow pilot down to a safe landing on an emergency strip after shell fragments had temporarily blinded him. As unusual as this was, less than a year later, while flying Panthers from *Boxer,* Thayer again played seeing-eye dog, this time to a wounded pilot who could see, but whose flight instruments had been knocked out by flak. Using only hand signals, Thayer led the pilot to a safe emergency landing in South Korea.[37]

• Some rescues involved fighting long odds. A two-seat Fairey Firefly from 817 Squadron aboard the Australian carrier H.M.A.S. *Sydney* operating in the Yellow Sea force-landed from flak damage in the midst of Communist troops. The plucky crew unlimbered the observer's machine gun, set it up, and held the Koreans at bay. *Sydney,* meantime, launched an American Navy HO3S-1 helo escorted by her Sea Furies to augment a land-based helicopter already on the way; some Australian Gloster Meteor jet fighters from the Royal Australian Air Force's 77 Squadron joined up as well in case any MiGs chose to interfere. But things soon looked bleak: the land-based helicopter had to turn back, and impending fuel starvation forced the Meteors to abandon their

CAP. *Sydney* reluctantly ordered the escorting Sea Furies home for the same reason, but the gutsy fighter pilots stuck around. Late in the afternoon, as dusk fell, the HO3S-1 crew spotted the wrecked airplane, alerted by the muzzle flashes from the Firefly's machine gun, and set down amid a hail of Communist ground fire. Helicopter crewman G. C. Gooding leapt out, gunned down two North Koreans firing at him from less than 50 yards away, and the beleaguered Aussies and Gooding scrambled back into the helicopter and took off. The Sea Furies covered the helicopter on its 107-mile flight back to the *Sydney;* the celebration is best left to the imagination.

• Not all stories ended so well. A heartbreaker in the same area involved five Marine Corsairs from VMA-312 embarked aboard the *Badoeng Strait*. Antiaircraft fire claimed one of their squadron mates, and he ditched in the Taedong estuary near Chinnamp'o. The rest of his flight, plus two other Corsairs on a gunfire-spotting mission, teamed up to cover the approach of rescue helicopters and a crash boat. But heavy Communist ground fire thwarted the rescue mission. Bespeaking the fierce loyalty of the Corps for its own, the five Corsairs fought a protracted dogfight with four MiGs that persistently attempted to strafe the would-be rescuers and the downed pilot. The Corsair pilots broke up the MiGs' attacks with head-on gun passes and even their air-to-ground HVAR rockets. The MiG drivers eventually abandoned the fight and retreated northwards, which made the subsequent loss of the pilot all the more bitter. The Corsairs stayed as long as they could, turning their lethal attention to targets on the ground. Finally, low fuel states forced their return to the "Bing-Ding," where they all landed safely with less than 30 gallons of fuel apiece.[39]

• A few months later, Major David Cleeland, who had led the gallant Corsair versus MiG fight, fell victim to flak over Haeju, in the same area. He managed to crashland on a frozen reservoir, and, as his anxious wingmen watched, he abandoned the plane and made a dash for safety. Out onto the ice charged a North Korean cavalry troop, complete with horses and flashing sabers. Down plummeted the angry Corsairs, their rockets and bombs breaking up the ice under the Koreans in a surrealistic 20th century replay of Pharoah versus the Israelites. A helicopter soon had Cleeland back among friends.[40]

• Marine fighter squadron VMF-311 had a reputation for being particularly aggressive. Flying Panthers on close air support and interdiction sorties, the Leathernecks proved the utility of jet fighters for CAS sorties, and, though it was not really their job, tangled repeatedly with MiGs, though without scoring any definite kills. Such aggressiveness brought with it corresponding losses. First Lieutenant Chuck Sewell took a flak hit north of P'yongyang while on a rail cutting mission and managed to reach the sea before ejecting; a convenient helicopter soon deposited him aboard a waiting destroyer. He eventually became one of America's most distinguished test pilots and a confirmed aquatic sports enthusiast.

• When Major John Glenn — later the first American to orbit the earth — arrived in Korea, fellow

Pacific War vets warned him the North Koreans "were a hell of a lot more serious than the Japanese." Glenn subsequently learned at first hand; he gained an unenviable reputation for repeatedly taking antiaircraft hits on his missions. Once a 85-mm shell hit his Panther as he rolled in on a target, blowing away a napalm bomb and a 3-foot section of wing. Glenn managed to limp back to P'ohang after cautiously determining that he could still control the airplane. On another sortie, he dueled it out on the deck with a 37-mm flak emplacement, and took a 37-mm hit from another emplacement that remained hidden. For one awful second, the F9F nosed down as if to dive into the ground. Glenn snatched the stick back, skimmed across a rice paddy, and then climbed to safety and home. That was still not enough for the future Senator from Ohio; in the closing weeks of the war he transferred on exchange duty to an Air Force Sabre squadron, shooting down three MiGs in nine days.

• Reservist Ted Williams, the finest baseball slugger of his time, nearly struck out in early 1953 while part of a mass strike against road traffic south of P'yongyang. Flak knocked out his hydraulic and electrical systems and set the Panther ablaze. Williams stuck with it, and led by a fellow pilot, the famed outfielder managed to make a safe emergency landing in the south. Williams returned to the Red Sox lineup in time for the 1954 season.[41]

Not all heroics occurred in the air. Groundcrews and flight deck personnel contributed more than their share. Marine squadron leader Lieutenant

Colonel Richard W. Wyczawski owed his life to Navy Hospitalman Charles Stalcup. After Wyczawski's F4U crashed on takeoff from Kimpo, the injured pilot staggered away, collapsing as the plane burst into flame. Loaded with napalm, the Corsair would explode at any moment. As others fled, Stalcup ran in, lifted the injured man, and carried him on his back to safety; they reached cover just as the Corsair erupted. Corporal Rene Wattelet, an ordnance technican, saved an F7F and a fellow mechanic when the other Marine accidently released a parachute flare. Wattelet grabbed the 30-pound flare, heaving it away just before it exploded. Ordnance technicians E. H. Forbush, Rod Courtney, and E. H. Rollf watched a Skyraider come aboard *Princeton* with an unreleased napalm bomb. Horrified, they saw that its igniters had somehow activated — perhaps from the shock of landing — and would fire at any time, covering the flight deck in flaming napalm. Without thinking of the risks, they removed the igniters and threw them overboard; one exploded as it fell into the sea. When another Skyraider on *Bon Homme Richard* dropped a million candlepower flare just before launch, smoke and flame from the sputtering firework threatened to engulf the airplane. Deck crewman James L. Seig raced across the deck, scooped up the flare, and tossed it over the side, possibly preventing a flight deck holocaust.[42]

Carrier operations always carry the potential for catastrophe; a flight deck, as anyone familiar with naval aviation is aware, is among the most hazardous spots in earth. As demanding as flight operations are in the era of modern angled-deck carriers equipped with steam catapults and sophisticated landing aids, Korean war operations in the era of the straight-deck carrier with hydraulic "cats," and an LSO waving paddles at the pilot, held even greater danger. The capricious weather added challenges. From October 13 through 15, 1951, for example, Typhoon *Ruth* disrupted Seventh Fleet air and surface operations in the Formosa-Korea-Japan area. H.M.A.S. *Sydney* was hit particularly hard: 50% of that carrier's Fireflies and Sea Furies sustained storm damage. But "routine" day-to-day flight operations posed the greatest danger. On September 16, 1951, a damaged F2H-2 unable to drop its hook landed on *Essex,* leapt the barriers, and trundled forward of the island, on its way to an inevitable collision. Its pilot presumably guessed that deck crews had already refueled and rearmed the fighters neatly parked along the port side of the flight deck, for the Banshee veered sharply to starboard, ramming four unarmed and unrefueled aircraft and disintegrating in a huge fireball. The pilot's decision plus prompt damage control and savvy shiphandling that took advantage of the winds localized the damage and *Essex* resumed flight operations the next day. But the accident claimed seven men, injured 27 others, and destroyed four airplanes. The following November 4, an errant Panther bounced over *Antietam*'s barriers, killing four, injuring 10, and leaving two aircraft destroyed and six others damaged. Such accidents expedited efforts to develop the angled deck; for more immediate impact, the Navy introduced a newly designed nylon tape and cable barricade to snag and halt a runaway aircraft. This new design, first employed on *Antietam,* superceded the older and less effective Davis barriers in use throughout the fleet.[43]

Unlike Vietnam, where the carriers *Oriskany, Forrestal,* and *Enterprise* all experienced disastrous hangar or flight deck fires with consequent heavy casualties, only one major fire plagued TF 77 during its operations off Korea. On August 4, 1952, the *Boxer* with Air Group 2 rendezvoused with TF 77 in the Sea of Japan to begin another round of air strikes. Under command of Captain Marshal B. Gurney, the ship commenced flight operations the next morning, launching 106 sorties against Korean targets. At 6:16 on August 6, after having launched eight predawn hecklers, *Boxer* fell prey to a portside hangar deck fire. For some reason, a plane's fuel tank exploded on the hangar deck, igniting other aircraft; explosions tossed some on their backs. On the flight deck, nearly 60 more planes, loaded with fuel and weapons, awaited launch. Captain Gurney wisely rejected thoughts of trying to launch them as quickly as possible, and, instead, reduced speed from 30 knots, directing deck crews to respot as many planes forward of the island as possible and jettison their ordnance over the side. The flames raced from portside throughout the hangar deck, forcing fire crews to attack it with foam and water from the number two elevator; *Boxer* came about to starboard so fire crews would have the winds at their backs. Hangar deck officer Lieutenant W. J. Norton lowered the elevator with fire control teams and a plane, starting the plane's engine so that its propeller

173

could clear the smoke. Meanwhile, the fire drove 63 crewmen over the side (*Boxer*'s consorts picked them all up), trapping others below and forcing the abandonment of some engineering spaces, including two fire rooms.[44]

Captain Gurney subsequently wrote:

It was at this point that considerable doubt existed as to our ability to control the fire. A further loss of power would have left us dead in the water and without water pressure for the fire hoses. Fortunately, tenacious men in the engineering department hung on to the point of exhaustion until the flames could be controlled. The Damage Control Central Station functioned throughout and was in constant communication with its four repair parties. Every man not trapped below unhesitatingly entered the inferno without regard to personal danger from exploding ammunition and bombs. The performance of the crew was magnificent and was a most impressive demonstration of selflessness, determination, and teamwork. While the fire fighting was progressing on the hangar deck, crews on the flight deck removed bombs and ammunition from aircraft and ready service lockers thus eliminating a terrible threat against the life of the ship. After having accomplished this Herculean task in a matter of minutes, these men turned to the business of fighting the fire.[45]

This fire triggered memories of the *Franklin*'s

ordeal in 1945. As escorts watched, great rolling clouds of smoke billowed from the stricken *Boxer*. On the flight deck, jersey-shirted deck crews and aircrews in flight suits manhandled aircraft and weapons. On the hangar deck, damage control teams fought in their own Dante-like Hell of thick smoke and lurid flames. Seaman R. W. Chapman sprayed a fire hose over airman Ralph Finley, preventing him from being burned while Finley lay injured on the deck amidst flaming wreckage. Then Chapman took advantage of a lull in the flames and pulled him to safety; the two men took refuge before rescue in *Boxer*'s photo lab. Cady Leib donned an oxygen mask and rescued nine men from smoke-filled spaces; fireman John Lewis, without a mask, bravely rescued at least 11 others before he was overcome himself. Medical teams worked alongside their damage control counterparts; fragments from exploding shells killed Hospitalmen Richard Taylor and James Wark, as well as Air Group 2's medical officer, Lieutenant James Shropshire, as they tended to injured men. After five hours, the efforts of these men and their comrades had saved the ship, at the cost of nine dead, 30 others injured, and 18 aircraft damaged or destroyed. *Boxer* steamed to Yokosuka for temporary repairs, then returned to the task force in mid-August for another month of operations.[46]

By this time the nature of the naval air war against North Korea had again begun to change from the single-minded pursuit of interdiction toward a more balanced employment of naval air power against a variety of more significant targets.

The last year of Korean conflict witnessed a movement back toward the days of the Pusan pocket and the drive to the Yalu, when naval aviation — both ship and shore based — had struck at diverse targets, and made its presence felt over the battlefield. Now, however, naval aviation would strike at North Korea with the weapons, tactics, confidence, and maturity that accompanied the experience accumulated in two years of air war.

5/AIR PRESSURE

Starting the summer of 1952, the Korean air war shifted from interdiction for its own sake to an increasing number of creative and well-considered "air pressure" strikes aimed at the heart of North Korea's new direction of the air war, and, with the *Cherokee* strike program, launched one of its more important aspects. The seeds of this change had long been germinating, and required only the watering of experience to blossom. Indeed, they had existed almost from the moment of the first naval involvement in the Korean War, starting with the raid on P'yongyang and the Wonsan oil refinery in July 1950.

One of the most productive and unusual Navy strikes was Air Group 19's assault on the Hwachon dam in May 1951. As Allied troops turned to offense after Communist fortunes ebbed in 1951, the Hwachon dam and reservoir assumed critical importance. The dam, located approximately 50 miles northeast of Seoul (midway between that city and the sea) impounds the waters of the Pukhan river. As Allied forces moved doggedly forward, the

Communist-held dam threatened the advance. The waters behind the dam could flood roads and destroy bridges. If necessary the Communists could close its floodgates entirely, reducing the Pukhan's depth downstream, setting the stage for a counteroffensive. Either way, the Hwachon dam had to be put out of commission. B-29s using guided bombs proved unsuccessful, and in early April, tipping their hand, the Communists released some of its waters, flooding the lower Pukhan and destroying some bridges. A hastily organized Ranger operation failed to seize the dam; then, frustratingly, towards the end of April the Allies did hold it briefly, relinquishing it to a Chinese counterattack before they could destroy its floodgates.

On the afternoon of April 30, Rear Admiral Ralph A. Ofstie, then TF 77 commander aboard *Princeton,* received an urgent Eighth Army request that the Navy destroy two or more of the dam's sluice gates to release the waters in piecemeal fashion, thus preventing any hostile attempt to flood the lower Pukhan with a massive release. Later that day, *Princeton* launched six ADs from VA-195 armed with a mix of 2,000-pound bombs and 11.75-inch Tiny Tim aerial rockets, accompanied by five Corsairs for flak suppression. But bombs merely chipped the face of the dam, and rockets hit it but skittered off. TF 77 had found a target even more difficult to destroy than a bridge. Annoyed but not dismayed, *Princeton* skipper Captain William O. Gallery suggested destroying the sluice gates with Mark-13 aerial torpedos, holdovers from the Second World War. *Princeton* had a small stock of Mark-

13s, and the air group had practiced antishipping torpedo attacks, though some pilots had never flown with a torpedo, much less launched one. But with enthusiasm running high, Gallery's aviators took up the challenge, and on May 1, *Princeton* launched eight Skyraiders, five from VA-195 and three from VC-35, with 12 flak-suppressing F4Us for escort. The ADs looked odd with the long cylindrical "fish" loaded under their bellies. As had Guy Gibson's Lancaster raid against the Möhne and Eder dams in the Second World War, the ADs from *Princeton* had to couple special tactics with superlative flying. They threaded their way through craggy terrain, dropped down at precisely the right moment over the irregularly shaped reservoir, held a constant speed, course, and altitude, and aimed for a target only 40 feet wide.

The attack group reached the dam and had a pleasant surprise: light and inaccurate flak. The Corsairs quickly made their runs, then circled around to watch the fun. By twos the ADs came, blue airplanes against dark waters, holding steadily on course as the pilots drew on prewar training exercises. Finally, the long torpedos dropped clear, slipped beneath the surface, and then, like miniature submarines, ran purposefully to the gates. The lightened ADs roared over the edge of the dam; its face dropped away steeply beneath them as they cocked their noses at the sky. Eight times the torpedoes splashed into the still waters of the dam, and of the eight, seven ran true to their targets. Six of the seven exploded, sending columns of water and rippling shockwaves across the surface, blowing away one sluice gate and ripping a gaping hole in another. As a circling Panther from VC-61's *Princeton* detachment took photos, the waters fell in long, white, seething columns to the river bed below. Air Group 19 had knocked the Hwachon dam out of the war. *Princeton*'s action report mentioned the attack along with CAS and interdiction strikes made the same day, lumping it with buildings, trucks, railroad cars, and gun emplacements, as if the dam strike was a most natural and mundane occurrence. VA-195 thought differently, however, taking the nickname *Dambusters.*[1]

Relations between the Navy and the Air Force, characterized by occasional hostility in prewar years and suspicion and mutual criticism (especially over the CAS question) in the war's early months, steadily improved. Both services grew to recognize each could offer strengths the other lacked for special purpose missions or urgent situations demanding closely coordinated strikes. On April 25, 1951, during the start-up of FEAF's interdiction campaign, Fifth Air Force requested TF 77's help in interdicting North Korea's west coast rail network in the vicinity of P'yongyang. In early May, Rear Admiral George R. Henderson, who had just succeeded Admiral Ofstie as TF 77 commander following the brilliant Hwachon dam strike, had his staff undertake a targeting survey. The staff recommended hitting four bridges in a triangular area northeast of the Communist capital that connected P'yongyang to Sonch'on, the rail net running east to Sunch'on, and thence via Yangdok to Wonsan. Willing to help, Henderson nevertheless recognized that he had insufficient forces to guarantee interdiction of Korea's east coast rail network, let alone the west coast lines as well. He could only call on *Princeton* and *Boxer* to support the strike, as *Philippine Sea* was in Yokosuka for replenishment, with *Bon Homme Richard* enroute from San Diego to Pearl Harbor in preparation for its own Korean deployment by the end of the month. Accordingly, on May, 11, *Princeton* and *Boxer* launched a massive 80-plane raid composed of 32 ADs from *Princeton*'s VA-195 and *Boxer's* VS-702, accompanied by 32 Corsairs and a top cover of 16 Panthers. Each Skyraider lugged two 2,000-pound bombs, and the Corsairs carried a mix of 100-pound and 250-pound bombs for flak suppression. By day's end, the sweep had damaged three out of the four bridges. *Boxer*'s airmen alone dropped three spans on one bridge and one span on another. Jubilant, the Fifth Air Force requested additional west coast strikes, but Henderson, who recognized TF 77's limitations and the necessity of concentrating on east coast lines, politely declined, a position COMNAVEFE not only endorsed but strongly reiterated.[2]

The Navy and the Air Force got together again, however, in August 1951, with a spectacularly successful attack on Rashin. Rashin (now known as Najin) lay far up Korea's east coast, an important rail and port city. Its extensive marshaling yards and petroleum storage facilities made it a particularly attractive target. Only 17 miles from the Soviet Union's Siberian frontier, Rashin posed a difficult problem for Allied airmen. During the Second World War, bombers of all nations had often missed their targets by wide margins, a commentary on training and the state of navigational and bombing aids at that time, particularly in the war's early days. Though conditions had dramatically improved by Korea, FEAF could not politically afford navigational errors that resulted in the intrusion of Soviet airspace. The Department of State looked upon proposals to bomb Rashin with the greatest of skepticism, and, predictably, reacted strongly when a B-29 strike against Rashin in August 1950 went slightly awry; most of the Superfortresses dropped their loads into the countryside, though still well away from the Soviet border. As a result, in September, the Joint Chiefs of Staff declared Rashin off-limits, and it remained so until mid-1951.

Much as Hanoi took advantage of the misguided and one-sided restrictions that the United States placed upon its air war in Southeast Asia over a decade later, North Korea shrewdly exploited the Rashin decision. Rashin expanded into a formidable supply point with ever larger facilities and capacities. The furor that followed General MacArthur's recall from Korea, including charges that the Rashin decision constituted a "flagrant example of political interference in military decisions," forced reconsideration in the late summer of 1951. General Ridgway asked permission to strike Rashin, and President Truman and the Joint Chiefs issued clearance to do so. Planning began at once.[3]

Survivability questions compounded the targeting and flight path problems. By the summer of 1951, the MiG had demonstrated its mastery over the B-29, even when a top cover of Sabres and slower

straightwing F-84 Thunderjets escorted the Superfortresses. Flown on daylight raids, the slow Superfortresses proved vulnerable to MiGs that dove
through the fighter screens, made a single pass, and
then ducked back across the Yalu, much as the
Luftwaffe's Me 262 had against B-17s and B-24s
escorted by Mustangs and Thunderbolts during the
late months of the Second World War. On April 12,
for example, FEAF lost four B-29s out of 39 during
another futile attack against the Sinuiju railway
bridge spanning the Yalu. Eventually such losses
forced FEAF to switch from daylight to night raids.
Planners feared a Rashin strike might stir up a
hornets' nest of fighter opposition, perhaps even
including Soviet MiGs from fighter fields around
Vladivostok. Rashin lay approximately 375 miles
northeast of the Sabre base at Kimpo; Sabres had
problems enough operating at roughly half that
distance to MiG Alley, a roughly trapezoidal area of
about 3,250 square miles bordered by the Yalu and
Ch'ongch'on rivers, northeast from Antung-Sinuiju
to Ch'osan, southeast to Huich'on, southwest to
Sinanju, and then northwest along the Yellow Sea
coast to the mouth of the Yalu. Many times they
returned to Kimpo's landing pattern with just minutes of fuel left, and were forced on occasion to
make powerless gliding approaches down to "dead-
stick" landings. Expecting Sabres to escort B-29s to
Rashin and possibly to engage in fuel-consuming
dogfights, represented an inconceivable optimism.
Conversely, committing B-29s without escort was
totally out of the question. Here, then, lay an
opportunity for TF 77, operating off Korea's east

coast, to furnish fighter escort for the Super-fortresses.[4]

On August 22, 1951, the carrier *Essex* (CV-9), first of her class and the possessor of an old and honorable name among American fighting ships, arrived for duty with TF 77, carrying VF-172, a squadron assigned the task of proving McDonnell's big F2H-2 Banshee in combat. The Banshee, a larger and more powerful design outgrowth of the earlier pre-Korean FH-1 Phantom* that launched the Navy into the jet age, lacked the Sabre's speed, but otherwise possessed excellent high-altitude performance which, when piloted skillfully, could make it a deadly foe. VF-172's pilots looked forward to guarding the B-29s as they made their way to sack Rashin.

On August 25, 1951, 35 B-29s from three bomb wings took off on the raid. Eighty miles from Rashin, 11 Panthers from VF-51 and 12 Banshees met the Superfortresses. The Banshees took position well above the bombers, since they had better altitude performance than the Grumman jets. The Panthers remained with the B-29s at lower altitude; the two sets of Navy fighters wove over the formation; all eyes turned northwards for a telltale glint of sun on metal that might betray a MiG attack. None came. In clear, beautiful skies, the silver B-29s placed over 300 tons of bombs squarely in the midst of Rashin's marshaling yards and, unmolested save for "considerable" but ineffectual flak, flew out to

*Not to be confused with McDonnell's subsequent F4H-1 Phantom II of 1958, which fought with distinction in Southeast Asia.

sea, the escorting Panthers and Banshees staying along until the obsolescent bombers reached safety, and then peeling off, curving down to the *Essex*. This raid, the first time that Navy jet fighters had escorted Air Force bombers over hostile territory, set the tone for future cooperation between the Navy and the Air Force in pounding North Korea's war machine. B-29s and Banshees flew together again on October 8, 1952, when *Kearsarge*'s VF-11 escorted Superfortresses raiding the Kowan rail center just north of Wonsan, part of an Air Force-Navy operation, including simultaneous strikes by *Princeton* and *Essex*. Such joint efforts worked well, fulfilling the expectations of both Air Force and Navy officials, particularly Admiral Arthur Radford, who had directed his Seventh Fleet and TF 77 commanders to work closely with their Air Force counterparts to develop joint targeting and operational plans for combined strikes.[5]

A very different kind of operation took place on October 30, 1951, when aircraft from *Essex* and *Antietam* raided Kapsan. Throughout the war, the UN command supported anti-Communist guerrillas fighting in the mountains and coastal areas of North Korea, small teams that often extracted airmen shot down over the north and furnished valuable intelligence information at great risk. Such bands came under control of a shadowy organization known as JACK: Joint Advisory Commission Korea. Through the Eighth Army, JACK fed targeting information to the Navy, thanks to the efforts of Lieutenant Commander James A. Scholes, a graduate of the Army's jump school at Fort Benning who met JACK personnel during his Airborne training, and who was now Flag Lieutenant to Rear Admiral J. J. "Jocko" Clark. On October 29, Eighth Army had informed TF 77 commander Admiral John Perry that senior political, security, and military representatives of Chinese and North Korean forces would meet the next morning at 9:00 a.m. in Kapsan, a town high in a valley by the Hoch'on river, amidst northeastern Korea's desolate mountains. A Kapsan strike seemed a good opportunity to kill a large number of high-level enemy decision makers. Precedent existed for such an attack; similar raids against senior enemy officials had characterized Allied air operations during the Second World War, notably the Royal Air Force's spectacularly successfully Mosquito raids against various Gestapo headquarters in Occupied Europe in 1944 and 1945. Perry immediately ordered high-altitude (and hence unobtrusive) photo reconnaissance of the site. Taken by a VC-61 Panther, the photographs clearly showed the meeting compound, a cluster of 12 buildings to the east of Kapsan, complete with records archives, security center, and troop barracks.[6]

At 7:30 on the morning of October 30, a specially selected strike group of eight VF-54 (an attack squadron, despite its "VF" designation) ADs led by C.O. Commander Paul Gray (the Navy's own flak magnet and Wonsan harbor ditching expert) launched from *Essex*. Each plane carried two 1,000-pound bombs; one had a proximity fuse set to explode above ground and inflict maximum casualties among antiaircraft crews, and one was set to explode instantaneously when it hit its target. Each

AD also carried a napalm tank on its centerline stores station, plus no less than eight 250-pound general purpose bombs and full belts of 20-mm ammunition (half incendiary and half high explosive) for its cannon. Air Group 5 augmented this force with four Banshees from VF-172 and eight Corsairs from VF-53. *Antietam*'s Air Group 15 contributed four Panthers from VF-831, eight Corsairs from VF-713, and eight other ADs from VA-728.

Gray's small band crossed the coast, stayed low under North Korean radar, and allowed approximately 15 minutes for conference attendees and late arrivals to get comfortable. They popped up to 8,000 feet over the ridgeline behind Kapsan at 9:13 a.m., rolled in on the compound and dropped their proximity-fused bombs; all eight exploded over the compound. Confusion existed over the level of flak. Gray's group reported none, presumably due to the bombs, but probably also because they were concentrating on the target so intently that they missed it. On the other hand, *Essex*'s action report cited intense antiaircraft fire. Both may be true: there may have been intense fire at the beginning as the flak crews, perhaps alerted by the growing roar of the Skyraiders during their approach, took them under fire, dwindling away as the bombs did their grim work. In any case, Gray's group zoomed back to their perch and dived down again, unloaded their remaining "thousand pounders," and followed with selective strafing, napalming, and, finally, attack runs with their 250-pound bombs. They left Kapsan "a smoking mass of rubble." Two days later, JACK's guerrilla service reported that the strike killed over

500 of the conference attendees and security force, as well as destroying all records of the North Korean Communist Party! Communist radio subsequently referred to Gray's team as the "Butchers of Kapsan," an inflammatory choice of words, though not an altogether inaccurate description. (Disarmingly, Gray's pilots took their call-signs from Walt Disney's dwarfs, Gray, naturally, being known as Snow White.) The Kapsan strike was JACK's swansong. Because of JACK's undoubted success, North Korean internal security forces pursued the guerrilla bands with tenacity. "Eventually," Jocko Clark recalled, "we lost contact with them as they either were captured or had to merge back into the population." Some prudently retired to await another day. As late as 1964, historian David Rees concluded that "the story of the underground war in North Korea still remains largely secret as some of the clandestine networks and groups are still in existence."[7]

As the Korean War progressed, the ratio of naval jet aircraft sorties to naval propeller aircraft sorties changed dramatically. In the first year of the war, TF 77 had averaged nearly 3,300 sorties per month, the ratio of jet-to-prop being 1:2. By the end of the second year, TF 77 flew an average of over 4,000 sorties monthly, with a jet-to-prop ratio of 2:3. Thereafter a rapid change occurred; by the end of February 1953, TF 77 averaged nearly 4,500 sorties per month at a 1:1 jet-to-prop ratio, and by the armistice in late July, TF 77 flew nearly 5,200 sorties per month at a jet-to-prop ratio of 4:3. Early in the war some carriers with TF 77 had one jet squadron and three propeller squadrons, with a few all-propeller air groups. By the middle of the war, carriers typically had two jet squadrons and two prop squadrons. By war's end, some air groups had three jet squadrons and only one propeller squadron. (The Navy would not complete the transformation to an all-jet fighter and attack force until the Skyraider retired from the fleet in 1968.) The increasingly Korean jet sortie rates reflected both the infusion of new jet aircraft into TF 77 (though at a persistently slower rate than desired) and the use of carrier-based jet fighters as strike aircraft that delivered bombs from ship to shore.

Unlike the Air Force, which went to war in 1950 with its F-80s carrying bombs and rockets as well as guns, the Navy, from June 1950 through March 1951, operated its Panthers armed only with full ammunition for their cannon and up to six HVAR or ATAR underwing rockets. This constraint stemmed from the performance of available hydraulic catapults aboard unmodified *Essex*-class carriers, as well as from the propulsion limitations of early jet engines. Under these circumstances, relative wind across deck assumed critical importance; how much is evident from a chart (based on the experienced of *Bon Homme Richard*) listing the permissible amount of ordnance (rockets, or an equivalent weight of bombs) that could be carried by a Panther operating with full internal and tip-tank fuel, and assisted by a maximum permissible 3,500 pounds per square inch of available catapult pressure.[8]

Wind (in kts)	Ordnance load
30	None
31	2 rockets
32	4 rockets
33	6 rockets

Occasional breakages of catapult bridles, which attached jets to the catapult, compounded the problem of wind across deck. Because of the low wind margin, any breakage immediately threatened disaster; if a pilot could not stop his Panther by chopping power and riding its brakes, the jet would wallow off the end of the flight deck and "splash." In most such accidents the plane guard helicopter or destroyer quickly recovered the pilot, but in some distressing cases, both pilot and plane were lost. One *Philippine Sea* pilot had an especially close call following a bridle breakage: his Panther slid to a stop, its nose wheel already on the ramp at the bow.[9]

Despite such difficulties, naval airmen were eager to evaluate the F9F as a carrier-based fighter-bomber. Such problems with flying from the fast carriers did not bother the Marines flying the Panther ashore; the Leathernecks treated it much as they would one of their beloved Corsairs, carrying anything they could fit. On April 1, 1951, for the first time in naval aviation history, a bomb-loaded jet strike left a carrier. On that day, with especially favorable winds, VF-191 replaced the rockets of two Panthers with bombs, and squadron skipper Lieutenant Commander George B. Riley and Lieutenant Arthur R. Hawkins catapulted from the *Princeton* carrying four 250-pound and two 100-pound bombs apiece. They attacked a small bridge, demolishing it in an encouraging display of precision bombing. Thereafter, air groups increasingly treated their jets much as they would any other strike airplane. The advent of the hefty Banshee gave TF 77 a superb fighter-bomber for bridge and rail strikes. Always the second fiddle in Korea (for the more numerous Panthers carried the bulk of the Navy's jet war to the enemy), the Banshee, in the words of an evaluation report, "proved to be superior to the F9F in every respect" but one: deck crews could not fold its wings if its tip tanks contained fuel. Accordingly, because of its size (the "Banjo" had nearly a 45-foot wingspread), if one scrubbed before launch, it was difficult to respot it and keep a launch schedule proceeding smoothly.[10]

The Banshee was ideally suited for rail interdiction. Easy to maintain, ruggedly built, and very resistant to flak damage, the F2H-2, with its twin jets, had a high rate of climb that permitted multiple attacks on a target. The plane's 30-minute endurance advantage over the Panther also impressed pilots from a flight safety standpoint. Banshees attacked rail lines in 30- to 40-degree dives, using 250-pound bombs. An F2H-2 could carry four 250-pound bombs (much more if operating from land), and sometimes lug four HVAR or ATAR rockets as well. After VF-172 completed its *Essex* tour, posttour analysis indicated that 35% of all the bombs dropped by the squadron had actually managed to cut a rail line. Since this involved hitting a target no more than 60 inches wide while moving at well over

400 mph, the Banshees' performance and that of its pilots was extraordinary.[11] An excerpt from an Air Group 5 dispatch concerning the Banshee gives a good idea of how it performed and how it fit into the pattern of attacks by other TF 77 aircraft:

One flak suppression mission was flown semi-coordinated with an AD [and] F4U bridge strike. The target, three bridges in a valley, was about two miles long [and] one-half mile wide, bordered by 3,000 foot mountains. About forty-eight active gun mounts of 40 mm to 5-inch with radar control were in the area. Eight Banshees loaded with four 260 lb. VT fused frag bombs, four ATAR's and 600 rounds of 20 mm, made six runs each and achieved eighty percent suppression. The runs were made by sections simultaneously on four gun positions each time. The first run was made from 12,000 feet altitude in forty-five degree dives with strafing from 8,000 to 5,000 feet and bomb release at 3,000 feet. Airspeeds of 480 to 500 knots were indicated in the pullouts at 1,500 to 2,000 feet. Succeeding runs were begun at about 10,000 feet and all runs were completed within a period of fifteen minutes. No effort was made to escort the strike group and the coordination was simply timing to complete the last Banshee attacks while the conventional aircraft were in their first dive. The mission was considered a success in that the bridges were knocked out and only one Banshee and one AD received damage.[12]

The use of jets as ground attack aircraft forced changes in doctrine, primarily because of speed. VMF-115, operating Panthers ashore, found its jets more susceptible to damage from their own bomb-blast during dive recoveries than Corsairs or earlier attack aircraft such as the famed SBD Dauntless. For example, a Panther required three times the recovery altitude of a Second World War Dauntless, since it moved well in excess of 500 mph in its dive compared to 300 mph for the older airplane. Both the Fifth Air Force (flying F-80s and F-84s) and TF 77 (with Panthers and Banshees) established a policy that pilots should not release bombs lower than 3,000 feet, lest they get caught in bomb-blast or succumb to target fixation and fly into the ground. Quite naturally, at higher drop altitudes, bombing accuracy deteriorated. VMF-115's pilots experimented with much lower drops, using delayed bomb fusing to get away. In a summary position paper, Major John Bolt, subsequently the Marine's only Korean ace, gaining all six of his MiG kills while on exchange duty with the Air Force, explained the tactics. VMF-115 favored attacks from 35 to 40 degree dives, entering a dive at 12,000 feet at about 260 mph, with speed brakes deployed and engine power reduced to 75%. The pilots dropped to 1,800 feet before bomb release, made an abrupt 5-g dive recovery, simultaneously went to 100% power, retracted the speed brakes, and "jinked" to avoid antiaircraft fire. Such low release altitudes enabled them to get excellent accuracy, but also exposed them to greater risk from small arms and light flak.

Though VMF-115 generally had an acceptable loss rate despite such tactics, critics noted that this ran counter somewhat to the Navy and Marine Corps' experience.[13]

In mid-1952, with Navy and Marine jets fully integrated into the ongoing interdiction campaign, there was a fundamental shift in the pattern of air operations against North Korea. By this time, events had overtaken and discredited Operation *Strangle;* its successor *Saturate* continued with greater effectiveness, though it did not produce the abrupt reduction in North Korean capabilities that interdiction proponents had hoped. TF 77 still averaged an impressive 133 rail cuts per day, but increasingly turned to combined air strikes and naval gunfire sorties against coastal targets, as well as attacks upon North Korea's small boat fleet, which attempted to land parties on offshore islands in Allied hands by night. In June, there was a new direction to the air war: the beginning of strikes aimed at increasingly enemy costs and reducing enemy efficiency by hitting at North Korea's electrical power network and remaining industry.

This new tack arose primarily from frustration with the interdiction campaign, from the inability to achieve a settlement via armistice talks, and from the efforts of key people in the Air Force, Navy, and Army. Brigadier General Jacob E. Smart, a brilliant planner appointed as FEAF's Deputy for Operations in January 1952, recognized a need to change the direction of air strategy. He believed that interdiction should continue at a level sufficient to prevent North Korea from significantly increasing its capacity to wage an offensive, but that the Allies should employ air pressure to convince the Communists to seek a negotiated settlement. At his direction, Smart's staff presented a plan in April 1952 for a more aggressive and selective air strategy, starting with a proposed series of raids against North Korea's power generation system. UN commander General Ridgway had resisted pressure from the Air Force for such raids up to this point. But as the truce talks at Panmunjom moved towards stalemate, Ridgway reluctantly recognized that the power strikes provided an excellent opportunity to pound the North. In May 1952, Army General Mark Clark assumed the duties of UN commander, replacing Ridgway. Clark strongly endorsed the proposed strikes in mid-June and ordered FEAF and Seventh Fleet to formulate a coordinated attack plan. Its final conception rested in the hands of two key men, both newly appointed to their positions: Fifth Air Force commander Lieutenant General Glenn O. Barcus, and Seventh Fleet commander Vice Admiral J. J. "Jocko" Clark. They worked well together; in fact, they were close friends. Clark, who had taken charge of Seventh Fleet on May 20, wasted no time in getting to work, and impressed all who came into contact with him. "Jocko Clark was a 'can-do' type of naval officer," General Smart recalled over three decades after the war. "Others might wait and see, but not Jocko."[14]

The power generation strikes involved attacks on four major hydroelectric generating facilities, three of which supplied an east coast power grid, with one responsible for a west coast grid. The three eastern facilities, comprised of hydroelectric generating stations at the Chosin, Fusen, and Kyosen reservoirs, supplied power from as far north as the Soviet frontier down to Wonsan and almost across the Korean peninsula. The west coast grid depended upon the huge Suiho hydroelectric facility, the fourth largest in the world, located on the Yalu river at the base of the Suiho (now the Sup'ung) reservoir. Suiho, Chosin, Fusen, and Kyosen all had multiple generating stations built during the Japanese occupation. Fusen, the oldest at two decades, generated over 80,000 kilowatts. Chosen, the next oldest, generated 150,000 kilowatts. Kyosen, the youngest and largest of the east coast complexes, generated upwards of 300,000 kilowatts. Designed with a capacity of 700,000 kilowatts, Suiho generated 400,000 kilowatts because the Soviets, during their occupation of North Korea, had removed two generators and three turbines from the dam, shipping them back to the Soviet Union. In May 1948, North Korea cut off South Korea from a Suiho-fed substation at P'yong-yang; increasingly Suiho sent much of its production across the frontier into China. Destroying or seriously damaging these plants, then, would essentially pull the plug on North Korea's power supply—and much of Manchuria's as well.[15]

Until the summer of 1952, political constraints dictated that the North Korean hydroelectric system be left alone. During the opening phase of the war, planners hoped that after the liberation of North Korea, the grids would be in place for friendly use. Then, as that hope faded, they thought that China's dependency upon Korean-supplied power might cause the Chinese to think twice about intervention, lest the Allies destroy the network. That did not work either. Once China entered the war, there was little reason not to attack the power network. In retrospect, it appears the hydroelectric strikes could have taken place at least a year earlier, and probably with greater effect. But no matter: with all the key players committed to striking the power network, from UN commander Mark Clark through the Air Force's Weyland and Barcus, and the Navy's Briscoe (then COMNAVFE) and Jocko Clark, North Korea's moment of truth had come. Clearly, any attack upon Suiho involved special risks, for Suiho lay perilously close to the major MiG bases at Antung and Tatungkou; MiGs often used the airspace above the reservoir as a forming-up area for their "trains" south of the Yalu. Accordingly, FEAF planned to saturate Suiho with a strike force of F-80s and Republic F-84s, all under cover of protective Sabre flights that allowed the fighter-bombers to operate unmolested. The Navy would take care of the easternmost grid.

In fact, plans changed significantly before the actual attacks. FEAF had scheduled the strikes for June 23 and 24, with intensive planning between the Navy and Air Force commencing only two days earlier. In preparation, TF 77 staggered carrier arrival and departure times so that all four of its carriers—*Boxer, Bon Homme Richard, Philippine Sea,* and *Princeton*—could participate, the first time four carriers had operated together on Korean strikes since the fall of 1950. Jocko Clark offered General Barcus the use of 36 Skyraiders for the Suiho attack, since the devastatingly accurate ADs, with their prodigious bomb loads, could guarantee maximum destruction of the generating facility. Barcus agreed. But, fearful of MiG intervention, he decided to go with the speedier jets, and, accordingly, cut the ADs down to 20. When Clark heard this, he immediately arranged to see Barcus in person, catapulting in a COD (Carrier Onboard Deliver) liaison plane from the *Philippine Sea* to shore. He persuaded Barcus that the ADs, escorted by Panthers at low level and with a Sabre top cover, could do the job. For the first time since the Yalu river bridge strikes nearly 18 months before, TF 77 would be launching a trans-Korean strike into MiG Alley.[16]

The strike came off without a hitch. Following several hours delay for inclement weather, TF 77 commander Rear Admiral Apollo Soucek (one of the Navy's most distinguished early test pilots) launched 35 of the planned 36 ADs early on the afternoon of June 23, employing planes from VA-65, VA-115, and VA-195. Each AD carried two 2,000-pound bombs plus a single 1,000-pound bomb. Four aircraft had a special "survival bomb" package in place of the thousand pounder that carried rescue and survival equipment for any aircrew unfortunate enough to be shot down. Thirty-six Panthers from VF-24, VF-112, and VF-191 covered the ADs; each Panther carried full ammunition for its 20-mm cannon as well as two 250-pound bombs suitable for flak suppression. By following a circuitous route that avoided populated areas and sticking to low altitudes, the strike force avoided detection; clouds helped. At 4:00 p.m. precisely on the revised schedule, the ADs arrived over Suiho, the Panthers nosing over to strafe flak positions. Overhead watchful Sabres noted a flurry of MiG activity at Antung. But those MiGs that did take off flew away northwards, into Manchuria! Not one rose to challenge the strike force. The ADs rolled into their textbook dives; unlike the Hwachon torpedoing of the previous year, the target this time was not the dam itself but rather its adjacent powerhouse and transformers. The F9Fs took much of the sting out of the flak, which was predictably intense and accurate until the jets unloaded on the Korean positions. Flak continued to stream up from the Manchurian sanctuary, and one VA-115 AD took a serious hit that necessitated a wheels-up landing at Kimpo. As the ADs pulled off target, having dropped 85 tons of bombs in a little over two minutes, bright flames billowed from the ruined powerhouse and dust and rubble filled the air. Then, hot on the heels of the ADs came 124 F-80s and F-84s, that added another 145 tons to the conflagration. Suiho was out of the war.

Commencing shortly after the ADs rolled in on Suiho, other Navy, Air Force, and Marine aircraft struck at the remaining three hydroelectric facilities. Attacks continued over the next day, and when it had ended, North Korea was virtually powerless. Ninety percent of its generating capacity had been destroyed, lost in the ruins of 11 — and possibly all 13 — of the generating stations in place of the four hydroelectric complexes. The surviving 10% power available came from small and relatively insignificant generating stations such as the Funei system near the Tumen river. Unlike the costly and morale-debilitating interdiction campaign begun over a year earlier, this sort of air-pressure seriously damaged North Korea's fighting potential. And, perhaps even more importantly, it solidified the growing cooperation between the Navy and Air Force on joint strikes, leading to other such team efforts during the remainder of the war. "My hat's off to the Navy for a terrific job," General Barcus had signaled Jocko Clark after the raid. "We must get together again sometime."[17]

And they did, less than a month later. On July 11, in conjunction with Marine, Air Force, British, and Australian aircraft, TF 77 hit military concentrations in and around P'yongyang. The strike group formed up over Wonsan harbor and proceeded across the Korean peninsula, receiving sporadic flak along the way, particularly near the Yangdok rail center. For humane as well as psychological reasons, the Allies dropped thousands of leaflets warning civilians of the attack, and flak was predictably intense, claiming two ADs of the 91 aircraft TF 77 dispatched from *Princeton* and *Bon Homme Richard*. Nevertheless, TF 77's raid resulted in heavy Communist casualties and destruction of numerous buildings, supply areas, and railroad facilities. On the return, lowering ceilings, precipitation, and fog forced the Panthers escorting the strike force to land at bases in South Korea, though the slower propeller aircraft pressed on. Guided by radio homing, they descended by four-plane divisions. They broke out of the overcast at an altitude of 300 feet, and trapped successfully aboard ship. The fickle weather forced

200

cancellation of remaining carrier strikes against the capital, but three other waves of land-based aircraft continued to pound the city as Sabres and Australian-flown Meteors maintained a barrier patrol against marauding MiGs, though none showed. By the end of the day, Operation *Pressure Pump* had passed into history; 1,254 sorties flown made it the largest air attack of the Korean war up to that time. The next month, the Allies bettered that, when, on August 29, UN planes again returned to P'yongyang, this time in 1,403 sorties (including 216 from *Boxer* and *Essex*) with equal success. For all practical purposes, P'yongyang lost its military value for the rest of the war.[18]

At Smart's suggestion, Navy-Air Force strikes next turned to the remnants of North Korea's industrial base. For the past year, North Korea's industry had shown an increasingly tendency to move northwards, closer to the Manchurian and Soviet frontiers. FEAF particularly thought that North Korea's extensive mining facilities—in service primarily for the Soviets and the Chinese—should be put out of commission by attacks against their vulnerable above-ground installations. Accordingly, FEAF and the Navy planned a series of strikes aimed at specific mining targets as well as related industrial facilities, such as cement plants and the power stations then undergoing hasty repair from the devastating strikes of June. On July 27, *Bon Homme Richard*'s ADs and Corsairs blitzed the Sindok lead and zinc mill, which reportedly shipped 3,000 tons of processed ore to the Soviet Union each month. The next day, *Princeton*'s Corsairs and Skyraiders destroyed a magnesite (MgCO³ a magnesium carbonate) plant at Kilchu in a deluge of bombs. On August 20, *Essex* and *Princeton* aircraft teamed up with Air Force F-84s in a concerted raid against Changp'yong-ni, a major west coast supply center.

On September 1, the largest Navy strike of the war (consisting of 142 aircraft from *Boxer, Essex,* and *Princeton*) destroyed the Aoji oil refinery, a target only eight miles from the Soviet frontier and out of range of most Air Force strike aircraft: B-29s could not hit it for fear of trespassing across Soviet territory, and it lay too far away for FEAF's F-80s or F-84s. The Aoji strike, and a simultaneous raid against industrial and power plant targets at Munsan and Ch'ongjin, came off without loss, a testimony to the fact that the raids caught the North Koreans so by surprise that they did not even throw up appreciable flak. On October 8, as mentioned, Banshees escorted the last great Superfortress daylight raid of the war to the Kowon rail center. As the B-29s left, *Princeton, Essex,* and *Kearsarge* followed up with an 89-plane strike against any remaining targets untouched or only lightly struck by the B-29s. Well established by the fall of 1952, the air pressure strategy, joint Air Force and naval aviation strikes against selected North Korean targets, remained productive until the armistice nine months later, though the number of suitable industrial targets quickly dwindled.[19]

In mid-October, the Allies sought to bring a different sort of pressure to bear on the North Koreans: a psychological gambit with the threat of an amphibious landing. Subsequently known as the "Kojo

202

feint," the operation centered on a 25-mile belt around the tiny coastal community of Kojo, just below Wonsan. Naturally, to be successful, such a feint would demand massive displays of naval air power against shore targets, and planners hoped it might serve to draw in troop and equipment reinforcements that carrier- and land-based strikes could hammer in concerted attacks. For its part, the Navy planned supporting air strikes and a mock amphibious landing. FEAF planned a mock airborne assault, and Eighth Army planned an attack in force northwards from the front near Kumwha. Only senior-level commanders knew the operation *was* a feint. At the working level, planners envisioned the operation as another Inch'on, and, brightened by the prospect of turning the war of stalemate into a war of movement (as well as fearful of the results of a beachhead failure), they worked hard to ensure that the landing would be a success. Fall weather off Korea is seldom pleasant and 1952 was no exception. During a practice landing, for example, four landing craft succumbed to heavy seas and pounding surf, fortunately without loss of life. TF 77's maintenance personnel and aircrews worked especially hard, taking extra risks. On "D minus 3," they flew 667 sorties against targets in the vicinity of Kojo. Even the escort carriers had moved into the Sea of Japan to support the "landing"; *Sicily* conducted spotting operations and *Badoeng Strait* furnished antisubmarine patrol (at one point, in fact, "Bing-Ding's" airmen actually thought they had detected a sub, but the mysterious contact disappeared).

Terrible weather plagued the actual "invasion,"

and though the landing craft, fortunately manned by skilled sailors and not containing troops, drew desultory shorefire, there was no other perceptible enemy response. "It seems proper to conclude," the official Navy history of the Korean War states, "that an enemy incapable of quick response cannot be very profitably hoaxed." But if the Communists had not bitten, the aircrews of TF 77 had, and they resented being used in such a fashion. Brisk antiaircraft fire had claimed five carrier aircraft, and the carrier commanders, who were also left in the dark, criticized the reasoning behind a plan that had their pilots taking risks appropriate to a potentially war-winning landing, but entirely inappropriate to what was increasingly referred to as a "training exercise." The Kojo feint, however well-intentioned, left a sour taste in the mouths of most of TF 77's aviators, and FEAF's as well. It did little to frighten the North Korean and Chinese forces in Korea into strengthening their seaward defenses at the expense of their frontline deployments, and while it did demonstrate that UN forces could land virtually where and when they wished if they chose to, the Communist high command shrewdly realized that (given the nature of the war) such a "go for broke" stroke was unlikely.[20]

The Kojo feint coincided with the beginning of an imaginative strike program instituted by Jocko Clark, and dubbed the *Cherokee* effort in honor of his American Indian ancestry. *Cherokee* strikes marked a return to the strategy of attacking on or near the battlefield, not by wishful interdiction, but rather by strikes behind the front, beyond CAS range. In some respects, ironically, the *Cherokee* effort recalled the Air Force conception of CAS back in the grim days of 1950: strikes beyond artillery range in front of friendly forces. These *Cherokee* strikes complimented the deeper air pressure missions aimed at the heart of North Korea. The enemy was becoming increasingly weary of fighting a protracted war that he had no ability to win by force of arms on the battlefield.

In May of 1952, Jocko Clark made an inspection trip to the Korean front. As he flew along behind the front, the diversity and concentration of supplies impressed the admiral, who recognized that if the North Koreans and Chinese had the ability to use their air power over the front, such open display of Allied supplies simply could not be tolerated. He likewise realized that maintaining supplies close to a fighting front was as necessary for the Communists as for the Americans and their Allies. Therefore, there must be a large number of suitable targets in North Korean territory, placed far enough behind the front so as not to be within artillery range, yet not as far back as the main supply routes. Clark had hit on an important means to ravage the North Korean military effort. Supplies at the front represented the product of costly, time-consuming, and dangerous road, rail, pack animal, and human transportation down the Korean peninsula, and were thus lucrative targets. If they could be found, they were Kim Il Sung's Achilles's heel.

After his return to the fleet, Clark had Rear Admiral John Perry, then commander of TF 77, arrange for photographic reconnaissance of enemy territory lying behind the range of Allied artillery.

As Clark suspected, the photos turned up many suitable targets, especially storage tunnels and supply concentrations burrowed into hillsides. Clark's operations officer, Captain Ray M. Pitts, met with Eighth Army and Fifth Air Force representatives to begin coordination of a strike plan. Meanwhile, at sea, Clark met with Rear Admiral Robert F. Hickey, who as COMCARDIV 5 had succeeded Perry* as Commander TF 77, to begin planning the initial assaults. Over the fall of 1952, the pace of fighting at the front had intensified, a measure of the attempts by both sides to expand their territorial control in anticipation of an armistice agreement that would bring fighting to a halt. Both Eighth Army and Fifth Air Force expressed strong support of the concept though Fifth Air Force initially considered the *Cherokee* strikes—the name was bestowed by Pitts in honor of his boss—to be little more than "normal" close support.[21]

Given the differences between the conception of close air support held by the Air Force, and that of the Navy and Marines, such confusion was understandable; as discussed in Chapter 2, aspects of the Air Force approach to CAS—specifically the notion of striking beyond the range of artillery but if

*Though a total of 13 rear admirals served as commander of TF 77, the position changed frequently among these men. Each additionally served as commander of Carrier Division 1, 3, or 5. The position of commander of TF 77 changed roughly every two weeks, ultimately involving no less than 56 changes of command among these 13 men over the length of the war.

necessary below the bombline—closely approximated the initial form of *Cherokee* strikes that TF 77 employed. Unlike the earlier debate, however, the *Cherokee* effort engendered little if any rancor between the services, and a conference held on November 17 between Army, Navy, and Air Force representatives quickly ironed out standard operating procedures. Numerous specifics differentiated CAS strikes from *Cherokee* strikes:

CAS	Cherokee
Spontaneous	Thoroughly planned
Not prebriefed	Prebriefed before takeoff
Eight aircraft maximum	Unlimited; typically 50
No flak suppression escort	Flak suppression escort
Primarily antipersonnel	Ordnance appropriate for target
Loiter "on call"	Fly in, hit target, fly out
Controlled by TACP/Mosquito	No TACP/Mosquito control*
Within bombline	Inside and outside bombline*

TF 77 launched its first *Cherokee* strikes on October 9, 1952, and by the end of the month, the Navy's Korean air operations for October had set a new wartime record of 13,000 flights. By mid-October, *Cherokee* strikes constituted fully 50% of TF 77's missions. However, by month's end, the employment of large Navy strikes near the front and within the bombline that severely taxed the abilities of forward air controllers, together with confusion about the purpose of the *Cherokee* missions, led to the November conference. As a result, the Navy

*Prior to coordination meeting of November 17.

agreed to operate *Cherokee* strikes above the bombline only, coordinate the strikes with Fifth Air Force and Eighth Army, and rely upon T-6 Mosquitoes to mark the targets for the strike force. For its part, Eighth Army agreed to move the bombline as close as 300 yards, if necessary, so that the raiders could do their job. Thereafter, until the armistice, the *Cherokee* strikes proved especially valuable as a means of destroying the Communists' ability to undertake a major offensive.

Complementing the *Cherokee* effort were *Call-Shot* strikes: a resumption of CAS missions in support of men confronting masses of Chinese and North Korean troops attempting to seize territory in assaults that resembled the pathetic human wall of carnage at the Western Front in 1916-1917. Pilots got used to taking heavy flak from strikes in the *"Cherokee* strip," as naval aviators dubbed the band running across Korea from just above the bombline of resistance to a depth approximately 20 miles further north. Losses, however, remained encouragingly low, and they dropped even lower as fighting continued into 1953. In October through December 1952, for example, the Navy and Marines lost 43 tactical aircraft compared to 65 for the same period in 1951. Losses for January through March 1953 dropped to 34 compared to 46 for the same three months in 1952. Losses for April through June 1953 fell to 32, compared to 58 for the same period in 1952, the last months of the interdiction effort.[22]

Only one brief cloud obscured the bright horizon of the *Cherokee*. On several occasions, strike aircraft — not all of them on *Cherokee* missions —

dropped bombs on friendly territory; combined casualties from all these instances totaled 4 dead and 12 injured. The outcry obscured the success of the strikes in a wave of self-recrimination that led to an edict threatening air group commanders and pilots involved in future incidents with being relieved of command or, at worst, court-martial. Such Draconian measures tempered the enthusiasm of naval aviators for *Cherokee* missions "for several weeks" (as Jocko Clark subsequently recalled) so that the *Cherokee* effort in 1953 was not quite as productive as it might otherwise have been. What is surprising is how little impact the *Cherokee* effort made on historians studying the Korean War; as the official Navy history of the war states boldly:

> It was a strange type of warfare in which naval aviation was now engaged. . . . For want of something better to do the carrier air groups were hauling explosives in and dumping them in the general neighborhood of the front. Volume had been substituted for accuracy, and the only indisputable dividends were the approval with which the Army greeted the effort, and the morale boost provided the frontline troops by the noise and smoke which rose from the enemy's back yard.[23]

That assessment is entirely too critical, and would certainly have caused its share of raised eyebrows among those on the scene at the time.

That the *Cherokee* strikes had an impact is undoubted; as difficult as it might be to measure, it was evident from circumstantial and direct evidence. One strike in early December resulted in no less than 27 secondary explosions. On an average, three *Cherokee* missions per day pummeled Communist positions along the front. Secondary explosions and billowing clouds of smoke signaled the destruction of supplies, and necessitated hasty resupply efforts. Accordingly, the amount of road traffic, including risky daylight convoys, rose appreciably as the North Koreans and Chinese strove to replace supplies blasted by the *Cherokee* attacks. For the first time in nearly two years, strike groups reported excellent truck and vehicle hunting, and night hecklers found more targets than they could conveniently handle. *Cherokee,* coupled with FEAF's ongoing air pressure campaign, forced the North Koreans and Chinese into a logistical nightmare and threatened them with exhaustion. As General James Van Fleet perceptively noted after the war, if the UN command combined *Cherokee* with a major ground offensive, the result might have so drained the Communists that they would have fallen back before an Allied advance. Given the political climate at the time of the *Cherokee* effort, such an assault is as inconceivable as, say, a "real" Kojo landing.[24]

As fighting escalated in the last three months of the war, the already intense pace of the air war itself picked up. A good indication of this is found in the action report of Air Task Group 1 embarked aboard U.S.S. *Boxer.* Air Task Group 1 was in action from May and most of June, 1953. ATG 1 consisted of three Panther squadrons (VF-52, VF-111, and VF-151), an AD squadron (VF-194), and small three-

and four-plane detachments of VC-3 (F4U-5N), VC-11 (AD-4W), VC-35 (AD-4N), and VC-61 (F2H-2P). The air task concept envisioned unified use of a carrier's air group for single-purpose missions, such as attack, or fighter. *Boxer* soon found the problems of operating three Panther squadrons from an unmodified *Essex*-class carrier prohibitive and eventually swapped one of its F9F squadrons (VF-111) for a Corsair squadron (VF-44) from *Lake Champlain*. But throughout the time period, the "Busy Bee" waged war with its Panthers and ADs in an impressive demonstration of one TF 77 carrier's contribution to the Korean war effort on the eve of the armistice. The following excerpt from the action report is included to give a feeling of the intensity of carrier operations during this time:

5-10-53: Departed Yokosuka 0700 enroute to the operating area.

5-11-53: Enroute to the operating area. 63 refresher sorties were conducted.

5-12-53: Joined TF 77. No air operations due to fog and rain.

5-13-53: 63 sorties. Familiarization flights were flown with planes from the *Valley Forge*. Hecklers hit transportation facilities around Pukchong. There were eight missions in close air support of our troops by AD's. Other offensive operations, mostly jets, were scattered from Wonsan to within a few miles of Songjin.

5-14-53: 109 sorties. AD's successfully performed CAS on the central and eastern fronts, knocking out artillery and trenches. Several

Cherokee strikes near Kosong were flown by AD's and F9F's alike. F9F's recce'd supply routes further north around the Hungnam-Hamhung area.

5-15-53: No air operations, due [to] replenishment.

5-16-53: 112 sorties. Seven Panthers destroyed ten railroad cars and damaged others in marshaling yards northwest of Wonsan. A truck park, supply buildings, and billeting areas near Hamhung suffered many direct hits from nine AD's about mid-day. F9F's also hit the general area with considerable success. Eleven AD's in two different strikes hit camouflaged billets and bunkers southwest of Wonsan. Hecklers found and destroyed several trucks on MSR's [Main Supply Routes] near Songjin and left a train burning after stopping it outside of the same city.

5-17-53: 124 sorties. Jets struck marshaling yards and other transportation facilities northeast of Songjin. A boxcar, [and] one large, and three small, buildings were leveled a few miles southwest of Tanchon. Many rail and road cuts were made and supply buildings destroyed in strikes from Wonsan to Hamhung. Panthers also hit a power building and strafed other large buildings and six transformers in the same general area. Meanwhile the Skyraiders were flying Rescap over a downed *Philippine Sea* pilot. Ens. G. M. Witters was hit by AA fire while flying the Rescap near Tanchon. He ditched at sea and was rescued by the U.S.S.

Manchester uninjured.

5-18-53: 44 sorties. Replenishment caused a late start in air operations today. Panther jets bombed personnel shelters and storage tunnels damaging the latter and destroying fifteen buildings northeast of Hungnam. Hecklers ended the day by hitting trucks, bridges, and gun positions near Songjin.

5-19-53: 107 sorties. In the vicinity of Puk-chong, F9F's destroyed fifty-two buildings and damaged others. AD's made forty runs on Hwae-do coastal defenses, saturating the island with ordnance. Ten buildings and three coastal guns were destroyed. In the afternoon Panthers made twenty-seven hits and near misses in destroying ten buildings and bunkers on the coast northeast of Songjin.

5-20-53: 80 sorties. Morning hecklers attacked transportation facilities leading to and from Wonsan. Besides destroying trucks and making road cuts, a train was left burning. An early jet strike hit a power station and industrial area near Oro-ri. AD's scheduled for CAS were diverted to a train stopped earlier by the morning hecklers. They made sure the train would stay stopped by destroying seven cars and damaging three more. The Skyraiders also hit coastal defense positions and assisted in naval gun firing, just southwest of Tanchon. Lt. (j.g.) W. J. O'Heren of VF-194 splashed off the port catapult and was recovered with minor injuries by U.S.S. *McCord*.

5-21-53: No air operations due to replenishment.

5-22-53: No air operations due to weather.

5-23-53: 89 sorties. A strike of AD's destroyed thirty buildings and damaged ten northeast of Hamhung. Lt. Howard Wolfe, an AD pilot, made a controlled ditch near Manyang-do and was soon picked up by a friendly minesweeper. The jets hit in the *Cherokee* area about fifteen miles north of the central front. Hecklers recce'd the MSR's along the northeast coast of Korea from Ch'ongjin to Wonsan.

5-24-53: 100 sorties. Two jet strikes between Songjin and Hungnam resulted in twelve rail cuts and damage to a train and tunnel mouth as well as trucks and troop concentrations. CAS missions by F9F's on the eastern front resulted in five road cuts, damage to three automatic weapons, and destruction to four personnel shelters. Lt. Wilfred Wheeler*, VC-3, while on a heckler mission was missing due to enemy action in [the] Pukchong area. Condition unknown.

5-25-53: No air operations due to replenishment.

5-26-53: 108 sorties. The hecklers led off an eventful morning by destroying half a dozen trucks and damaging many more. Two jet recce's were given a pre-dawn launch to attack the unusually heavy truck activity. At least nine trucks were destroyed and fourteen damaged, with heavy damage to rail

*Crashed in F4U-5N near Soho-ri; subsequently MIA.

facilities, by the pre-dawn jet launch. CTF 77 [message] 252046Z refers: "WELL DONE EVENT 2 AND 3 X REPORTING COORDINATION AIR DISCIPLINE AND RESULTS MOST GRATIFYING." The AD's of Air Task Group One destroyed twelve gun positions on the eastern front lines in a later event. Other Skyraiders put fifty bomb hits into a small supply and billeting area northwest of Kansong.

5-27-53: 104 sorties. The combination of jet and heckler aircraft was again used to damage a locomotive and to destroy five boxcars and the tender. The major effort of the rest of the day was concentrated on coastal defenses in the Wonsan harbor area. At least seven coastal defense guns were destroyed and two hundred yards of trench rendered unusable by the props and jets of Air Task Group One. Twenty-three buildings and bunkers were also destroyed.

5-28-53: No air operations due to replenishment.

5-29-53: No air operations due to adverse weather.

5-30-53: 107 sorties. With assigned targets in the bombline area weathered, ATG-1 planes hit targets in the Wonsan-Hungnam area. Forty-three supply and billeting buildings were destroyed and seventy-four damaged by the day's effort.

5-31-53: 53 sorties. In spite of marginal weather which caused cancellation of the day's activity by mid-morning, Skyraiders and Panthers flying from the *Boxer* hit rail facilities along the coast.

6-1-53: 55 sorties. Taking advantage of poor weather to replenish, TF 77 did not start air operations until afternoon. F9F's in two events hit *Cherokee* targets in central Korea. Thirty buildings were destroyed and thirty-five more were damaged with the aid of some seven secondary explosions. The hecklers finished off the day by destroying a locomotive just west of Kowon.

6-2-53: 102 sorties. A Skyraider strike made Hamhung West airfield non-operational with some fifty-five hits [on] the runway. The AD's also performed NGF [naval gunfire] spotting for the U.S.S. *Manchester* and the U.S.S. *New Jersey*. On the bombline the props also knocked out mortar positions and bunkers during a CAS mission. The jets hit *Cherokee* targets in eastern Korea. While on a *Cherokee* mission Lt. (j.g.) J. J. Chambers† was wounded in the left wrist and right leg by shrapnel, necessitating a crash landing at K-18. His condition was reported as "good" after treatment. He has been transferred to a hospital in Japan.

6-3-53: 122 sorties. Marginal weather continued in the bombline area causing all *Cherokee* missions to be diverted to targets further north. AD's and F9F's teamed up to crater Yongp'o

†Listed as "F. Chambers" in action report; flew F9Fs with VF-52.

Airfield into a non-operational status. The Sky-raiders were able to get in on a CAS mission, destroying at least three troop shelters and digging up four hundred yards of trenches.

6-4-53: No air operations due to replenishment.

6-5-53: 45 sorties. Jets, flying all today's sorties, ranged from Ch'ongin to Wonsan in strikes against Communist supply and rail facilities. Thirty-four buildings, most around rail transfer points, were destroyed and some fifty-six damaged.

6-6-53: No air operations due to weather.

6-7-53: 38 sorties. Diverted Panther jets hit a supply area south of Wonsan, destroying seventeen buildings. Two coastal defense guns were destroyed by the jets.

6-8-53: 61 sorties. Again, all jets strikes were weathered out of their assigned targets and forced to hit targets of opportunity in the *Cherokee* area. The AD's were able to give some support to our troops on the MLR [Main Line of Resistance] before weather forced a cancellation of the remainder of the day's flights.

6-9-53: 88 sorties. Again Air Task Group planes were forced to attack targets of opportunity south of Wonsan. However, two flights caught troops on the move with the result of some eighty-five troops KIA for the day.

6-10-53: 95 sorties. The AD's destroyed one and damaged one artillery [piece] in caves, with a large secondary explosion testifying [to] some unobserved damage, in front of friendly lines. Radar drops and diversions were again the order of the day for the jets. However, one F9F flight was diverted to a lucrative target of some one hundred boxcars in a marshaling yard near the Anbyon reservoir. The result was ten cars destroyed and thirty damaged.

6-11-53: 130 sorties. The AD's proved exceptionally effective in a CAS mission on the central front. The Mosquito controller reported five hundred yards of trench destroyed, fifteen mortar positions destroyed, and twelve secondary explosions. The jets attempted to aid the UN ground forces but were again hampered by weather and had to resort to radar drops and [divert to] targets further north. Ens. W.W. Spear, VF-194, was forced to ditch at sea due to engine failure on the way to the target. He was picked up in good condition by an Air Force helo from K-18.

6-12-53: 22 sorties. The only offensive missions were a CAS and two MPQ [radar-controlled bombing] flights. All flights dropped under radar guidance and the results were not observed. All air operations were cancelled by 1000, due to weather. [TF 77 replenished at night].

6-13-53: 139 sorties. Taking advantage of assigned northern targets and MPQ drops. ATG 1 flew a record-breaking number of sorties. The Panthers flew all the way to the Manchurian border to hit the airfield at Hyesanjin. Sondok and Kilchu airfields were also cratered. Damage assessment on the radar drops is not available. The props hit bunkers and trenches on the far-eastern end of the front line.

6-14-53: 131 sorties. Jet *Cherokee* strikes hit supply buildings near the eastern front line near Anchor Hill. AD's and jets were both used on CAS on the eastern and central MLR. 1,625 yards of trench, eight mortar positions, and nine gun emplacements were destroyed by the CAS missions from the *Boxer*. The main effort was placed on Anchor Hill which had recently been taken by the Communist forces.

6-15-53: 147 sorties. Today's strikes were part of a maximum effort put out by TF 77 in support of a counteroffensive by the UN forces to retake ground lost the previous week in the vicinity of Anchor Hill. ATG 1 placed 102 sorties [of] either *Cherokee* or CAS in the Anchor Hill sector. In the effort, 650 yards of trench, three machineguns positions, seven mortar positions, and seventy-three buildings were destroyed. "Well Dones" were received from CG Eighth Army, COMSEVENTH-FLEET, CTF 77, CINCPACFLEET, and COM-NAVFE. Jet recce in the northeastern section of Korea destroyed supply buildings and transportation facilities.

6-16-53: 124 sorties. Jets destroyed sixteen large buildings and set a coal dump ablaze in northeast Korea [and] killed eighty sheep. Others damaged two buildings and caused two secondary explosions. A jet *Cherokee* strike hit a truck park where six buildings were destroyed and seven damaged. Seven Panthers diverted to a train in the Anbyon valley, where they made a rail cut fore-and-aft of the train, then went to work and destroyed four cars and damaged six others. The Skyraiders on a CAS mission north of Panmunjom destroyed seven mortar positions, two automatic gun positions, eight personnel shelters, and 150 yards of trench.

6-17-53: 64 sorties. Eight AD's on CAS destroyed eight bunkers, 100 yards of trenches, and caused three secondary explosions on the eastern MLR. Other AD's of ATG 1 were equally successful throughout the day in the same area.

6-18-53: No air operations due to weather.

6-19-53: 78 sorties. Although marginal weather hampered operations, the Skyraiders hit troop areas and trenches on the central front. A building was destroyed, one hundred and fifty troops KIA, and four large secondary explosions were caused. Jets attacked transportation facilities and supply areas in the Wonsan-Hungnam area. Lt. D. H. Opsahl, VF-111, while flying a photo escort mission, was forced to ditch due to fuel exhaustion. He waited four hours in the water before being picked up by the U.S.S. *St. Paul*. He was found to have back injuries the extent of which is not known at this time. At 1730 the U.S.S. *Boxer* departed the Task Force enroute Yoksuka.

6-20-53: No air operations. Enroute Yokosuka.

6-21-53: No air operations. Moored port side to Piedmont Pier, Yokosuka, Japan, at 1545.[25]

No carrier had done more, or suffered more, than *Boxer* during her four Korean deployments. The pace of *Boxer's* flight operations in the last frantic months of the war is indicative both of her crew's dedication to duty, and the unceasing demands upon TF 77 for tactical support of Allied ground forces under renewed and relentless assault.

In a sense, the fighting in the summer of 1953 brought TF 77's experiences full circle; as in the summer of 1950, the carriers found themselves supporting ground forces under attack as the North Koreans and Chinese attempted to seize territory before signing at the armistice table. So intense was the pace, that TF 77 resorted to nighttime replenishment at sea every second day, so that as much of its striking power as possible could be brought to bear during the day. Fog, rain, and low ceilings plagued the task force, which pressed on with operations until absolutely forced to keep its strike aircraft on the deck. Taxed and fatigued by the cycle of flying and nighttime replenishment, maintenance crews did their best to keep up with the demands of the flying schedule, but, as might be expected, there was an increase in breakdown of both ships and aircraft under the stress of operations. One carrier, *Lake Champlain,* lost use of both its catapults for a time, and propulsion problems curtailed flight operations on *Princeton* and *Philippine Sea*. *Boxer* returned from Yokosuka to help fill in, serving through the armistice on July 27.

Daytime flight operations took precedence over night heckling, but it would not be accurate to state, as some have, that "the hours of darkness were conceded to the enemy."[26] Ashore, the night-fighters of VMF(N)-513 flew a variety of night B-29 escort missions (as is discussed later), and night strike and close air support missions as well. While not as extensive as the Air Force's use of B-26 night intruders, the Marine effort, which started with F4U-5Ns and progressed to twin-engine Grumman F7F-3N Tigercats, was no less professional. A night sortie might involve a so-called "MPQ" mission, a radar-controlled bombing sortie. MPQ targets typically lay within five miles of friendly front lines. The Tigercat crew would take off from their base at Kunsan (K-8), climb out, and after contacting appropriate ground stations, finally report to a Marine Ground Control Interception (GCI) unit. The GCI controllers assigned the Tigercat a speed and altitude (typically 160 knots and 15,000 feet), and the F7F pilot set his autopilot appropriately. Following a path parallel to the front lines, the Tigercat held the desired course, speed, and altitude; at the ground controller's command, the crew would arm their ordnance, and, again on his command or by a radio signal from the ground, the Tigercat would salvo its load on the target. MPQ attacks did not generate precision bombing, but, on a large enough target, such as a storage area or troop position, its results could be devastating.

Another typical night mission had Tigercats escorting Air Force B-26s on strikes and, if no enemy aircraft turned up, turning their attention to ground targets such as trains and road traffic. In April 1953, the Marines experimented with two intersecting beams from 24-inch searchlights located in Marine infantry frontlines to pinpoint targets on the battlefield, and guide attacking strike aircraft on night CAS sorties. Between April 12 and May 5, 1953, VMF(N)-513 flew 58 night CAS missions "with excellent results." (Earlier in the war, the squadron had relied on "mud Marines" firing converging tracer from two widely placed machine guns to achieve somewhat the same effect.) Already war weary, the Tigercat quickly gave way to the Grumman F9F in the Marine night-attack program, though VMF(N)-513 itself never operated the Grumman jet, progressing from Corsairs in 1950-1952 to Tigercats and Douglas F3D-2 Skyknights in 1952-1953, to all Skyknights by the end of the Korean War. The squadron, nicknamed the "Flying Nightmares," flew its last Tigercat sorties on May 5, 1953, when a section of F7Fs, *Greasecup* 3347A and 3347B, attacked troop, bunker, mortar, and automatic weapons positions ahead of the Marine front with a mix of bombs and 20-mm strafing, causing numerous fires and secondary explosions. When they landed back at Kunsan (K-8), the two crews had the honor of flying the last combat mission completed by this rakish (though obsolescent) design.[27]

The Marines and their Air Force counterparts were not the only ones roaming the skies over North Korea at night, for TF 77's heckling effort continued to the armistice. In late March, three Corsair pilots from *Oriskany* volunteered to attack a "hotly defended" highway bridge at Hamhung; they snuck up on it in bright moonlight and dropped its center span before flak crews could fire a shot. VC-35, parent squadron to night heckling detachments of AD-4NL Skyraiders deployed on TF 77's flattops, played a particularly active role. In April, "Team Mike," aboard *Philippine Sea,* evaluated the 2.75-inch *Mighty Mouse* rocket. An AD-4NL could carry six pods of "mice," each pod holding seven of the small but deadly unguided rockets. Combat tests proved conclusively that the rockets devastated North Korean and Chinese road convoys; the podded weapon functioned much like a shotgun, blasting a broad area with shrapnel. At last, night attack aircraft had a weapon that somewhat offset the problem of firing accuracy. Eventually, the *Mighty Mouse,* developed originally for air-to-air combat, became a standard ground attack weapon, serving in subsequent conflicts as well.[28]

Perhaps the most interesting heckler mission of the war involved night heckling Skyraiders from *Valley Forge* that hit the Chosin No. 1 power plant on the night of May 3, 1953. Hotly defended during the day, the Chosin plant's antiaircraft gunners ignored overflying Navy aircraft at night, a fact not lost on the skipper of the "Happy Valley's" hecklers, Lieutenant Commander W. C. Griese of VC-35's Team Baker. Griese had three ADs raid Chosin; they launched at 3:00 a.m. and navigated to the plant by radar. The leader flew over the plant and dropped an illuminating flare, allowing the other two aircraft to run in and each drop a 1,000-pound bomb. Then the aircraft alternated as flare droppers and bombers until each had unloaded two 1,000-pound bombs. The three intruders returned to the *Valley Forge,* their crews having the satisfaction of seeing the plant showering sparks. In many ways, this strike against a heavily defended power plant—intelligence estimated it as ringed with over 30 37-mm cannon and a dozen ones of larger size—calls to mind VA-85's epic night raid by two Grumman A-6 Intruders against North Vietnam's Uong Bi power plant in April 1966, an equally successful strike that was alleged to have been carried out by B-52s. This was a Radio Hanoi charge that drew appropriate chuckles from the "Black Falcons" of VA-85.[29]

Boxer's ATG 1 contributed its own unique approach to night heckling, when Lieutenant Commander James J. Kinsella, C.O. of VF-52, known as Kinsella's Fellas, instituted a program of night heckling with the squadron's F9F Panthers. Convinced that the Panther could operate more effectively because of its relatively silent approach and higher speed, Kinsella picked three experienced pilots on their second Korean tour to accompany him. Early in the morning darkness of May 26, 1953, the four launched from *Boxer*, sweeping over the coast and prowling the road from Pukchong to Ch'ongjin. As Kinsella hoped, the Panthers caught Korean road traffic by surprise, and, once defenders did shoot back, the speed of the jets threw off their aim. Kinsella's strike destroyed 9 trucks and damaged 14 others, an unusually successful heckling mission by any standards. Had the Korean War continued beyond July 1953, night employment of jet aircraft for heckling purposes would have become a standard feature of TF 77's operations.[30]

In May 1953, Fifth Air Force launched a series of attacks against North Korea's irrigation dams, assisted by Marine air. Designed to impede North Korea's west coast transportation net by flooding or otherwise damaging roads and rail lines, the attacks were also aimed at destroying North Korea's ability to grow rice; they reasoned that North Korea would have to switch from exporting to importing rice. China did not have that much to spare, and with North Korea's logistical network already sorely taxed, transportation of rice to the front would be difficult, leading to possible food shortages among front-line forces and a drop in morale and efficiency. The strikes succeeded brilliantly, another example of a long-overdue measure that might have shortened the war considerably had it taken place earlier. As North Korean crews worked frantically—no other word seems adequate to characterize their response to the raids—fighting at the front reached a crescendo. In June and July, TF 77 found itself supporting I and II ROK Corps against fierce attacks, despite weather that severely hampered efforts to help UN forces. Exclusive of the hotly demanded *Cherokee* strikes, Eighth Army required no less than 48 CAS sorties per day in June. On July 14, Jocko Clark ordered all TF 77 activity to support either CAS or *Cherokee* missions. Fearful that the Chinese and Korean offensive might carry the day, Clark

> hastened to Tokyo to plead with Mark Clark to assign nuclear bombs to be placed on board my carriers as a precautionary measure. He concurred and took immediate steps. Task Force 77 was then equipped with nuclear capability.[31]

Fortunately, it did not come to that. Marine F9Fs flew numerous MPQ missions, 20 on July 14 alone. On July 26, TF 77 launched 649 sorties against Communist targets. At 10:00 a.m. on July 27, the representatives at the truce talks signed the Korean armistice. With 12 hours to go before it took effect, naval aviators continued to fly and fight, concentrating on transportation networks but also hitting airfields to render them unserviceable at the time of the truce. On that last day, TF 77's airmen destroyed or damaged 23 railroad cars, 11 railroad bridges, a railroad tunnel, 9 highway bridges, 69 buildings, and 100 yards of trenchworks. They made 40 rail cuts and 3 highway cuts, cratered runways at 5 airfields ranging from Hyesanjin on the Manchurian border to Hamhung, and dropped leaflets over the north as well. At 9:25 p.m., Marine Captain William J. Foster of VMA-251 rolled into a dive and planted three 2,000-pound bombs amidst Communist positions. Slightly more than a half-hour later, the Korean War was history.[32]

6/THE STRUGGLE FOR AIR SUPERIORITY

FEAF's Korean experience evokes images: Sabres dueling with MiGs, prowling B-26s striking by night, noisy little FACs, and stately B-29s pressing on to their targets despite MiGs and flak, in the grand tradition of Schweinfurt and Regensburg. The Navy and Marine air war conjures different ones, mostly of Corsairs on CAS strikes, and ADs, Panthers, and Banshees going after bridges and rail lines. In fact, the naval air war, like FEAF's, was far more complex than these convenient images suggest.

The naval air war did not demand the constant struggle for air superiority that confronted FEAF. First, the air superiority war had fairly strict geographical boundaries. After being drubbed in the first six months, the Communist air forces generally restricted operations to MiG Alley. As the war went on, MiGs sometimes sortied across to Wonsan or, more typically, south to P'yongyang, Haeju, and the vicinity of Sok-to and Ch'o-do islands. But these aside, opportunities for MiG fights by and large eluded naval aviators, as they seldom flew where the MiGs operated. Second, FEAF had remarkable success in dealing with the MiG threat, leaving the Navy free to carry on an air-to-ground war. The graceful but heavy Sabre had deficiences in acceleration and firepower as compared to the somewhat chunky MiG; for example, to FEAF's annoyance, the Sabre had to make do with six .50-caliber machine guns because the muzzle blast from a more desirable package of four 20-mm cannon distorted airflow through the Sabre's inlet, compressor stalling the plane's J47 engine. It compensated, however, by having better high-Mach (Mach 0.85 and above) handling qualities than the Soviet fighter, in part because the Sabre had hydraulically boosted ailerons for faster roll (lateral control) response and an adjustable horizontal stabilizer that gave its pilots greater longitudinal (pitch) control authority as the plane neared the speed of sound. This advantage when coupled with the great experience of American fighter pilots—and the Sabre wings in Korea featured a galaxy of veterans who had blasted the *Luftwaffe* and the Japanese air services out of the skies during the Second World War—ensured that most MiG drivers had their hands full, and thus stayed close to the Yalu. This, of course, frustrated the eager Navy and Marine fighter pilots in slower straight-wing Panthers and Banshees that possessed no advantages over the MiG, except in the courage and training of their pilots and the lethality of each of these fighter's excellent four-gun 20-mm armament systems. Prop pilots expressed fewer reservations, however. "Sure, I saw MiGs in Korea," one

Navy attack pilot recollected after the war, "and I thank God I saw them through an umbrella of Sabres."

The MiG's use of Chinese sanctuary from Antung and other airfields scattered through Manchuria, such as Tatungkou, Takushan, and Mukden (Shenyang), vexed and infuriated Allied fighter pilots, the majority of whom showed commendable restraint in not violating the self-imposed sanctuary across the Yalu. Others, however, succumbed to temptation. Sabre pilot Colonel Walker "Bud" Mahurin, a distinguished ace from the Second World War, recalled a memorable incident when his patrolling wing heard two Americans in a big tangle with eight MiGs north of the Yalu, calling threats, covering each other, and shooting MiGs down. For obvious reasons, the two Sabre jockeys did not use identifying call signs; the grunting and exclamations over the air gave a graphic picture of the desperate high-g swirling furball they must be in. Repeatedly, Mahurin, using his call sign "Honest John," radioed the unknown duo asking where they were so his own Sabres could come to their rescue. No answer. Finally, at the end of his patience, Mahurin radioed:

'Listen you bastards, this is Honest John. If you guys want help, tell me where the fight is and tell me now.' Another moment of long silence, and then a sober voice came back to me: 'To hell with you, Colonel. Find your own damn MiG's.'

The question of who flew the MiGs in Korea

furnished hours of bar and ready room conversation. Allegedly, during 1951-1952, Colonel Ivan N. Kozhedub, the Soviet Union's leading fighter ace from the Second World War, commanded a Soviet MiG division in Korea. As aggressive as his opposite numbers in the Sabre wings—pilots like Colonel Francis "Gabby" Gabreski, Colonel Harry Thyng, and Bud Mahurin—Kozhedub could easily have served as the model for the fictional "Casey Jones," the masterful Russian "engineer" of the Yalu MiG "trains" in Sabre pilot James Salter's fine novel *The Hunters*. Clearly many pilots *were* Soviet: communication intercepts picked up Russian language broadcasts between controllers at Antung and MiG leaders over the Yalu. Later, with increasing frequency, Chinese and Korean language intercepts turned up, indicating the growing strength of China's air power and the rebuilding of North Korea's shattered air force. Sabre pilots divided the MiG pilots into two broad categories: tyros (a vast majority, usually Chinese and Korean) and honchos (presumably selected Soviet veterans of the Russian Front as well as occasional gifted newcomers such as Chinese aces Li Han, Chang Chi-wei, and Wang Hai). The latter could be very dangerous indeed. Naturally, the Soviets were as eager to prevent the capture and subsequent identification of any of their airmen as the UN Command was to secure one; in any event, UN forces never captured Soviet personnel in Korea.

Some encounters had humorous aspects; others reflected the grim nature of the struggle. During one notable dogfight, Sabre ace Major Frederick C. "Boots" Blesse (subsequently the author of an influential post-Korean fighter manual entitled *No Guts No Glory*) shot down a MiG whose pilot ejected. As Blesse circled his descending foe, and took photos to authenticate the victory, the MiG's red-haired, red-bearded, and obviously Caucasian pilot shook his fist at the Sabre. Blesse, a strict follower of the fighter pilot's code, let the MiG driver descend in peace and limited his response to shaking his own fist back at the parachutist. Another case turned out quite differently. For months FEAF attempted to capture ejecting MiG pilots, putting a Sabre CAP over them and alerting air-sea rescue. Each time, the MiG pilot so targeted escaped into the countryside. One day, a MiG went down over the coast, its pilot ejecting and then landing safely in the Yellow Sea. Alerted, a rescue helicopter left Ch'o-do island, heading north to pick him up. Meanwhile, a Sabre CAP orbited the downed airman, floating safely in the water, obviously alive and well. Suddenly, four flights of MiGs jumped the Sabres, triggering a fierce dogfight. While the Sabres fought for their lives, four other MiGs suddenly appeared, diving down and strafing their erstwhile comrade in the water, a telling comment on Stalinist Russian's regard for human life.[2]

UN forces eagerly sought opportunities to acquire a MiG itself. Early in the war, technical intelligence forces shipped a captured Il-10 and a Yak-9 to the United States for evaluation, but those aircraft were old technology. Capturing a MiG offered a chance to examine current Soviet design practice. Accordingly, at the beginning of April 1951, FEAF's intelligence branch assembled an American-Korean team to snatch a MiG if a suitable "candidate" turned up. The team consisted of specialists hastily trained to dismember the MiG with small explosives and hand grenades and take selected pieces, such as instrumentation and engine parts, back for analysis; heavily armed and highly skilled ROK Rangers would accompany the intelligence specialists for protection. After several false starts, Operation MiG finally got underway on April 17, 1951. Three days before, fighter pilots reported spotting a wrecked MiG on a hillside near Sinanju, well north of the front but near the Yellow Sea coastline. Follow-up photo reconnaissance confirmed the sighting, and on the morning of the mission, the team left Taegu in a small Beech C-45 transport. They landed at Seoul and added members before transferring to a Sikorsky H-19 helicopter. The helicopter left Seoul and made its way to the small offshore island of Paengyong-do, headquarters of a South Korean guerilla team. Early in the afternoon, after refueling, it lifted off for North Korea. It stayed low over the Yellow Sea, and an escort group of Mustangs rendezvoused as it passed over Ch'o-do island.

This strange armada crossed the North Korean coast, the helo clattering at low level up the Ch'ongch'on estuary. At 4:20 in the afternoon, its crew spotted the MiG and set down in a barley field 600 yards away. The Rangers scrambled out and set up a defensive perimeter, and the snarling Mustangs circled and strafed the area. Luck stayed with the team. No North Koreans appeared, though "a fresh, well-beaten path" surrounded the MiG. The team leader photographed the wreck thoroughly; disappointingly, the forward fuselage and cockpit area had burned out, preventing recovery of cockpit instrumentation. Two other team members then blew the MiG apart with a hand grenade, extracting other engine parts, and slicing off its horizontal stabilizer. The team carried its booty back to the waiting H-19 as the Rangers withdrew as well. The stablizer's size precluded closing the helo's hatch, and with the team and Rangers intact, the helicopter crew lifted off for a drafty return flight. Flak near Sinanju damaged one rotor blade, fortunately not seriously, and, still protected by circling F-51s, the H-19 landed back at Ch'o-do for refueling. Afterwards it returned to Paengyong-do, where a waiting Navy amphibian picked up the cargo and team, returning them victoriously to Seoul. Two days later, the wreckage left Korea, on its way to Ohio and technical intelligence experts at Dayton's Wright-Patterson Air Force Base.[3]

A very different and in some respects more remarkable MiG recovery took place three months later, in mid-July 1951. Like FEAF, the Navy sought to plunder a MiG shot down over the Korean coast, but despite false alarms, no opportunity presented itself. Then, on July 9, the Joint Operations Center passed word to Task Element 95.11 (the light carrier H.M.S. *Glory* and the escort carrier *Sicily*) that a damaged MiG had splashed in shoals off the Ch'ongch'on river. Korean guerrilla teams led by "Leopard" and "Salamander," (two American intelligence officers) swung into action in an attempt to locate the wreckage, while Corsairs from *Sicily* and *Glory*'s Fireflies flew reconnaissance. *Glory*'s airmen located the MiG on a sandbar under 17 feet of water, several miles off shore and 30 miles north of the Taedong estuary. This location, more than 15 miles from its reported position and on the fringes of MiG Alley, lay a mere 10 minutes' flying time from Antung, which seemed to place the wreck beyond salvage. Nevertheless, the spirited commanding officer of the light cruiser H.M.S. *Ceylon* remained convinced that a team could carry it off, and with the urging of COMNAVFE and an enthusiasm worthy of Lord St. Vincent, went ahead with his plans. The Landing Ship Dock U.S.S. *Whetstone* (LSD-27) brought up a Landing Ship Utility (LSU) equipped with a crane. July 19 dawned fair and the plan moved into high gear; the LSU grounded itself on a sandbar, then worked itself free.

Early on July 20, with weather worsening (fortunately, as things turned out), *Glory* launched its Sea Furies for air cover, while *Sicily*'s Corsairs struck at a variety of targets, keeping the Communists busy. The cruiser H.M.S. *Belfast* stood by for last-ditch antiaircraft protection, with the little frigate H.M.S. *Cardigan Bay* on call for additional fire support if necessary. A U.S. Navy H03S-1 from *Glory* marked the MiG with a buoy, the LSU plodded to the spot, and the recovery began. The LSU's crew worked for the rest of the day and through the night, and by the morning of July 21, had recovered much of the MiG including its entire engine.* Now weather forced restrictions on *Sicily*'s operations. *Sicily*'s Corsairs had assumed CAP duties from *Glory*'s Sea Furies, and that afternoon, the Leathernecks noted no less than 32 MiGs stooging about. Fortunately fog and low visibility prevented contact, and nothing came of it. The next day, the LSU carrying bits and pieces of MiG docked with the U.S.S. *Epping Forest* (LSD-4). *Epping Forest* then made its way to Inch'on and safety and brought this tale of Anglo-American cooperation to a happy end. In 1953, after the armistice, a North Korean pilot defected with a brand-new MiG-15bis. Subsequent intensive flight testing at Okinawa by a crack test team consisting of Major General Albert Boyd, Major Charles E. "Chuck" Yeager (the first pilot to fly faster than sound), and Captain Tom Collins ridded it of the last of its secrets as well as its remaining mystique.[5]

Though the naval air war remained largely air-to-ground, there were enough exceptions to make life interesting and force Navy and Marine pilots to constant vigilance. On April 21, 1951, four Yaks bounced two Corsairs from *Bataan*'s VMF-312 near Chinnamp'o. The Yaks apparently noticed only the section leader, Captain Philip DeLong, a veteran ace from the South Pacific. Their attack took DeLong by surprise, and the Yaks holed his plane, though not seriously. His wingman, Lieutenant Harold Daigh, slipped behind and hammered one of the

---

*Subsequent analysis at the Cornell Aeronautical Laboratory, Buffalo, New York, revealed the MiG as an early production model (serial number 120147) manufactured in Factory No. 1, Kuibyshev, U.S.S.R., in 1948. Interestingly, it had a two-gun armament of one 23-mm and one 37-mm cannon, in contrast to the type's standard three-gun armament of two 23-mm cannon and one 37-mm cannon.

Yaks, blowing away its wing and sending it earthwards where it exploded. DeLong, surprised no longer, rolled into a split-S, dove to pick up speed and energy, recovered into a high-speed climb and, still climbing, shot down a Yak while in a turn. He saw Daigh flying east, pursuing the Yak leader, but tailed by another; DeLong quickly radioed a warning. Daigh broke hard, turning under the trailing Yak and then opening fire upon it as it overran him. His burst left the Yak streaming a thick banner of smoke, and though Daigh subsequently received credit for damage, it is probable that the Yak never made it home. Meanwhile, DeLong caught up with the Yak leader who Daigh had chased before breaking off. During a short, intense dogfight, DeLong riddled the Yak, whose pilot took to his parachute. Both Corsairs returned safely to their carrier. Intelligence's final verdict on the affair credited the Yak pilots with generally good air discipline; they had stuck together, attempted mutual support, and pressed home their attacks with determination. But their tactics and marksmanship (aside from the opening shots) were another matter entirely.[6]

MiGs embodied a much graver danger. On July 21, 1951, 15 jumped three Panthers from VMF-311 as the Marines returned from a mission; they shot one F9F down and sent its pilot into captivity for the rest of the war. The following September 25, eight of the same squadron's Panthers tangled with 12 MiGs north of P'yongyang near Sunch'on while on a rail cutting strike; the MiGs bounced the Panthers before they hit the target and forced them to drop their bombs. Having disrupted the mission, the MiGs contented themselves with half-hearted passes and, not wishing to press the angry Marines too closely sped back to MiG Alley.[7]. On November 27, 1951, two MiGs wandering near Wonsan attacked four Corsairs and two ADs from *Bon Homme Richard* as they flew a rescue CAP over a downed *Essex* pilot. Communist marksmanship saved the Navy from serious losses, though one AD sustained slight damage. As a result of this particular encounter, TF 77 doubled CAP flights over the fleet and instituted daily reconnaissance flights over North Korean airfields.[8] Not surprisingly, perhaps, the MiGs took after the recon detachments: on March 10, 1952, a MiG flight bounced two F2H-2Ps from VMJ-1 and inflicted major damage (despite violent defensive maneuvering) on both photo Banshees before breaking off the engagement; the Marines returned safely with their film, but squadron commander Lieutenant Colonel R. D. Gould's plane had sustained so much damage that it was fit only for salvage.[9]

On April 30, 1952, in the same general area as their September 1951 encounter, seven VMF-311 Panthers came under attack from eight MiGs as they dove on a rail line. This time, the Panthers stuck to their runs, turned into the MiGs after bomb release, and traded fire; one MiG and one Panther sustained damage before the MiGs broke off.[10] The next month, on May 11, two MiGs attacked a VP-42 Martin PBM-5 Mariner as it droned its way over the Yellow Sea, tearing its wing with 23-mm cannon fire, but otherwise causing no damage; the affronted patrol bomber returned safely to its base at Iwakuni,

Japan. Two months later, on July 16, another patrol plane over the Korea Bay escaped without damage from a MiG that made "six or seven" unsuccessful passes. But at the end of the month, tragedy struck one of the Reserve "Patrons." On July 31, two MiGs coming from astern shot up a Mariner from VP-731. Cannon fire killed two defensive gunners, aircrewmen H. G. Goodroad and Claude Playforth, and wounded two others. Pilot Lieutenant E. E. Bartlett, Jr. nosed downwards, taking the Mariner as low as he dared, and then zigzagged his way to a safe emergency landing at Paengyong-do.[11]

The superior training and marksmanship of American and British naval aviators occasionally turned the tables, however. Late in July 1952, MiGs attacked and damaged two Fireflies from 825 Squadron aboard H.M.S. *Ocean*. Then, on August 9, eight MiGs bounced a formation of Sea Furies from *Ocean*'s 802 Squadron while they covered a group of Fireflies near Haeju. The Sea Fury pilots, itching for action, turned into the MiGs smartly. The MiGs stuck around to fight — a big mistake. Flight leader Lieutenant Peter "Hoagy" Carmichael promptly riddled one with his four 20-mm cannon and sent it crashing to earth. Two other MiGs broke off with heavy damage, and the rest promptly fled north. The next day, 802 Squadron fought a protracted battle with much more skillfully handled MiGs ("They must have sent the instructors down," Carmichael speculated), but the agile Sea Furies shot down yet another, upholding the Fleet Air Arm's deserved reputation for fearlessness.[12] On August 20, six MiGs warily toyed with 12 VF-191 Panthers from *Prince-*

ton during a coordinated Air Force-Navy-Marine raid on the west coast's Changp'yong-ni supply center; the Navy pilots subsequently commented on the poor shooting of the Communist fighters, who broke off combat as suddenly as they had begun it.[13]

Increasingly concerned by the rapidly growing MiG risk, the Marines had launched an intensive air-to-air training program for Corsair pilots operating near Haeju and P'yongyang. Now it paid off. On September 9, 1952, four MiGs attacked two Corsair flights from *Sicily*'s VMA-312 near Chinnamp'o. The wary Corsair pilots kept turning into them, forcing the MiGs to break off their attacks; next they probed the flanks of the Corsair formation as the F4U pilots dove westwards, towards Ch'o-do island, but the same response compelled the MiGs to give up and turn back north. The following day, eight MiGs bounced three of VMA-323's Corsairs, but the Leathernecks evaded every attack, and, after 10 clumsy passes, the MiGs sped for the Yalu.

That same day, Captain Jesse G. Folmar and Lieutenant Willie L. Daniels launched from *Sicily* on a ground support mission. East of Sokto island, the two Marines began a cautious weave. Folmar then spotted two MiGs closing fast in a "loose deuce" formation, called the threat, and the two Corsair pilots began fighting for their lives. They jettisoned all external ordnance to lighten and clean up their planes, and kept weaving and covering each other. Like marauding sharks, two more MiGs joined the fight. Fighting light and clean, the Corsairs (like Britain's Sea Fury) could outmaneuver the MiGs if the enemy chose to play the F4U's game.

One foolishly did, winding up in front of Folmar in a climbing turn; Folmar hosed it with a five-second burst of 20 mm, sending it down in flames: one gone. Now four more MiGs jumped in, and still Folmar and Daniels fought on, struggling to get back to friendly territory. A burst of 37-mm fire destroyed Folmar's left wing, and he bailed out after transmitting a hurried Mayday; one MiG followed the stricken Corsair all the way down and fired at the spinning plane until it hit the water. Sok-to's antiaircraft gunners and, presumably, low fuel forced the MiGs off at last. Folmar, unharmed, spent 15 minutes in the Yellow Sea before an Air Force SA-16 Albatross amphibian rescue airplane picked him up. Daniels, having performed his duties as wingman brilliantly, returned safely to ship.[14]

Thereafter, the number of MiG encounters off Korea's west coast decreased dramatically. The MiGs now turned their attention to the Wonsan and Hungnam areas, and, for the first time since the war began, TF 77 lost aircraft to enemy fighters. On October 4, four MiGs ganged up on a VF-884 Corsair from *Kearsarge* (CVA-33), shooting it down near Yongp'o and killing its pilot, Lieutenant Eugene F. Johnson. Three days later, MiGs attacked a mixed formation of ADs and F4Us south of Hungnam, fortunately without incident. That same day, however, *Princeton*'s airedales had three MiG encounters of their own; VF-193 lost a Corsair with Ensign John R. Shaughnessy north of Wonsan. But a month later, the Navy got its revenge and more when *Oriskany* Panthers clashed with Soviet-flown MiGs in the most dramatic and significant of the

Navy's Korean dogfights.[15]

New to war, the U.S.S. *Oriskany* (CVA-34), an *Essex*-class carrier, had arrived for its first Korean tour in late October with veteran Air Group 102 (an all-Reserve outfit) embarked. It launched its first air strikes on November 2, and by the middle of the month, had already lost two ADs to flak. November 18 found TF 77's aviators busily striking industrial targets in the northeast corner of Korea, close by the Chinese and Soviet borders. Steaming approximately 100 miles south-southwest of the major Soviet naval complex at Vladivostok, TF 77 lay within easy range of the many Soviet fighter bases ringing that area. As a precaution, *Oriskany* launched a CAP consisting of two divisions of Panthers from VF-781. The eight planes orbited slowly over the fleet while shipboard radar kept track of bogies. The CAP consisted of new F9F-5 Panthers, the first to arrive in the Korean theater. The F9F-5, a longer, taller model of the Panther, had a 6,350-pound static thrust Pratt & Whitney J48 jet engine that offered greater power than earlier models. It also had an APG-30 radar-ranging gunsight that significantly improved the Panther's probability of kill if the pilot could maneuver into a firing position. The key to any successful fighter, however, is the man in the cockpit, and *Oriskany*'s VF-781 were among the best. A Reserve unit, VF-781's pilots had earned the nickname "Pacemakers" for volunteering in their entirety for activation when war broke out in 1950.[16]

All morning long the task force had tracked large numbers of bogies flitting about the radar screens 40-100 miles ahead of the fleet. The heavy cruiser

U.S.S. *Helena*, on search and rescue duties with a destroyer midway between the fleet and the Korean port city of Rashin, believed the contacts to be some sort of barrier patrol under positive ground control, a typical Soviet approach to air defense. At 1:29 in the afternoon, radar picked up "Raid 20," a group of 16-20 aircraft, approaching from the north. Whether the estimates ran high, or a smaller group broke away from this contact is unclear, but *Oriskany* detected approximately eight bogies at a range of 83 miles on a direct course for the fleet. Throughout the Korean War, the Navy lived in fear of a surprise MiG assault on the task force, with MiGs streaking out before radar could give adequate warning. They might overwhelm the technologically inferior straightwing Panthers and Banshees, strafing the decks of the carriers, and setting them up for a devastating assault by conventional bombers or torpedo aircraft or, perhaps, by the new Ilyushin Il-28 twin-jet medium bomber. The Il-28 was known to be in Manchuria and was believed spotted on one occasion over central Korea itself.

Oriskany's Combat Information Center (CIC) wasted no time, detaching one of the Pacemaker divisions to intercept. The four-plane division consisted of two two-plane sections: division leader Lieutenant Claire R. Elwood and his wingman Lieutenant (j.g.) John D. Middleton, and section leader Lieutenant E. Royce Williams and his wingman Lieutenant (j.g.) David M. Rowlands. Unfortunately, Elwood's Panther chose this moment to act up; fuel boost pump failure crippled it and negated its combat value. In response to CIC's call, Elwood detached William's section, and Williams and his wingman Rowlands began a steady climb from 13,000 feet to intercept the incoming bogies. Few doubted the origin of the bogies; the location of the contact precluded any possibility of them operating from a known Korean MiG base, the direction of the contact pointed at the heart of the Vladivostok naval and air complex, and — the clincher — radio intercepts picked up Russian being spoken by the pilots. The bogies closed fast, their condensation trails clearly visible to the climbing Panthers. The trails passed overhead — CIC reported that they had overflown the intercepting Pacemakers — and then, removing any doubts as to their intentions, the bogies themselves turned to close with the Panthers; they wanted some sort of confrontation. Still far below, Royce Williams tallyho'd the bogies while climbing through 15,000 feet, identifying them as seven MiGs "flying very high."[17]

The following is *Oriskany's* own after-action report:

In a loose abreast formation, they came approximately overhead, made a descending turn and split into two groups, as though to bracket.

At this point the Pacemakers lost contact as the MiG condensation trails had ceased.

Because of his engine trouble Lt. Elwood and his wingman, Lt. (j.g.) John D. Middleton, remained at 13,000 feet. Meanwhile, Lt. Williams and his wingman Lt. (j.g.) David M. Rowlands, continued their climb to 26,000 feet under CAP control since visual contact had been lost. As they leveled off, the two Panther jets spotted four MiGs initiating a flatside firing attack from the ten o'clock position. Lt. William broke his section 'hard left' in a defensive counter and spoiled the effectiveness of the run, although he could not bring his own guns to bear. The MiG's recovered to the right in a strung out position with the fourth plane especially far back. Lt. Williams continued his wrapped-up turn and brought his section around for a tail-end shot at the last MiG. Firing from 15° off the tail, his first burst from the four 20-mm guns put the enemy jet into a smoking, uncontrolled spiral. Lt. (j.g.) Rowlands followed the crippled MiG down to 8,000 feet where it was last seen smoking in a steep graveyard spiral. Gun camera film confirmed the kill.

When the straggler was shot down, the three remaining MiG's pulled away rapidly in a climbing turn from Lt. Williams. When out of range, they split and once again attempted to bracket the lone F9F-5. The [MiG] section made a high-side run in loose formation. Williams rolled into a sharp counter and got a head-on burst at the second MiG. The Communist pilots seemed reluctant to press home a head-on attack and fired from far out. In the dogfight that followed, Williams continued to counter and succeeded in exchanging short bursts at various angles of deflection, largely head-on.

At one time he found himself dead astern of

a MiG. Immediately after he fired, the MiG dropped his dive brakes and Lt. Williams had to break sharply to the right and pull up to prevent collision. The MiG may have been damaged by this burst.

During this dogfight, the MiG's were able to turn and maneuver with the F9F-5 with apparent ease. The fight was fought with the F9F-5 at a continuous 100% RPM. When a MiG wished to break away, he pulled away in a rapid, climbing turn to recover the advantage for another pass.

Lt. (j.g.) Rowlands climbed up to rejoin his section leader and the air battle turned into a melee. It may be that the three MiG's unaccounted for had now joined in the fracas. The pilots had extreme difficulty keeping track of the MiG's. As Rowlands reached the scene of action, a MiG made a head-on run, firing from far out and breaking sharply to the left in a steep climbing turn. With planes all around him, Rowlands found himself in an advantageous position with a MiG in his sights. Firing a long burst, he started it smoking but was diverted by another jet attacking him. The MiG and the F9F-5 ended up circling with neither jet gaining the advantage. The MiG finally leveled his wings and climbed away rapidly.

Another MiG turned inside Williams and scored a hit, seriously damaging the F9F-5. A high explosive shell severed rudder controls and knocked out the aileron boost. [i.e.: Williams no longer had directional control (yaw control), and his lateral control (roll control) became exceedingly sluggish.] With the MiG still firing on his tail, Williams dove for a cloud bank 10,000 feet below him and approximately ten miles away. Rowlands followed, although out of ammo by this time. He flew almost a loose wing position on the enemy jet in an effort to drive him off.

About this time Lt. (j.g.) John D. Middleton was vectored up to aid his two squadron mates. His indoctrination to aerial combat was a head-on run by one of the sweptwing jets who came in from the two o'clock position. Lt. Middleton countered him and simultaneously saw Lt. Williams, a MiG, and Rowlands diving toward the cloud bank. As he dove to render aid, a MiG made another run on Middleton. On breaking away, the enemy plane reversed course and apparently lost the F9F-5 in the sun, for he remained in perfect position for a ninety degree deflection shot. Middleton tracked him, fired from far out, and continued firing as the MiG's superior speed caused the Panther to tail in behind him. The pilot bailed out and Middleton saw the plane crash into the sea and the pilot land in the water.

Meanwhile, Lt. Williams and Rowlands reached the safety of cloud cover and after flying in the 'soup' for about five minutes received a steer to the Task Force which was under the overcast. They made individual letdowns breaking out in the clear at 1,200 feet. The crippled Panther made a successful landing

aboard, followed by the other three Pacemakers.

As Lt. Williams was returning to the Task
Force, a standby CAP was launched from the
Oriskany. Led by the skipper of the Pacemakers, LCDR. Stan Holm, the division broke
through the overcast at 11,000 feet in time to
see two MiG's high make a sweeping turn and
disappear to the northwest at high speed.[18]

Things did not end quite so smoothly. An escorting destroyer fired at Williams's crippled Panther
until a good glimpse of its straight-wing planform
left no doubt as to its identity. Then, as he approached *Oriskany,* Williams experienced an increasingly difficult time lining up on the carrier; small
wonder, since, for all practical purposes, he had a
rudderless airplane. *Oriskany's* skipper, Captain
Courtney Shands, obligingly turned the ship slightly
out of the wind to accommodate the ailing Panther,
and, with the help of LSO Lieutenant Robert
MacKenna, Williams trapped safely aboard.[19]

Probably only one or two of the seven MiGs made
it back to shore; officially the Navy credited Williams and Middleton with kills, and Rowlands with a
damaged. Though sweet, small disappointments
marred the otherwise excellent show. *Kearsarge* had
a division apiece of Banshees from VF-11 and Panthers from VF-721 within two minutes flying time of
the dogfight yet, for some reason, controllers failed
to vector them in. Faulty plotting led to the downed
Russian airman being lost at sea; the one certain
chance the UN had to pick up a Soviet MiG pilot

had been lost. Approximately an hour and a half after the dogfight ended, radar detected a slow-moving bogie, presumably a Soviet amphibian rescue plane, operating in the area where the pilot went down. It is doubtful, however, that he could have survived in winter waters where lifespan is measured in minutes, not hours. Once again, the superior training of naval aviators had turned the odds from defeat into victory. Once again, the dogfight affirmed the Panther's inferiority to the MiG. But for the moment, all attention rightly turned to the Pacemakers' gallant fight. Williams and Middleton each received the Silver Star and Rowlands a Distinguished Flying Cross. Shortly afterwards, when President-elect Dwight D. Eisenhower visited Korea on a preinaugural tour, Admiral Arthur Radford, Vice Admiral J. J. "Jocko" Clark (then commanding Seventh Fleet), and Vice Admiral Robert P. Briscoe (who had succeeded Admiral Turner Joy as COMNAVFRE) arranged for Eisenhower to meet and chat with the three pilots in General James Van Fleet's private suite in Seoul. The President-elect and his son, Army Major John Eisenhower, mixed highballs for the flyers and then, together with General Mark Clark, listened enthralled as the three described the fight "complete with hand gestures and body English." The interservice squabbles of the 1940s must have seemed far away.[20]

Why had the Soviets struck TF 77? Was it the rash act of a local commander in response to the raids close to the Soviet and Chinese frontier? Was it an attempt to teach a "lesson," to inflict heavy casualties on the CAP to flex muscle? Was it intended as an actual prelude to a more direct Soviet participation in the war against the fleet? The answers to these questions will likely remain unknown. In fact, the strike may have resulted both from a desire to "teach a lesson" and a need to lash out, born of growing frustration on the part of the Communists over the rising effectiveness of new Allied air strikes. By November 1952, as has already been mentioned, the Allied powers in Korea changed the nature of the air war. With the "air pressure" and *Cherokee* campaigns taking tolls in a way that the previous interdiction effort had not, the MiG attack might simply have been a frustrated lash at the source of the torment.

In the early months of 1953, there were sporadic encounters between MiGs and Corsairs and Sea Furies on the west coast. No further American or British aircraft, and no MiGs, were lost, though a Corsair from the ever-aggressive VMA-312 got in a good burst that damaged one of the Communist jets during a dogfight between six MiGs and four F4Us near Sok-to on February 4. Aside from these inconclusive engagements, the naval aviators who had the greatest chance of encountering MiGs were those serving on exchange duty with the Fifth Air Force's Sabre squadrons then doing daily battle above the Yalu. Most successful of these were Marine Majors John Bolt, A. J. Gillis, and John Glenn; Bolt destroyed six MiGs, becoming the only Marine ace of the war, and Glenn and Gillis each destroyed three. Glenn scored all in a nine-day period, flying a Sabre suitably emblazoned with the legend "MiG Mad Marine," and almost certainly would have bagged two more but for the intervention of the Korean armistice. A list of Navy-Marine MiG killers together with the number of MiGs they shot down indicates the success enjoyed by some of the relatively small number of naval aviators serving on exchange duty, and may be taken as an indication of how well naval aviators in general might have done if they had had an opportunity to confront the MiG on a more routine basis with a naval airplane possessing performance akin to the Sabre:

Pilot	Score
Maj. John F. Bolt, USMC	6
Lt. Simpson Evans, USN	1
Maj. A. J. Gillis, USMC	3
Maj. John H. Glenn, USMC*	3
Maj. W. F. Guss, USMC	1
Capt. H. L. Jensen, USMC	1
Capt. V. J. Marzello, USMC	1
Lt. Col. J. Payne, USMC	1
Lt. Cmdr. Paul Pugh, USN	2
Maj. R. L. Reed, USMC	2
Lt. Walter Schirra, USN*	1
Maj. T. M. Sellers, USMC	2
Capt. R. Wade, USMC	1

But if daytime encounters between Communist

*It is interesting to note that this select group included two fighter pilots, Glenn and Schirra, later chosen for the first group of Americans in space.

aircraft and those of the Navy and Marines remained a relative rarity, during this time VMF(N)-513 and small detachments from VC-3, VC-4, and VMCJ-1 waged a quite different kind of air war against the NKAF. Nightly encounters with MiGs and (at the end of the performance spectrum) small and light aircraft that were difficult to intercept (used by the North Koreans for their own night-heckling program) characterized this phase of the air war.

Night air missions against North Korea fell into two broad categories. First, of course, were the offensive attack missions flown by a variety of aircraft that ranged from B-29 medium bombers to B-26 road- and rail-cutting missions, the night-heckling effort of TF 77, and night strike sorties by land-based Marine Corsairs and Tigercats. Second came night air defense missions, using night-fighters to escort and protect nightbombers from interception by Communist aircraft, or using night-fighters to protect airfields and targets in South Korea from North Korean night-hecklers. Much of the night air war against North Korea rested in the hands of the Marines, who wielded their Corsairs, Tigercats, and, later, Skyknights against North Korean forces with a skill and record of accomplishment that had received too little attention.

In 1950, Lieutenant Colonel Max Volcansek's VMF(N)-542 had instituted the Marines' night air war against North Korea, flying from Kimpo in their big Grumman F7F-3N Tigercats. Soon, Major Hunter J. Reinburg's VMF(N)-513, the "Flying Nightmares," joined with F4U-5N Corsairs. Reinburg preferred the larger two-place Tigercat to the single-seat Corsair, since night flying a single-place aircraft, especially one having such a high level of workload as the Corsair, took a particularly skillful pilot. Both the Marines made do with the Corsair until late 1952. Meanwhile, VMF(N)-542 left Korea for El Toro Marine Corps Air Station in California, to serve as the training squadron for the new twin-jet Douglas F3D Skyknight night-fighter. Its Tigercats went to -513, which subsequently operated a mix of the F4Us and F7Fs.[21]

In March 1951, VMF(N)-513 began a trend-setting series of night operations in conjunction with Air Force Douglas C-47 transports. The Air Force had embarked on a program using flare-dropping C-47s (aptly dubbed "Fireflies") in partnership with roving B-26 intruders. The C-47s took off, flew to a target area, and dropped flares as soon as scanners spotted a North Korean convoy. Down roared the B-26s, bombing, strafing, and rocketing. The project involved tremendous danger for aircrews, not merely from antiaircraft fire, but from weaving at low level and high speed among canyons and mountains, with inadequate external visual references, and ever-present risk of vertigo. The B-26, though it possessed reasonably good speed and payload, lacked the agility and survivability necessary to be completely successful in this role. One such night mission claimed Army General James Van Fleet's son, an exceptionally aggressive Air Force pilot. Colonel George S. Brown, then Fifth Air Force's Director of Operations, would complain in the summer of 1952 of "trading B-26's for trucks in a most uneconomical manner."

Intrigued, the Flying Nightmares decided to try the approach using their more nimble Corsairs, and by June, VMF(N)-513 claimed upwards of 1,4000 trucks destroyed at night. That month, in an attempt to improve their effectiveness, the squadron experimented with two flare-dropping Convair PB4Y-2 Privateers on loan from VP-772, a Reserve squadron based at Atsugi, Japan. The Privateers worked quite well, and, thereafter, teamed Corsairs and Tigercats and Privateers became commonplace. Commander Charles S. Minter, Jr., skipper of VP-28 based at Itami, Japan, took a detachment of four flare-dropping Privateers (dubbed "Lamplighters") to Korea. He recalled subsequently that the Korean road strikes were

> an interesting thing to watch. It was like ants running from an anthill. The minute the flare burst, the fellows all started pulling off and trying to get under trees or whatever, but we had them many times.[22]

A typical Tigercat sortie involved a Privateer Lamplighter flying over the North, its scanners looking for lights that might betray a Korean convoy. Throughout the war, the North Koreans ran their convoys with headlamps lit and relied on ground observers to hear the drone of Allied intruders, and signal the vehicles with flares or radio to douse their lights. Often strike aircraft could sneak up on road traffic, the drivers oblivious to the planes' approach because of the roar of their own engines. When scanners spotted a convoy, the Privateer radioed the Tigercat, dropping illuminating flares, and stood by to drop more as the F7F dove in on the vehicles. Night intruder crews disliked HVARs, and usually did not carry them; the flash from the rockets temporarily blinded them—a dangerous business in hill country. Accordingly, a Tigercat strike usually involved three passes, the first with bombs the second with napalm, and the third with 20-mm strafing. Ordnance expended, the F7F would return to base. But the PB4Y-2, equipped with as many as 250 flares, would remain on station for a total of six hours, working with a succession of night-fighters. Lamplighter crews lived with the certainty that if they took a hit from antiaircraft fire (as Minter recalled) "we'd have made the biggest, brightest star in the sky." None did. A bigger danger was collision. One dark night Minter saw a Tigercat, pulling off target, coming head-on at the ungainly patrol bomber. "We each did the reverse thing," he remembered; "I dove and he climbed. We missed by feet, literally feet."[23]

In 1951, North Korea began flying night-heckling sorties against the south and Allied-held islands; they used a variety of light aircraft but, most typically, the two-plane open-cockpit Polikarpov Po-2 biplane, already nearly a quarter-century old at the time of the Korean war. A workhorse comparable in many ways to the American Stearman biplane, the Po-2 had performed a variety of roles, from pilot training to agricultural crop-dusting to night nuisance raider. During the Second World War, Soviet female pilots, dubbed "Night Witches," had scored some singular successes dropping small bombs from Po-2s over Nazi-held territory. Now, in North Korean hands, the plane proved to be an annoyance out of proportion to its apparent worth in combat. Often flying well under 100 mph at very low altitude in hilly or mountainous terrain, the nimble and pesky Polikarpov posed difficult challenges to intercepting night-fighters. Its construction gave minimal radar return, and, once a heavier, faster night-fighter committed itself to attack, the biplane could easily sidestep, if flown by an experienced and nervy crew. In June 1951, near Seoul, a B-26 crew returning from a night interdiction mission closed on one Po-2, throttled back, and with gear and flaps down, hung in long enough to shoot it down. Jet night-fighters, with their high stall speeds and lack of low-speed maneuverability, had an especially difficult time. One unfortunate Air Force F-94B crew overran their target; both crews perished in the ensuing collision.

Despite the difficulties, night-fighters took up the Po-2 challenge. They relied if possible on vectors from Kimpo's Tactical Air Control Center *Dentist* to position themselves where their own radar could detect the little biplanes. On July 1, 1951, Captain Edwin B. Long and Warrant Officer Robert C. Buckingham made three firing runs on a Po-2 and sent it crashing to earth with their 20-mm fire as the biplane's rear seat occupant gamely shot back at them with a hand-held machine gun. Less than two weeks later, on July 12, VMF(N)-513 got a second Po-2 kill when Captain Donald L. Fenton, flying a F4U-5N, pressed in despite return fire from a ma-

"Carlson's Canyon" after the final strikes of April 2, 1951 had left only the battered concrete piers standing. (U.S. National Archives)

Deck crews manhandle a F9F of *Princeton's* VF-191 into position, 1951. (Grumman archives)

A pilot of *Princeton's* VA-195 checks a detonator on a 2,000-pound bomb, preparatory to an April 1951 strike. In addition to two 2,000-pound bombs, this AD carries ATAR rockets. (U.S. Naval Institute)

Two F4U-5Ns piloted by flight leader Lieutenant (j.g.) John D. Ely and wingman Lieutenant (j.g.) J. G. Stranlund from *Boxer's* VC-3 detachment return from a predawn heckling mission over North Korean rail lines. (U.S. Naval Institute)

Two *Boxer* Panthers from VF-721 (armed with four ATAR and two HVAR rockets apiece) overfly Wonsan during a July 1951 strike: in the distance is the infamous trans-Korean "Death Valley." (U.S. National Archives)

With his Panther damaged on a November 22, 1951 raid over North Korea, this fighter pilot returned to complete a successful landing on the U.S.S. *Bon Homme Richard* (CV-31) with his port landing gear retracted, saving a valuable airplane. (U.S. Naval Institute)

Two-seat AD-3Q Skyraiders served in small detachments aboard TF 77 carriers, and proved very useful for electronic reconnaissance and countermeasures duties. Indistinguishable to the untrained eye from a standard Skyraider, the "Q" featured a small midships cockpit for an ECM operator. Here five from VC-35 fly in echelon in March 1951. (McDonnell-Douglas archives)

Lieutenant (j.g.) John A. Chalbeck of *Boxer's* Reserve squadron VF-721 nears the North Korean coastline while returning from a strike against supply lines, August 29, 1951. (U.S. National Archives)

Emergency on the flight deck: The external belly tank of this AD ruptured from the force of the landing, and the hot engine exhaust quickly ignited escaping fuel. Here fire crews rush to contain and smother the fire, as the pilot runs to safety across the starboard wing. Note the firefighter over the port wing working to remove 20-mm ammunition from the gun bays. The prompt response saved the plane to fly another day. (U.S. Naval Institute)

Aftermath of tragedy: Weary fire crews on the U.S.S. *Essex* (CV-9) fight the lingering fire left from the deck-landing accident of a VF-172 Banshee on September 16, 1951 that killed seven men and destroyed four airplanes. (U.S. National Archives)

Fire crew mop-up hot spots left from *Boxer's* near-disastrous fire on August 6, 1952. Note the remains of the F4U-4B, blown over on its back and ripped apart by the explosions that rocked the hangar deck. (U.S. Naval Institute)

As *Princeton's* Ads pull off target, the Hwachon dam is rocked by torpedo blasts that rupture its sluice gates, releasing its impounded waters and sending ripples of shock waves across the reservoir. (U.S. National Archives)

A Douglas AD-2 from *Boxer's* Reserve squadron VA-702 nears the North Korean coast at Wonsan bay in mid-1951 on an armed reconnaissance sortie. *Boxer* had the first all-Reserve air group to see action in Korea. (U.S. Naval Institute)

A VF-172 McDonnell F2H-2 Banshee returns to *Essex* from a mission over North Korea, September 1951. (U.S. National Archives)

Happy to be back, Lieutenant (j.g.) William T. Barron of *Philippine Sea's* VA-95 explains how his AD-4L got hit by flak to Commander Thomas D. Harris, skipper of Air Group 9. The rugged AD took a 37-mm shell hit that blew an 18-inch hole in the horizontal stabilizer (*see above Barron's head*) and peppered the tail section with over 200 holes from shrapnel during a strike in March 1953. (McDonnell-Douglas archives)

This dramatic photograph taken by another Panther catches a rare pilot's view of an attack typical of TF 77's interdiction sorties. Having dropped a bomb and fired a rocket from under his port wing a moment before, this VF-71 Panther pilot from *Bon Homme Richard* drops another 250-pound bomb from under the right wing as he dives towards a small highway bridge in November 1952. Note the extended speed brakes, and the craters left from previous attacks. (U.S. Naval Institute)

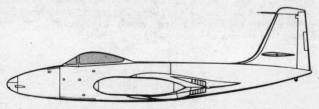

McDonnell F2H-2 Banshee

The three-man AD-4NL played a major role in TF 77's night attack effort. Here are the four comprising *Valley Forge's* VC-35 detachment, each carrying radar and searchlight pods. Aircraft 03 (*at top of photograph*) was subsequently lost to 37-mm flak; the two aircrewmen and pilot Lieutenant (j.g.) Harry Ettinger parachuted into captivity for the remainder of the war. (McDonnell-Douglas archives)

Boxer's last recce mission of the war returns to the ship. Here a F2H-2P photo plane (lacking the standard wingtip fuel tanks) from *Boxer's* VC-61 detachment and two escorting F9F-5s from VF-52 go "feet wet" over the North Korean coastline. (U.S. National Archives)

Another example of Anglo-American fraternity. British deck crewmen of the carrier H.M.S. *Glory* cluster around Major John Dexter's F4U-4 Corsair from *Sicily's* VMF-323. The *Death Rattler's* pilot diverted to *Glory* when *Sicily* had a fouled deck, and his fuel state prohibited waiting it out. (U.S. Naval Institute)

Marine ground crews refuel two ATAR-armed F9F-2B Panthers of VMF-311 at P'ohang in the summer of 1952; note the pierced steel planking taxiway—a feature of Korean airfields during the war. (Grumman archives)

Two of *Glory's* deck crewmen pull the chocks on this Hawker Sea Fury, launching on a strike against the Haeju peninsula, as other rocket-armed Sea Furies, wings still folded, warm up aft. With a distinctive five-bladed propeller, the powerful Sea Fury performed admirably as a naval fighter-bomber. Flying a Sea Fury over the same area, H.M.S. *Ocean's* Lieutenant Peter "Hoagy" Carmichael shot down a MiG-15 in August 1952. (U.S. National Archives)

Grumman's sleek radar-equipped F7F-3N Tigercat saw extensive service as a night intruder and interceptor over Korea, armed with bombs, rockets, and cannon. (U.S. Naval Institute)

Convair's four-engine PB4Y-2 Privateer, a navalized derivative of the wartime B-24 Liberator bomber, served in Korea on maritime patrol, electronic intelligence gathering, and nocturnal "Lamplighter" flare-dropping sorties. (U.S. National Archives)

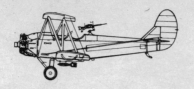

Polikarpov Po-2 (U-2VS)

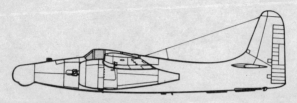

Grumman F7F-3N Tigercat

An F3D-2 Skyknight of VMF(N)-513 during an engine run-up at Kunsan, South Korea. Note the inlet screens to protect the engine from FOD (foreign object damage) during ground runs. The size of this all-weather fighter is readily apparent. (McDonnell-Douglas archives)

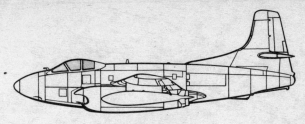

Douglas F3D-2 Skyknight

A "Flying Nightmares'" Skyknight in flight. Note the large size of the tail warning radar housing; the relative size of the pilot in the cockpit offers an indication of the Skyknight's dimensions. (McDonnell-Douglas archives)

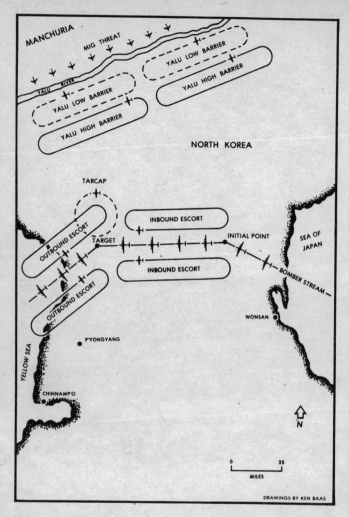

Night escort over Korea 1952-1953

Major William T. Stratton (*left*) points to the red star painted on his Skyknight as radar systems operator Master Sergeant Hans C. Hoglind (*right*) looks to the camera; on the night of November 3, 1952, while patrolling over Sinuiju, they emerged triumphant from the world's first jet versus jet night combat. (U.S. Naval Institute)

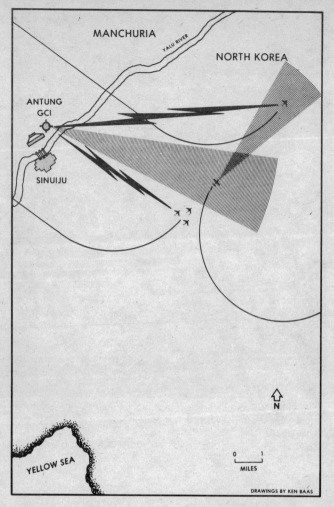

MiGs versus Skyknight: Jousting with North Korea's night interceptors.

As radar systems operator Master Sergeant Lawrence J. Fortin (*left*)
looks on, Major Elswin P. "Jack" Dunn (*center*) points out an aeronautical chart to a debriefer where they shot down a MiG-15 over Sinanju,
sticking with the Communist fighter during extensive night maneuvering.
(McDonnell-Douglas archives)

Mission accomplished. A fine study of a Marine Corsair piloted by
Lieutenant Colonel T. J. O'Connor coming aboard in the days of the
paddle-armed LSO. Note the flight of Corsairs entering the pattern.
(U.S. Naval Institute)

A relic of the past but a portent of the future: A Grumman F6F-5K drone catapults from the *Boxer* during the experimental strikes undertaken by Lieutenant Commander Larry Kurtz's GMU-90 in August and September 1953. Awaiting its turn at launch is the AD-2Q drone controller (on the starboard catapult) and an AD-3Q from *Boxer's* detachment. (U.S. National Archives)

The prototype Vought XF8U-1 Crusader flying on a 1955 test mission from Edwards Air Force Base, California; this fine aircraft (which exceeded the speed of sound on its maiden flight) benefited from the technological fallout of the supersonic breakthrough as well as the lessons of Korea, and became a fearsome "MiG-master" in its own right during the Vietnam War. (U.S. Air Force)

The Douglas F4D-1 Skyray interceptor underwent accelerated development as a result of the Korean War; this particular example of the distinctive modified delta-wing fighter flew with the National Advisory Committee for Aeronautics, the predecessor of today's NASA. (National Aeronautics and Space Administration)

A Grumman F9F-7 Cougar of VF-21 photographed in October 1953; the previous model, the F9F-6, entered service too late to see combat in Korea. (Grumman archives)

The second production McDonnell F4H-1 Phantom II on a flight test sortie at Edwards Air Force Base (note the pylon mounted cameras to record external stores separation). This versatile multimission interceptor and strike aircraft exemplified the application of Korea's lessons to naval combat aircraft design. (U.S. Air Force)

The prototype Grumman A2F-1 Intruder, predecessor of the outstanding A-6 family of all-weather attack aircraft, during an early contractor test flight. (Grumman archives)

Ed Heinemann's outstanding A4D Skyhawk attack bomber landing after a test mission at Edwards Air Force Base in 1954. (U.S. Air Force)

Early flight refueling tests off the California coast between a Douglas A3D Skywarrior with a drogue and reel refueling system and a probe-equipped North American FJ-4B Fury from VA-116. (U.S. Air Force)

A Sikorsky HO3S-1 lands on the heavy cruiser U.S.S. *St. Paul* (CA-73) after having spotted naval gunfire against Communist shore positions during the ongoing siege of Wonsan, April 1951. (U.S. Naval Institute)

A Sikorsky HRS-1 of HMR-161 delivers supplies after having participated in shuttling a Marine company to new frontline positions. (U.S. Marine Corps)

Whimsey at sea: *Bon Homme Richard's* VC-61 detachment of F9F-2Ps poses for a photograph, October 1951. Note that each airplane is named for a prominent photo-journal of the day: *Life, Look,* and *Pic.* (U.S. Naval Institute)

No peace on earth this year: a striking photograph of the superlative long-nose McDonnell F2H-2P Banshee photo recce aircraft and its short-nose F2H-2 fighter stablemate flying over the convoluted mountains of North Korea. Here a F2H-2P of the U.S.S. *Kearsarge's* (CVA-33) VC-61 detachment is trailed by a Banshee fighter from the carrier's VF-11 during a Christmas Eve reconnaissance mission, 1952. (U.S. National Archives)

chine gun-wielding observer and blew the biplane apart. In mid-September, *Dentist* and the Flying Nightmares again demonstrated their desire to pull the teeth of the Po-2s when Major Eugene A. Van Gundy and Master Sergeant Thomas J. Ullom destroyed another; the Tigercat crew's combat report offers a glimpse of this cat-and-mouse war:

I was standing strip alert when scrambled on the morning of 23 September. My ground controller vectored me to a point northeast of Kimpo airfield. Upon reaching an altitude of 10,000 feet I was instructed to orbit while the ground controller vectored us on station and released the other plane. He then changed our altitude from 10,000 feet to 5,000 feet and commenced their controlling of the intercept.

Although the bogey made frequent changes in headings, the controller accurately changed our vectors to correspond. As we began to close on our target our controller instructed us to reduce speed to 160 knots, then to 140 knots, and then to 120 knots. At 140 knots we lowered our gear and flaps in order to get as slow as possible. My radar operator, MSgt. Ullom, then established contact on our own radar gear. He directed me to a point where I established a visual contact of the bogey at approximately 500 feet. I made a firing pass expending 100 rounds of 20-mm ammunition. The bogey instantly burst into flames. As we pulled away we observed that the entire enemy aircraft was ablaze. . . . The total interception took about

25 minutes, and was completed at 3,000 feet altitude.[24]

VMF(N)-513's next victim was a bird of quite a different feather. Throughout the Korean War, the Flying Nightmares mixed night ground attack and night air defense sorties, and on June 7, 1952, Lieutenant John W. Andre had a unique opportunity to blend them. The North Koreans had decided to do some night intercepting of their own, perhaps to bag one of the Lamplighters or its intruding consorts. In any case, Andre, working over seven trucks with a mix of napalm and 20-mm strafing while under flares, suddenly saw tracers passing over his left wing from behind, then streaking under the plane and over the right wing—an unnerving experience, to say the least. The attacker passed Andrew to starboard; it moved only a little faster than the Marine's F4U-5NL, and the Leatherneck identified it as a Yak-9, cloaked in dark camouflage. Andre lined up on the enemy fighter, riddled it with 20-mm fire, and watched it stream flames from beneath its engine. He pulled up as the Yak dove away, and as he circled back, the Lamplighter reported an explosion on the ground: scratch one Yak.[25]

By the summer of 1952, VMF(N)-513 consisted of combat-tested veterans, proud of their status as "red ink" Marines. Many strove to have only red ink— night flight—entries in their log books, rather than blue ink—daytime—ones. As a result, they felt increasingly confident of their ability to take on the NKAF at night and win. So far, throughout the Korean War, the NKAF had shown itself reluctant to

258

commit itself to night air combat, with the exception of the Po-2s and the occasional odd sortie of a Yak or two. That changed rapidly in the winter of 1951-1952 as North Korea began integrating its radar early warning network with radar-controlled searchlights and radar-directed ground controlled interception of American Boeing B-29 Superfortresses. Because the B-29s had proven so vulnerable to MiGs during daylight raids, FEAF's Bomber Command switched to night bombing, flying slightly over 1,000 sorties in the last three months of 1951 and nearly 1,500 sorties in the first three months of 1952.

In late December, radar-vectored night-fighters, working in conjunction with radar-guided searchlights, damaged two B-29s. A B-29 stream generally moved toward its target at an altitude of approximately 25,000 feet, and at a speed averaging only about 265 mph. Using the SHORAN (Short Range Radio Navigation) bombing technique, whereby bombers navigated along a SHORAN "arc" signal and dropped their bombs when they intercepted an intersecting signal, the B-29s followed constrained flight paths. Experience soon taught the North Koreans where the suitable arcs lay, and they concentrated flak and searchlights accordingly.

But the clear indication that Superfortresses could no longer operate with impunity over the North came on the night of June 10-11, 1952, when 11 B-29s set out to raid a railway bridge complex at Kwaksan, outside Chongju, in MiG Alley. That night, searchlights coned 10 of the B-29s as they approached the target. A night interception force estimated as high as 12 MiGs, operating in conjunction with an airborne attack coordinator who flew parallel to the bomber stream, shot down two B-29s and severely damaged another; it made an emergency landing at Kimpo. Admittedly, none of the bombers had dropped chaff against the searchlight radars, and only one attempted frequency jamming: the 11th and last aircraft, which evaded the searchlights. Nevertheless, Kwaksan shook FEAF Bomber Command to the core, and instilled great appreciation for chaff-dropping and active ECM, including the need to upgrade electronic intelligence. Eventually, RF-50G ferrets escorted the B-29s on their bombing mission. The "Crows," electronic intelligence gatherers, captured as much information about enemy radars as they could. Often signal intensity in target areas proved so dense that "ECM operators in the ferret aircraft could not hope to Direction-Find them all."[26]

The greatest apprehension, however, was engendered by the obvious increase in North Korea's night-fighter capabilities. FEAF had no desire to find itself locked in the kind of seasaw war that RAF Bomber Command had seen with the *Luftwaffe's* night-fighter force during the Second World War. Since the Air Force had made a conscious decision not to employ the later B-36, the all-jet B-47, or even the upgraded piston-engine B-50 Superfortress, FEAF Bomber Command had to make do with the older B-29. The command had several options it could exercise: execute diversionary or low-level approaches behind shielding terrain including feints, jam GCI and VHF-GCI communications, employ ECM jamming of enemy early warning and GCI radar frequencies, and rely on night-fighter escort to take care of the MiG threat.

FEAF rejected feints and diversions because they would result in B-29s spending even longer over North Korean territory, and a MiG suckered away by a feint had such an overtaking speed that it could quickly reposition itself for an attack on the true bomber stream. FEAF rejected jamming VHF-GCI communications because of the value of listening-in for intelligence-gathering purposes, an undoubted but perhaps overrated value understandably questioned by the harrassed bomber crews. But it cleared the B-29s to jam GCI communications other than VHF on strikes along the Yalu, where MiG opposition could be expected to be fiercest. FEAF rejected out of hand any suggestion of jamming early warning radars, since such activity might give away the state of Strategic Air Command's capabilities in the ECM field, but it did approve jamming specific GCI radar frequencies (with the exception of S Band, again for fear of compromising SAC's ECM capabilities). Inadequate training and antiquated equipment complicated FEAF's problems.

FEAF Bomber Command constantly found it had greater need for trained ECM operators than it could fulfill. The need for SHORAN equipment aboard the bombers limited the amount of power available for jamming equipment, and hence the amount of jamming equipment that could be carried along. The jamming equipment itself all dated to the Second World War, and, in fact, FEAF received its first jammers of post-World War II vintage in May 1953: AN/APT-9 systems. In the meantime, FEAF

261

Bomber Command opted for widespread use of chaff, avoided altitudes where weather forecasters predicted the Superfortresses would stream heavy contrails, painted the underside of the bombers black — a "tactic" (if it may be called that) dating to bomber operations in the First World War — and, most significantly, relied on escorting night-fighters to fend off the MiGs.[27]

The status of North Korea's night-fighter force engendered almost as much speculation as the question of who flew the MiGs. An intelligence summary issued in January 1953 listed 10 different kinds of fighters thought to have been encountered at night, four jet-propelled and six powered by piston engines and propellers:

Jet	Propeller
Mig-15	La-5
Yak-15	La-7
"Type 8" [La-150]	La-9
"Type 15" [La-15]	Yak-9
	Yak-11
	Il-10

Of the 10, the Type 8 existed only as a prototype and the Type 15, a shoulder-wing Lavochkin jet fighter subsequently known as the La-15, served as a ground-attack aircraft; it was extremely doubtful that it had shown up in Manchuria or North Korea as a night-fighter. The Soviet Union's Yakovlev design bureau built the Yak-15 (a jet-propelled derivative of the wartime Yak propeller-driven fighter family) in small numbers, using this interim design with a "tail dragging" landing gear as a jet fighter-trainer. A successor, the tricycle-gear Yak-17, distinguishable from its predecessor by a taller vertical fin and a bulge under its nose engine inlet for the semi-retractable nose landing gear, served in larger numbers, but the higher performance MiG-15 quickly superseded it in service.

A VMF(N)-513 crew shot down a fighter they identified as a Yak-15 on November 3, 1952, but it is probable that they had shot down a later Yak-17 instead; there are no other reliable encounter reports between this early Soviet-built jet fighter (designed for day use only) and other Allied aircraft. The La-5, -7, and -9, and the Yak-9, served in varying numbers with North Korean and Chinese forces, and did appear occasionally as rudimentary (and ineffective) night-fighters in much the same fashion that the *Luftwaffe* used day-fighting Bf 109s on so-called "Wild Boar" night interception missions over Europe. It is doubtful that the Yak-11, a trainer, served as a night-fighter itself, though it might have flown sorties as an airborne controller of other night-fighters; it did appear, like the Po-2, as a nuisance raider. The Ilyushin Il-10 ground attack aircraft possessed a heavy 23-mm cannon armament that would have suited it for the role against slower Allied aircraft; again, a doubtful prospect as a serious night-fighting aircraft. Only one serious threat aircraft existed, then: the MiG-15.[28]

FEAF had "fairly positive reports" that two Soviet night-fighter units maintained standing patrols of seven to eight MiGs airborne between the Ch'ongch'on and Yalu rivers. While "no substantiation" of Communist use of airborne radar equipment existed, the night-flying MiGs clearly made use of good air-to-ground communications, possibly with an airborne controller "pacing" the B-29 formations, and with ground-based GCI radars. GCI was particularly effective along Korea's west coast and within a radius of 90 miles from Antung, where a major *Token* GCI radar facility existed. The enemy night-fighters made good use of coordination between searchlights and night-fighters (as at Kwaksan); they used contrails streaming from the B-29s to locate the bombers, dropped flares to illuminate the bomber stream, and apparently made use of aircraft to help direct flak. Communist night-fighters appeared primarily in MiG Alley, but also down the west coast as far as Ch'o-do island, and sometimes Allied intruders reported random encounters over all of North Korea. The Communist night-hecklers—a different breed of night pilot—routinely flew south of the front, but the night-fighters per se preferred to remain over water or over North Korean territory.[29]

Based at Antung, Tatungkou, and Takushan, the MiGs appeared to lack airborne radar; ferrets repeatedly failed to detect an airborne signal, though on at least one occasion, a monitoring aircraft did detect a radar signal that could have emanated from an airborne set. This is puzzling, for in Korea the Soviets had an excellent opportunity to evaluate the performance of new equipment under relatively secure and clinical conditions. In late 1949, the Mikoyan design bureau had flown a prototype of a single-seat radar-equipped MiG, the MiG-15SP-1.

The bureau also proceeded with a two-seat all-weather version of the MiG-15, the MiG-15SP-5, on the two-place MiG-15UTI conversion-trainer.

Eventually, Mikoyan produced in quantity a single-seat radar-equipped all-weather fighter based on the MiG-15bis, the MiG-15bisP. That plane, like its predecessors, utilized an S band fixed-scan radar known as *Izumrud* (Emerald). Portions of this system were mounted on the upper lip of the engine inlet and also in a cone located in the center of the inlet itself, that projected from the inlet's splitter plate (a vertical wedge that split the incoming airflow so that it passed on either side of the cockpit structure before being fed to the engine). *Izumrud* could pick up targets at a range of approximately 7½ miles, and could function as a gun-aiming radar at distances below 1¼ miles. Armed with twin 23-mm cannon, the MiG-15bisP entered Soviet service in time to deploy to Korea, had the Kremlin so desired. The carnage wrought against FEAF Bomber Command's B-29s might well have proven unacceptable.[30]

As the B-29s encountered increasing resistance to their nightly forays, FEAF examined suitable Allied night-fighter escort and barrier-patrol operations to blunt the effectiveness of the night-flying MiGs. FEAF had already deployed the Lockheed F-94B to Korea. Essentially an afterburner-equipped variation of the Lockheed T-33 trainer, the F-94B had an armament of four .50-caliber machine guns and featured a sophisticated Hughes-built fire control system known as the E-1, a modified derivative of an earlier defensive radar used on the massive B-36.

Concern over compromising its state-of-the-art fire control system forced FEAF to employ it initially on defensive missions over the south. With the F-94B thus restricted, FEAF's only other alternative consisted of having the Flying Nightmares of VMF(N)-513 escort the B-29 strikes.

The Marines eagerly accepted the challenge of furnishing night protection to the Superfortresses and used a twin-jet interceptor equipped with an older radar cleared for use over the North, the Douglas F3D-2 Skyknight. Designed by Ed Heinemann, the Skyknight (soon nicknamed the "Blue Whale") had a deceptively portly appearance. With conventional straight wing and tail section, side-by-side seating for its pilot and radar intercept operator, and two Westinghouse J34 engines placed low on the flanks of the fuselage under the wings, this large airplane looked more like a strike or attack aircraft. But it had an armament of four 20-mm cannon, coupled with no less than three onboard radars, which together comprised the AN/APS-35 fire control system: an AN/APS-21 search radar with a range of 15-20 miles, an AN/APG-26 gun-aiming radar able to lock onto a target at a range of 2¼ miles, and an AN/APS-28 tail warning radar that could warn of approaching fighters at a distance of 10 miles (though crews usually expressed few qualms until the bogeys got down to 4 miles or less). The first true all-weather jet fighter that the Navy had, the Skyknight had a maximum speed of 493 mph, but usually patrolled at about 390 mph.[31]

Since mid-1951, VMF(N)-542 had been working up in the Skyknight at El Toro, California, and in

June 1952, a detachment of 15 left El Toro for San Diego, subsequently being shipped as deck cargo to Yokosuka. After final prepping, including replacement of large-style white lettering, star insignia, and dark blue finish with smaller stars, red lettering, and flat black finish, the Skyknights arrived at Kunsan, Korea, their base for the next half-year. Known as "King-8" (K-8), Kunsan served as the home of VMF(N)-513's Tigercats and Corsairs, to which the Skyknights were assigned. Mechanical problems, including the radar shaking loose from its mounts when the battery of four cannon fired, took several weeks to correct. Pilots averaged about 152 flying hours in the type when they deployed to Korea, their radar operators only 25. On August 8, in conjunction with Fifth Air Force, Marine and Air Force planners drew up operational plans for the Skyknight's combat evaluation. Like the F7Fs, the F3Ds would operate under the *Dentist* control center; they would take off from K-8 and proceed to a "free area" bounded on the north by a line running from Sonch'on east to Tokch'on, south to a spot near Samdung, and then west through P'yongyang to a spot over the Yellow Sea due south of Sonch'on. The F3Ds would thus patrol a rectangular space including much of the territory frequented by Communist night-flyers, particularly the flak and fighter hotbeds near the Ch'ongch'on estuary. Radio transmissions were to be succinct, encoded, and infrequent. After receiving directions from a controller, an F3D crew would transmit "Roger Dee" if they had a contact. "Dishpan" meant an inoperative radar and signified breaking off a mission and returning to base. "Steer to Mama" ordered a crew to return to K-8. "Infield" signified the F3D had reached the free area, as tracked by *Dentist*. "Outfield" cautioned a crew it was headed outbound from the free area, and "Home Run" warned a crew they were about to cross the Yalu sanctuary.[32]

During a sortie, *Dentist* and a friendly GCI radar station located on Ch'o-do island vectored the F3D into a position where the big interceptor could use its own radar to detect bogeys. The airborne interception radar operator, usually a Marine NCO or (in Navy units) a Petty Officer, picked up a target blip on the AN/APS-21 radar and guided the pilot into range to lock-on the AN/APG-26 gun-aiming radar. Then the pilot would close range and (if the crew identified the bogey as a "bandit") open fire, as the AIO watched the AN/APS-28 tail warning radar to make certain the Skyknight remained free of hostile interceptors approaching from the rear. Altogether, then, the process required excellent coordination among the two-man Skyknight crew, and between the airborne team and ground controllers.

Even before conference attendees had drawn up plans for the Skyknight's operational evaluation. VMF(N)-513 flew its first combat sortie in the craft. The honor of making this first flight in anger fell to a Royal Air Force exchange pilot, Squadron Leader John R. Gardner, flying with a Marine AIO, Staff Sergeant R. G. Kropp. Launched as a training mission, *Dentist* had diverted it to combat when radar picked up several hostile contacts. In any event, a combat opportunity failed to present itself, and Gardner and Kropp returned to K-8 empty-handed.

On August 11, the first planned evaluation flight occurred, when *Dentist* controlled F3Ds on a night combat air patrol (NCAP) north of Ch'o-do island to the coast of North Korea.

The F3D's evaluation period did not go smoothly. The NKAF failed to rise to the bait against the F3Ds, and this eventually resulted in a change of plans: the F3Ds would operate only on nights when the B-29s raided the North, taking advantage of the bomber "bait" to go after the "fishing" MiGs. An accident claimed one F3D and its pilot, and the squadron C.O., Colonel Peter D. Lambrecht and Lieutenant James M. Brown, his radar operator, failed to return from a combat patrol and were listed as missing in action. Engine safety and maintenance requirements resulted in the grounding of the squadron (except for limited test flying) until mid-October 1952. For a while, VMF(N)-513 operated its older propeller-driven F7Fs as B-29 shepherds, but the complete unsuitability of these airplanes as MiG-duelers forced the Marines to relegate them primarily to night MPQ and CAS sorties, or to escort for B-26 strikers (the "Formula" and "Pacify" missions). F7Fs never met the MiG in night combat; we can only speculate on how this aircraft, a representative of the final evolution of the propeller-driven fighter, might have fared against the early Soviet night jet interceptor.[33]

The F3D was well-suited to escort the B-29s, largely because of the capabilities of its three radars. Eventually, the Air Force's F-94B would receive clearance to support B-29s over the North, but even so, the night-fighter war was for the most part fought by the Marines. The F3Ds flew two kinds of B-29 support operations. One consisted of low and high "racetrack" barrier patrols south of the Yalu to intercept any MiGs or other night-fighters heading south for a bomber stream, and the second of close escort of the B-29s. In the second, the F3Ds picked up the bomber stream as it reached its initial point (IP), a geographical spot usually about 30-40 minutes away from the target, and escorted the bombers to the target, "handing off" the bombers to another team of Skyknights that would escort them out of Korean airspace. In addition, -513 often stationed a so-called Target Combat Air Patrol F3D to act both as mission coordinator and to circle over the formation and attack any MiGs audacious enough to bounce the bombers during their runs. Occasionally, spare aircraft launched from K-8 in case one of the primary escorts "broke." Or, returning barrier flights no longer needed, spares might be stationed in another racetrack pattern near Ch'o-do island to intercept North Korean night-hecklers, dubbed "Lowboys." Ch'o-do flights could be extraordinarily boring, but occasional night MiG forays as far south as Ch'o-do demanded that both night-fighter crews and ground controllers keep on their toes.

In November, VMF(N)-513 quickly scored against Communist night-fighters. On November 3, virtually over Sinuiju, Major William T. Stratton, Jr. and Master Sergeant Hans C. Hoglind shot down a single-engine night-fighter they identified as a Yak-15:

On 3 November, 1952 at approximately 0107/I

at 14,000 feet contact was made on radar. Unidentified at same altitude heading approximately 330 degrees, speed 320 knots. Distance 7 miles. Contact lost, then again established, same distance. Closed to 2,100 feet. APG-26 [gun aiming radar] would not lock [and] visual sighting [was] made of single-engine jet-type aircraft identified as Yak-15 at 0110. After some delay, permission was given by *Dutchboy* [allied GCI] to "Bag Bandit." Opened fire at approximately 0113 at 12,000 feet altitude, 1,200 feet from directly astern. First burst hit port wing of bandit, second fuselage, third entered tailpipe, exploding therein. Three explosions in all were observed and plane smoked heavily as it went down. Last seen at 6,000 feet still on fire and smoking.[34]

So ended the first night air combat between opposing jet-propelled aircraft in military aviation history.

Less than a week later, on November 8, Captain Oliver R. Davis and Warrant Officer Dramus F. Fessler shot down the squadron's first MiG, in a classic example of the partnership between the ground GCI controller and the airborne fighter team. Flying as *Volleyball* 3338, Davis and Fessler responded to a GCI call that they had a bogey 10 miles dead ahead, at an altitude of 12,500 feet. Davis dove down from 19,000 feet, going to full throttle at 14,000 feet to catch the speeding unknown. Fessler picked up the contact on his set, asked for a gentle turn to starboard, then lost contact; Davis got a new heading from the GCI,

Fessler again picked up the contact, again asked for a starboard turn, and placed Davis close enough so that he could spot both the dark shape ahead of him and the glow of a jet exhaust. He asked the GCI controller to confirm that the bogie was hostile; the controller urgently radioed "Bag it, bag it!" Closing rapidly, Davis popped his rectangular speed brakes, surprised at his rate of closure and the brightness of the MiG's exhaust. Perhaps at that time the Antung GCI warned the MiG of its danger, for, as Davis subsequently reported,

> The bandit began a hard starboard. I turned with him and fired a short burst of about twenty rounds of 20-mm into the tail pipe. There was an explosion and parts flew past my plane. I was closing dangerously. I pulled hard back on the stick and since I was already in a hard starboard turn, I passed the enemy to his right. I observed flames and black smoke passing from the center portion of his plane. After reversing my turn, I picked up a visual on the flaming craft as it descended and crashed. There was another explosion upon impact.[35]

The rest of November and December passed without further MiG kills, though Lieutenant Joseph A. Corvi and Master Sergeant Dan R. George had a notable encounter on December 10 when, firing strictly by the gun-aiming radar, they shot down a Po-2, then closed and possibly shot down another. This was the first time, so far as is known, that a night-fighter shot down another aircraft without its crew first transferring from a radar-controlled approach to a visual firing run. VMF(N)-513 had some close calls and frustrating moments during this period; the Po-2s flew so slowly that, on several occasions, ground controllers simply could not position the F3D crews to attack the biplanes. One communications foul-up during a flight on December 2 nearly led to a shootout between a F-94B and F3D. When *Volleyball* 3385 took up station, the F3D crew received a positive "parrot" (Identification Friend or Foe) transponder check from ground control, which indicated that ground control should have known where they were and that they were friendly. Shortly afterwards, *Harpoon* 06, an Air Force F-94B called out that it had a contact. Ground control station *Dutchboy* cleared the F-94 to check out the contact as GCI "had nothing on their gear." Suddenly the F3D crew picked up a tail contact closing fast. They broke hard right, then left, and heard *Harpoon* 06 reporting the bogey was taking evasive action and requesting permission to fire! Putting two and two together, *Volleyball* radioed a frantic "Hold your fire"; *Harpoon* "Rogered," and *Dutchboy* lamely radioed "Standby." The F3D crew looked off their left wing and there was a F-94.

Fortunately, a nocturnal encounter among misguided friends never took place in Korea's night skies, though crews moved warily among understandably trigger-happy Superfortresses. More ominously, on several occasions, the hunters almost became the hunted. On December 15, while on a barrier patrol near Huich'on, a F3D had two close escapes with bogeys that closed suddenly, stuck with the F3D through evasive maneuvers, and then broke off contact of their own accord. On December 21, *Enrage* 87 experienced difficulties with its radar gear, and received a warning call from GCI of "Heads up, boy, look out!" followed by a stream of red balls, 37-mm tracers, from a MiG. The startled Skyknight crew resorted to one of the F3D's strengths: its lateral control. They rolled over on their back, and pulled full aft stick, diving downwards in a split-S, then doing a series of vertical diving rolls. Such maneuvers, in instrument-only flying conditions, are best left to the imagination. The crew recovered, and, unbelievably, received another "Heads up, boy!" called from ground control. The MiG had followed them down. Again they plunged into a series of diving rolls, noting a diving light following them. They remained at 5,000 feet in overcast, gingerly feeling out their aircraft, before returning to Kunsan. This particular encounter caused some concern that the MiGs used their own airborne radar. Again, ferret information discounted such a conclusion, but this and similar encounters disturbed both Marine and Air Force night-fighter crews.[36]

Despite the growing use of night-fighters over North Korea, B-29 losses continued. On November 18, a 98th Bomb Wing Superfortress went down under MiG attack; a 19th Bomb Group B-29 followed on December 30, with two others so badly damaged that they were fit only for scrap. On the latter mission, a F3D crew saw the B-29s hit and observed sustained airborne firing between the MiGs and the B-29s, but the F3D was too far away to intervene. On another mission, a MiG and F3D got into a classic circling tail chase in the midst of a B-29 stream. Things got worse in January 1953, a month one subsequent Air Force analysis referred to as "Desperate." FEAF Bomber Command lost four Superfortresses that month to MiG attack, statistics that were inconsequential by the standards of the Second World War, but ones that indicated all too well the growing vulnerability of the slow bombers to jet interceptors. By this time, aggressive use of chaff drops had minimized problems with flak and radar-directed searchlights, but the MiG threat continued. In January, the Air Force's 319th Fighter-Interceptor Squadron scored its first kill when a F-94 crew blew away a La-9 on January 30, and damaged a Yak-9 the next night. The big MiG killers, however, continued to be the Marines, and in January, the Flying Nightmares shot down no less than three. On January 12, Major Elswin P. "Jack" Dunn and Master Sergeant Lawrence J. Fortin shot down a MiG over Sinanju, despite desperate evasive maneuvering by the Communist jet. On January 28, Captain James Weaver and Master Sergeant Robert P. Becker closed behind another, opening fire at a range of 1,500 feet and shooting it down in flames. On January 31, squadron commander Lieutenant Colonel Robert F. Conley and Master Sergeant James N. Scott shot down yet another, sending it into a mountainside.[37]

Like "Bloody April" 1917, which sorely tested Britain's Royal Flying Corps but which stands as the turning point in that air war, January 1953 inflicted heavy losses on FEAF Bomber Command, but night-fighters also hurt MiGs. North Korea's night air defenses never approached the magnitude of Nazi Germany's during the Second World War, or the sophistication of North Vietnam's over a decade later. But what's intriguing is the almost "clinical" nature of the North Korean night air defenses effort. It was as if the encounters between B-29s and MiGs, and later between the F3Ds, F-94s, and MiGs, were laboratory experiments, with the Communists seeking to refine GCI control of intercepting fighters. FEAF did not lose another B-29 to MiGs for the remainder of the war after January, a tribute to the use of chaff, ECM, and, particularly, to the effectiveness of the Allied night-fighter effort over the North. But it was also a result of the nature of the small parcel-like deployment of hostile fighters against the bombers. FEAF Bomber Command had few illusions about the future of the B-29; it recognized that the Communists had chosen not to deploy radar-equipped all-weather interceptors to Korea. "Because of this providential unreality," a postwar analysis concluded, "the old and weary B-29s weathered the crisis of the last year of Korean hostilities."[38]

Unfortunately, while B-29 losses ended, January marked the last month that the Flying Nightmares scored against the MiGs. From that point on, the Skyknights often found themselves fighting for their lives over the North. Exacerbating VMF(N)-513's problems were personnel changes that left the squadron (now based at P'yongtaek, K-6) with little experience in planes and in Korea. On March 3, at least two MiGs teamed up to give a F3D crew some bad moments near Sinuiju, red balls of 37-mm tracer streaking all around the aircraft as it maneuvered violently and got away. On May 30, Captain J. B. Brown and Sergeant J. V. Harrell, crew of *Greascup* 1225, failed to return to K-6 from a mission. Another crew experienced six attacks from at least 12 MiGs. The pilot reported later that:

For a period of approximately ten minutes we constantly had at least one tail contact while taking hard and desperate evasive action. We went through the target area from 30,000 to 5,000 feet during these ten minutes, diving vertically, usually in a wrap-up turn and with the aircraft buffeting most of the time at its limiting Mach [number].[39]

Though convinced they had been bounced by radar-equipped MiG, the crew conceded that "the enemy GCI is becoming more efficient as the weeks go by."[40]

On June 7, the 319th FIS bagged its first known MiG when squadron commander Lieutenant Colonel Robert V. McHale and Captain Samuel Hoster, his radar operator, shot one down near the Yalu. But less than a week later, on the night of June 12, this same crew disappeared on a NCAP over Ch'o-do island after receiving permission to fire on an enemy aircraft. By this time, the MiGs had started playing a new game with the night-fighter forces. Relying upon their excellent GCI control out of

Antung, a MiG formation of four aircraft took off from Antung or any of the other major MiG fields. They would orbit, waiting for a moment to pounce on a F3D or F-94. When search radars picked up a patrolling night-fighter (for example, a F3D), jammers tried to break its communications with friendly GCI stations. One of the MiGs slowly positioned itself directly in front of the Skyknight, tantalizing the crew by flying just fast enough to encourage a tail chase. As the Skyknight picked up the MiG on its search radar and closed toward gun range, the other three MiGs, which flew low to minimize chances of their detection by airborne or ground radar, would suddenly pop up, vectored by the Communist GCI. They climbed swiftly and closed rapidly from the rear to catch the F3D by surprise. Oddly, the leading "bait" MiG would often flash a blinking strobe. Was this to attract the F3Ds and F-94s as a flame attracts moths? Or was it perhaps a beacon for the following MiGs, indicating that a F3D sat on a straight course between them and the light? If a Skyknight crew was not paying as much attention to their tail warning radar as they should, the MiGs could close and score.

The F-94 lacked tail warning radar—this despite the fact that tail warning radar had been a feature of night-fighter design even in the late stages of the Second World War—but it had one advantage the Skynight lacked: its jet exhaust was difficult to see from behind. In contrast, the F3D looked like two blazing stove jets moving through the air. The F3D's problem stemmed from the design of its engine: the J34 had a very short length from its hot turbine to the exhaust nozzle, and thus its exhaust, which lacked the shroud produced by conventional long tailpipes, glowed merrily and was visible at eight miles. At three miles, the exhaust clearly separated into two points of light. (In the mid-1960s, the Air Force operated pairs of Martin B-57 Night Intruders over the "Street Without Joy," below Vinh to the Vietnamese Demilitarized Zone, flying C-130 transports as flare ships on "Blind Bat" missions against Communist trucks. Aside from the sense of déjà vu to anyone familiar with Firefly/B-26 or Lamplighter/F7F operations from Korea, something else was familiar: a Marine Skyknight, now designated EF-10B and used for ECM protection, accompanied the odd task force, its exhausts still glowing brightly to the wonderment of accompanying airplanes. *Plus ça change*.)[41]

On June 23, Lieutenant Gerald G. O'Rourke, skipper of Detachment 44N of VC-4, arrived with four brand-new R3D-2s for duty with VMF(N)-513. O'Rourke, a keen and aggressive naval officer who would subsequently become one of the driving forces behind the superlative McDonnell F4H Phantom II, crossed the Pacific aboard *Lake Champlain*. Skyknights were not popular with carrier skippers or deck crews; their canted engine nozzles scorched, singed, and occasionally set fire to teak flight decks, and made deck plating red-hot. Determined that Det 44N should be useful, O'Rourke decided that VMF(N)-513 was where the action was, and requested permission to go ashore. On his flight from the carrier to Korea, the four Skyknights expended 21,000 rounds of 20-mm fire on road traffic near Wonsan, though O'Rourke frowned on wasting so valuable an asset as a F3D-2 on trucking. Later, operating over the west coast near Sinuiju, O'Rourke and his colleagues would marvel at the bright strings of truck lights wending their way from the Yalu south, one reason the west coast thoroughfare down to P'yongyang had earned the nickname "Highway 101." Det 44N set to work immediately, the Navy crews getting along well with their Marine counterparts. O'Rourke's detachment had originated at NAS Lakehurst, New Jersey, and consisted of a select group of volunteer pilots and enlisted airborne intercept radar operators, most of whom had no previous flying experience, but who had proven to be excellent aviation electronics technicians. Within days, the detachment had tangled with MiGs, and before the armistice brought a halt to its activity, it completed 12 bomber escort and 39 NCAP missions resulting in 55 radar contacts with enemy fighters, one victory, and, unfortunately, the loss of one of its own.[42]

O'Rourke himself had a close call with the blinking-light MiG and its followers. On one mission his radar operator, ATC L. C. Smith, Jr., picked up a MiG ahead of the Skyknight. Smith placed O'Rourke almost within range of the gun-aiming radar, O'Rourke looking up from his instruments to spot the MiG before opening fire. To his surprise, he saw the MiG flashing a strobe. Puzzled, O'Rourke closed slowly. Suddenly Smith let out a yelp: three MiGs closing fast, only a little over a mile behind the F3D. O'Rourke, aware the MiG "could go faster straight up than we could straight down," followed standard F3D escape procedure: "roll inverted and pull with all you've got." There were a few frantic minutes as the F3D dove, rolled, and turned with four MiGs visible as shadowy forms occasionally passing by the nose. At last they broke off, and O'Rourke and Smith turned for home and safety, where they briefed the other crews on the strange nocturnal encounter. Unfortunately, O'Rourke's episode came as a prelude to Det 44N's only loss. One of his most aggressive and keen airmen was Lieutenant (j.g.) Bob Bick. Determined to "get a MiG," Bick left with Smith on a Ch'o-do island NCAP on the night of July 2. There, 12 miles north of the island, Bick found his MiG, and three others. It is likely that he decided to press on, hoping to blast the bait MiG before his pals got within range. Listeners heard Bick radio that he had shot down the MiG, followed by "the red balls are streaming by," and then—nothing. Bick and Smith never returned to P'yongtaek. Two nights later, *Whipsaw* 1218 disappeared with Marine Captain Lote Thistlewaite and Staff Sergeant W. H. Westbrook during a patrol just north of the same area.[43]

For the rest of July, the night air war over the North continued, with no further victories or losses. The F3Ds and F-94s split the duties of escort and barrier patrol. Continuing the pattern begun after January, not a single B-29 fell to Communist interceptors during their nightly visits to North Korean targets. South of the deadly game near the Yalu, night-heckling Po-2 and other light aircraft continued their own forays. In June, "four or five"

Yak-18 trainers had attacked the Inch'on area; they hit a fuel dump and destroyed nearly 5.5 million gallons of fuel, the single most successful NKAF attack of the war. Determined to end the night-heckler menace once and for all, the Allies deployed increased antiaircraft protection, as well as special night-fighter flights of Corsairs detached from VC-3, a pair of Fairey Fireflies from the Fleet Air Arm, and two modified AD-4 Skyraiders of VMCJ-1 equipped with APS-31 radar in a belly radome. One night, Marine Major George H. Linnemeier and his radar operator kept their potbellied Skyraider at less than 100 mph, staying with a Po-2 long enough to shoot him down. Navy Lieutenant Guy P. Bordelon, a F4U-5N pilot on detachment from *Princeton,* received credit for five kills over night-hecklers, between June 29 and July 17, and was awarded the Navy Cross and recognition as the Navy's only Korean ace. While it would not be completely accurate to claim that these measures ended the "Bedcheck Charlie" menace, they certainly worked to curb the enthusiasm of any Communist pilots planning to visit Seoul.[44]

With the armistice, tranquility returned to the skies of Seoul and, for that matter, Korea as a whole. While North Korea rapidly moved to reassert its air power south of the Yalu once the war had ended, outright combat had come to an end. Occasionally a MiG would approach the armistice line, testing the South's defenses. One night in December 1953, a F-94B crew found itself locked into a series of canopy-to-canopy passes with a MiG that eventually turned back north. But such events only served to highlight an inescapable fact: peace had returned to Korea. It was not the decisive peace of a Tokyo Bay, but the uneasy peace of a no-win limited war: a kind of peace the world would see much more of in places far from the small peninsula jutting into the Sea of Japan.[45]

7/ THE KOREAN LEGACY

In August, the North Koreans released their prisoners, and gave the world another perspective on the war. To Western nations shocked at the treatment of prisoners by Imperial Japan during the Second World War, the outright brutality of the North Koreans and, to a lesser extent, the Chinese toward their captives offered appalling testimony to the moral bankruptcy of both the Kim and Mao regimes. The gaunt men were victims and witnesses to institutionalized brutality not equaled until North Vietnam demonstrated the savagery of its own system. As could North Vietnam, North Korea could count upon Western apologists willing to "understand" or otherwise rationalize such abuse, especially the notorious Australian journalist Wilfred Burchett. Burchett, it seemed, was always more willing to bend the truth than to honestly report on the war. But Burchett — as with some of North Vietnam's apologists subsequently — had his own hidden agenda. As an outright Communist sympathizer writing for *L'Humanite,* he participated in the interrogation of captured Allied aircrews and (as he would in Vietnam subsequently) "interviewed" them on their alleged "war crimes." Fortunately, such twisted reasoning as sprang from his writings and its ilk could not suppress the truth, and served only as shabby examples of post-Korean disinformation.[1]

As the prisoners returned to their homes, the war in Korea slowly slipped off the front pages, replaced by news from French Indochina where, in less than a year, France met a second Waterloo at Dien Bien Phu. On a much smaller scale than in Korea, France's *Armée de l'Air* and *Aeronavale* found itself operating B-26s, Corsairs, Bearcats, Hellcats, Helldrivers, and Privateers in an predictably vain effort to interdict the Viet Minh's supply lines from Communist China. Taiwan continued its uneasy existence, protected by the Seventh Fleet. The war had gone from hot to cold; the struggle between the U.S. Navy and Asian Communism flashed occasionally, as in July 1954, when Chinese La-7s bounced a mixed formation of F4Us and ADs from *Philippine Sea* searching (in vain) for survivors from a Cathay Pacific airliner shot down off Hainan island. The ADs much to the chagrin of the Corsair drivers, quickly bagged both attackers. The tables turned in August 1956 when Chinese fighters shot down a VQ-1 Mercator on a night patrol out of Iwakuni, killing all on board. By and large, however, the Navy's posture of wary readiness would remain unchanged until *Ticonderoga*'s airmen launched the first naval air strikes of the Vietnam war in August 1964.

Over 30 years have passed since the negotiators at

Panmunjom put their signatures to a document forever dividing Korea into two armed camps. Since that time, tension between the two nations has continued to run high, marked by verbal bellicosity and occasional armed clashes, including episodes — such as the seizure of the U.S.S. *Pueblo,* the downing of a EC-121, and the killing of soldiers in the zone between North and South — that involved American forces. With Korea well in the past, and Vietnam dimming in the nation consciousness, there is danger of losing proper historical perspective on the Korean conflict. Today, it is fashionable in some quarters to consider it an example of "low intensity conflict." In fact, during its periods of crisis, such as the first six months and the last three months, Korea was just as intense as most other American wars. In losses inflicted upon the North Koreans and Chinese, Korea approached the level of the First World War, particularly as the Communists tried desperately to seize real estate towards the end of the war. Certainly the losses of aircraft mark Korea as anything but low intensity.

During the course of the Korean War, direct enemy action resulted in the loss of 564 navy and Marine Corps aircraft, only five of which are known to have fallen before the cannon of rampaging MiGs. Operational causes not directly attributed to enemy action claimed a further 684, with 56 of the latter stemming from combat situations such as pilots flying into the target, or aircraft caught on their own bomb blast. In sum, then, the Navy and Marines lost a total of 1,248 aircraft during the war, more than one per day. A summary of losses from enemy action according to aircraft type presents an interesting perspective on the naval air war:[2]

Losses from Enemy Action, by Aircraft Type

Type	Number
Grumman F7F Tigercat	15
Grumman F9F Panther	64
McDonnell F2H Banshee	8
Douglas F3D Skyknight	1
Vought F4U Corsair	312
Vought AU Corsair	16
Douglas AD Skyraider	124
Lockheed P2V Neptune	2
Sikorsky HO3S	6
Bell HTL	2
Cessna OE Bird Dog	8
Convair OY Sentinel	4
Grumman/General Motors TBM Avenger	2
Total:	564

Fighter aircraft constituted 400 of the losses, followed by 140 attack aircraft, 12 observation aircraft, 8 helicopters, 2 patrol planes, and 1 patrol and 1 transport version of the TBM. In fact, almost all the losses of fighter and attack aircraft involved ground attack missions of one sort or another. During the Second World War, such losses would not have seemed at all unusual. Given the "limited war" in Korea, however, they are quite high, if for no other reason than the cost of the aircraft; during the Second World War, a typical fighter airplane cost approximately $60,000. By Korea, the cost had risen to over $250,000, and though a far cry from the

Vietnam era's $2 million or more, that was still steep enough to generate acute concern.

Losses of aircraft are nothing, however, compared to losses of people. The frustrations of fighting a war stalemated for political reasons, not by military necessity, increased the anguish of aircrew losses, pain that the years have not expunged. *Princeton*'s VF-153 gave rise to one of the more poignant examples. In 1953, Lieutenant Richard "Stretch" Clinite, an outstanding pilot and naval officer, landed back aboard with a badly damaged F9F. His Panther, with an experimental bare-metal finish, had a riddled tail section. Another pilot, Ensign William Wilds, returned aboard with a blue-finish Panther equally shot-up in its midsection. Maintenance crews took the two airplanes and made one whole one by joining the blue tail of Wilds's Panther to the silver fuselage of Clinite's. Dubbed the "Blue Tailed Fly," the plane completed 12 missions piloted by Clinite before being ordered back to the States for rebuilding. Clinite took off in a different Panther on another mission, was shot down near Wonsan, and, after ejecting, drowned in the Sea of Japan when stiff winds prevented him from collapsing his parachute. His squadron commander took the loss particularly hard:

> You didn't want to lose anybody. You wanted to have the best record in everything. But when I lost this young man, I literally came unglued. I really was emotionally shaken. I still remember walking the flight deck most of the night, crying like a baby. I stayed outside. I couldn't

go to my room. I couldn't go to the ready room or anything else. One man did it to me. And to this day, as you can see now, I start crying when I think about it.[3]

On average, a carrier air group sent to Korea could expect to lose 10% of its aircrew to combat and operational losses before it completed its deployment.

The Korean War marked a profound change in the way the Navy regarded use of carrier aviation. From the birth of the carrier in the midst of the First World War, through trial and error in the 1920s and 1930s and the wide-ranging carrier battles and strikes of the Second World War, the carrier had been the long-range striking arm of the fleet, the tool to reach out in swift raids to destroy enemy fleets, seize islands, devastate vital coastal and harbor installations. But in Korea, the demands on the carrier were quite different: it was a floating airfield operating within a relatively confined body of water close to hostile shores and for long periods. In 1950, the carriers had ranged from the Sea of Japan to the Yellow Sea, striking where they could do the most good. Time showed that this approach was unnecessary, and thereafter the CVEs of the support group and the CVs (later CVAs) of TF 77 remained, for the most part, in the Yellow Sea and the Sea of Japan, respectively.

Korea marked an important step in the evolution of the carrier as a force-projector: in addition to its expected role as the displacer of the battleship, the carrier would also have to operate on occasion as a mobile airfield, a source of air power in an environment where land-based air power might not be available or convenient. The post-Korean experience of the Navy, from Vietnam to the Indian Ocean and Mediterranean, has confirmed this basic evolutionary change in the use of the carrier. Those who drafted the Navy's fifth Korean evaluation report shrewdly recognized the change:

> The attempt to deprecate as exceptional and special the circumstances of carrier operations off Korea should be tempered. . . . Carrier task forces may, in the conduct of limited objective wars in the Far East, be forced hereafter to accept small and inadequate screens, the calculated risk of enemy submarine attack, and incessant danger from shore-based enemy aircraft. Forces may discover that operations within fifty to one hundred miles of an unfriendly coast are necessary to provide assistance to our forces or allies. Instead of terming these 'special' conditions, commanders must comprehend that future operations off Asia, from Indonesia to Kamchatka, may require actions not unlike those now a matter of daily routine off Korea.[4]

Given this change, the uneasiness of carrier commanders operating in close proximity to shore is understandable, particularly in light of the Panther's and Banshee's inferiority to the MiG-15. In 1953, the Navy employed an airborne Combat Information Center orbiting over TF 77, a modified Boeing

PB-1W Flying Fortress early warning aircraft, in an attempt to increase warning time available to the fleet and air defense efficiency in a strike against the carriers. After the Korean War, the Navy accelerated development of truly long-range early warning radar aircraft, starting with the four-engine Lockheed WV-2 Warning Star, a derivative of the Lockheed Super Constellation civilian airliner. With this came the introduction of more efficient shipboard airborne early warning aircraft, starting with the Grumman WF-1 Tracer of the mid-1950s and progressing onwards to the sophisticated Grumman E-2C Hawkeye of the present day.

Shortly after the armistice, the sweptwing Grumman F9F-6 Cougar entered squadron service with the Seventh Fleet, helping redress the technological imbalance between the straight-wing fighters then in fleet service and the sweptwing Soviet jet. The Korean impetus stimulated rapid introduction of another interim solution, the North American FJ-2, -3, and -4 Fury (a Sabre spin-off), as well as new and genuinely more capable interceptors and fighters, such as the Douglas F4D Skyray, the Vought F8U Crusader, and, ultimately, the McDonnell F4H Phantom II. Smarting under its inability to tangle with the MiGs on at least equal terms, the Navy vowed never again to face an adversary possessing a qualitative superiority in aircraft. (One Marine air commander put it bluntly: "Having the second-best fighter is like having the second-best hand at poker.") In Vietnam, Navy Crusaders and Phantoms performed well against the later MiG-17, MiG-19, and MiG-21 family and, indeed, the Air Force itself turned to the Navy-developed Phantom when it needed a multipurpose air-to-ground and air-to-air fighter in the 1960s.[5]

Hand in hand with fleet air defense fighter and interceptor development, Korea naturally influenced the development of surface-to-air, air-to-air, and air-to-ground guided missiles. Already under development by the time of Korea, surface-to-air missile systems such as the Terrier and air-to-air systems such as the Sidewinder surged ahead under high priorities. (Within two months of the armistice, both a Terrier and Sidewinder had destroyed Grumman F6F-5K target drones during test firings.) Since before the Second World War, Navy researchers had studied the potential of cruise missile-like weapons. In 1944, the Navy had launched 46 pilotless TDR assault drones using television guidance via a control airplane against Japanese fortifications in the Rabaul and Bougainville areas; 24 had actually hit in the target area with results ranging from satisfactory to excellent. After the war, the Navy followed up on this early operational evaluation with research that employed modified F6F-5K Hellcat drones. Used primarily as radio-controlled targets, the old Hellcats generated interest as possible weapons. During 1952, the Naval Air Development Unit at Johnsville, Pennsylvania, formed a special operational test unit, Guided Missile Unit 90 under the leadership of Lieutenant Commander Larry Kurtz, and dispatched it with six Hellcats and two AD-2Q drone controllers to Korea for a combat evaluation of the strike drone concept. Between August 28 and September 2, GMU-90 launched six Hellcats from *Boxer* against various bridges, tunnels, and power plants in the Wonsan-Chosin-Ch'ongjin-Hungnam area, inauspiciously scoring one hit, one abort, and four misses. Work continued after the war, particularly on smaller air-launched guided "stand-off" weapons; it resulted initially in the Bullpup, which entered fleet service in 1959. Though it certainly had its limitations and disappointments, Bullpup symbolized a post-Korean desire to get away from the conventional "iron bomb" approach to war. The drive, alas, was quickly slowed by malaise and not vigorously renewed until Vietnam.[6]

Memories of "Highway 101" and the inability to undertake persistent, sustained, and effective night attack goaded proponents of night, all-weather strike aircraft to push for specialized multiplace designs, typified by the Grumman A-6 Intruder, which performed so well in Southeast Asia, and which is still the backbone of the Navy and Marines' all-weather attack forces. Night interception experiences encouraged development of two-seat all-weather interceptors crewed by pilots and professional radar intercept officers: this resulted in the Phantom II and its heir, the contemporary Grumman F-14 Tomcat. For high-speed conventional and nuclear jet attack, the Navy turned to the little Douglas A4D Skyhawk and its larger, heavier, twin-engine stablemate, the A3D Skywarrior. The hefty AD continued in service, partly in tribute to its adaptability, but also because of the growing requirement for a heavy-payload non-nuclear bomber for the kind of limited-war environment that the Navy had faced in Korea and would face again in

Vietnam. Douglas and the Navy had planned to replace the AD with the A2D, a turboprop-powered Skyraider derivative, but propulsion problems prevented this promising aircraft from attaining service. The Skyraider soldiered on until the end of 1968 in Navy service, and through the end of the Vietnam war as a specialized "counterinsurgency" aircraft flying with Vietnamese and specialized Air Force squadrons. Its legendary reputation for lifting prodigious amounts of ordnance continued unblemished, but, alas, not so its loss rate. The need to provide an updated AD-like aircraft for the 1970s eventually spawned the present-day Fairchild A-10 Thunderbolt II.

The nature of carrier operations and equipment changed dramatically within a few years of the Korean War. The angled deck replaced the treacherous straight deck, ending the era of barrier leaps and jet tangles forward of the bridge. The steam catapult replaced the hydraulic cat, and the mirror landing system replaced the old LSO waving paddles as a jet came screaming down the groove. In-flight refueling eliminated many of the pressures of returning aircrew as they went "feet wet" back to the ship. By Vietnam the era of automated carrier landings had arrived. First tested by an experimentally equipped F3D in 1957, automatic carrier landing equipment — capable of providing "hands off" flight control and throttle manipulation — entered service in 1963, a decade after the end of the Korean War. Coupled with the newer-generation carriers entering service — specifically the *Forrestal* and its successors — such developments enhanced the safety and capability of naval aviation.

One of the major aspects in which the Korean air war differed from previous conflicts lay in the use of helicopters. In Korea, helicopters demonstrated their value in search and rescue, covert operations, minesweeping, liaison, gunfire spotting, medical evacuation, resupply, and combat insertion and extraction. Using Sikorsky HRS-1 helicopters (the equivalent of the Navy's HO4S-1 or the Air Force's H-19), Marine helicopter squadron HMR-161 demonstrated the helicopter's inherent versatility in a wide variety of missions, including counter-guerilla operations, search and rescue, and troop resupply. In Operation *Ripple* in August 1952, the squadron transported a 4.5-inch rocket battery in a test that included offloading the battery, setting it up and firing a salvo of rockets, transporting it to another site, and repeating the performance. By the war's end, HMR-161 had perfected the technique of shipborne assault helicopter operations; they launched from the escort carrier *Sicily*. The helicopter matured in Korea, and the lessons learned there, coupled with advances in technology (including gas turbine propulsion), furnished the basis for the routine large-scale employment of helicopters in Vietnam.[7]

During the Korean conflict, the Navy and Marines were fortunate that they could call upon their "Weekend Warriors," to augment the limited number of regular forces available for service. Activated in late July 1950, the Reservists soon arrived for combat overseas. Typical were those of VA-702 from NAS Dallas, Texas. Called up on July 20, 1950, this TBM outfit moved one week later to North Island,

San Diego, checking out in ADs. In March 1951, VA-702 joined the first all-Reserve air group to see action in Korea, embarked upon U.S.S. *Boxer*, and subsequently served with distinction. Unlike their Navy counterparts, Marine Reserves most often did not go to war in their squadrons. Because of the urgency of Korean requirements, Marine Reservists usually were distributed piecemeal among regular units as need arose. The Navy and Marine Reserves called up were members of the same communities — fighter, attack, and patrol — that existed in the "regular" services. They had to master new and unfamiliar aircraft; in some cases, pilots transitioned from propeller-driven fighters such as the F6F or F4U into much higher performance F9Fs. That they did so with few casualties and a fine combat record is a tribute to their ability and dedication. By November 1951, nearly 75% of all Navy Korean strikes were being flow by Reservists; in mid-1952, over 50%" of 1st Marine Aircraft Wing pilots were Reservists. Reservists, then, clearly contributed their share to the naval air war in Korea.[8]

Aerial reconnaissance in support of the fleet was a major difficulty for the Navy during the Korean War. Increasingly, TF 77 had to rely upon its own shipborne reconnaissance for intelligence, a situation that swamped the limited photo lab and darkroom facilities available on board the carriers. By mid-1951, TF 77 operated with a reconnaissance plan that provided photo sweeps over selected bridges and airfields every four days, and over selected cities every seven days. Whenever possible, recon aircraft photographed blitzed targets the same day as the strikes to furnish prompt damage assessment. To assist the ongoing rail campaign, TF 77's photo detachments mapped the east coast rail network in August and September of 1951 and used the results to produce "flak mosaics" distributed to attack crews to help minimize losses.

The Navy relied on F9F-2Ps from VC-61, equipped with two K-17 cameras apiece, with 6-inch and 12-inch lenses. *Bataan's* photo detachment modified F4Us to carry K-25 cameras facing aft from modified baggage areas that permitted strike photographs from altitudes as low as 100 feet. But the critical need was for high-altitude photography, and here the Banshee excelled. Equipped with K-38 cameras having a 36-inch focal length, a Banshee, in one run over a target at 15,000 feet, could obtain the same coverage as a K-17-equipped Panther in three passes at 5,000 feet. Thus the Banshee could do a reconnaissance job more safely (operating above most flak) and thoroughly, with fewer prints, which reduced the number of hours photo-interpreters needed to analyze the mission's results. As one carrier action report concluded, "The F2H-2P has proven to be the finest photo plane in service. Its speed, maneuverability, visibility, range, and endurance far exceed any other fighter photo [plane] in Navy use."[9]

VMJ-1, a land-based Marine Banshee photo unit commissioned in February 1952, performed most impressively; it completed 5,025 sorties before the armistice and contributed as much as 50% of all Fifth Air Force photo reconnaissance, a third of the entire UN effort in Korea. Occasionally shot at by

MiGs, the Banshee photo pilots relied on the speed and ruggedness of their twin-jet recce birds to get them back safely from missions as far north as the Yalu. By war's end, VMJ-1 produced enough exposed film to circle the earth at the equator six and a half times.[10] Korean reconnaissance experience caused the Navy to rethink its carrier-based fleet air reconnaissance for the future. The Navy's third Korean evaluation report stated:

> The prospects of similar requirements in operations of this nature in the future should be recognized and increased facilities provided. The ever-growing importance of aerial photography to the carriers for intelligence must be considered in planning for future operations in other theaters.[11]

There were some surprises in the experiences of naval aviation forces in Korea. The amount of tonnage dropped on targets quickly exceeded that of World War II standards. During the Second World War, the average naval sortie delivered .15 tons. In Korea, the figure shot up to 74 tons per sortie. In part, this resulted from the higher payload of the AD, the use of the F4U as an attack bomber and not as an air-to-air fighter (except in a secondary role), and the lack of air defense (counter-air) missions, so that more strike flights could be launched. By the summer of 1952, after only two years of war, TF 77 alone had dropped an amount of munitions greater than the combined total dropped by *all* Navy and Marine squadrons during the Second World

War. Not surprisingly, then, timely supply of ammunition to the fast carriers became a major logistical problem, and delivery rates soared to approximately five times the levels of the Second World War.

Equally surprising and much more disturbing were statistics on naval aircraft production and replacement. In his annual report to the Secretary of the Navy submitted in December 1951, Rear Admiral Thomas S. Combs, Chief of the Bureau of Aeronautics, noted with some relief (but with a sense of concern as well):

For something in excess of the first year of the Korean conflict, new production of aircraft was unable to keep up both with attrition and numbers required to commission new squadrons, much less obsolescence retirements. Aircraft of increased obsolescence had to be issued to some fleet units. Before the end of fiscal 1952, the efforts being made to accelerate new production achieved deliveries generally more than sufficient to counter attrition. Qualitative upgrading of the operating forces, particularly in Korea and the Far East, was being progressively achieved. . . . This is not to say that the Bureau of Aeronautics is in a position now to be complacent about any of its major responsibilities. The report shows that the margin of new production over attrition and obsolescence retirement is still far too small to achieve full operational readiness for a long time to come.[12]

In 1950, the Navy could count on 9,422 combat

aircraft on hand. Retirements, operational losses, and combat attrition reduced this to 8,713 in 1951. Thereafter it grew slowly, to 8,742 in 1952 and 8,818 in 1953. The number of carriers changed more dramatically, as ships left mothball fleets for active service once again. In 1950, the Navy had a total of 15 carriers, consisting of 4 *Essex* class, 3 *Midway* class, 4 light carriers (CVL), and 4 escort carriers (CVE). In 1953, this had changed to a total of 34: 14 *Essex,* 3 *Midway,* 5 CVL, and no less than 12 CVE. Likewise, the number of personnel on duty increased rapidly. In 1950, the Navy had 9,481 officer pilots and 920 enlisted ones; the Marines had 1,922 officer pilots and 255 enlisted ones. In 1953, the Navy had 17,612 officer pilots (the number of enlisted had dropped to 684), and the Marines had 4,484 officer pilots (with a drop of enlisted to 131).[13]

As surely as the Second World War was a victory, the Korean War was a draw. Neither side "won" in the traditional meaning of the term. Prompt assistance saved South Korea from being gobbled up by its aggressive northern brother, but when the war ended, the South remained as likely a target of expansionism as ever, preserved by massive American aid. The war resulted in an adjustment of the borders, from the unrealistic straight-across-the-parallel approach of 1945 to a more realistic and defensible border running roughly northeast from the Yellow Sea to the Sea of Japan. The war's outcome was an undeniable disappointment, especially for those who had participated in the painful days of 1950: from the fall-back to Pusan, through the Inch'on invasion, the drive to the Yalu, and the long retreat back down the peninsula before the new drive north—a drive stopped by diplomatic maneuvering.

Korea ended because, at last, it had become painfully clear to the Communists that they could not win: they could not wear down resistance to the point where the Allies would simply leave the South to its fate (as with South Vietnam in 1975). An important point not often mentioned is the growing and understandable impatience of Allied negotiators. By 1953, growing sentiment within the military community argued for use of tactical nuclear weapons if the fighting continued into 1954. Elected in 1952, President Dwight D. Eisenhower brought with him a willingness to employ nuclear weapons, even against Communist China, should it be necessary to force a settlement. Secretary of State John Foster Dulles, the father of the "Brinkmanship" notion, transmitted this indirectly to Mao via discussions with India's Jawaharlal Nehru held in New Delhi in May 1953. Thereafter events moved swiftly and inexorably towards the armistice agreement, probably also advanced by the death of Stalin the previous March.[14]

Distinguished American diplomat Robert McClintock has termed Korea "the archetype of limited war." It involved a clearly delineated geographical area, mutual sanctuaries, and a tacit understanding that nuclear weapons would not be used by the two superpowers. Those who complained of the war's limits, who argued for an expansion of the conflict to the Chinese and Soviet frontiers (and sometimes

301

for air strikes into Manchuria as well) missed the point: both sides had sanctuaries. As surely as the Chinese could rely upon their Manchurian sanctuary, the United States could rely on its bases in Japan and Okinawa. Only MiGs flew from Manchuria, not strike aircraft seeking out Allied troops, ships, or airfields. And, with the strange exception of *Oriskany's* MiG fight, Soviet forces refrained from flying from the Soviet Union against the Allies, or from using their already significant submarine power to confront the Navy at sea. Both sides, then, exhibited restraint, though it is certainly true that the United States and its Allies exhibited greater restraint than the followers of Stalin, Mao, and Kim.[15]

As a nation, Americans have traditionally favored decisive action; in part, this stems from the heritage of the frontier. We are a people who emphasize action over contemplation, and resolution over indecision. Thus, as with Vietnam over a decade later, the end of the Korean War left a disquieting feeling that something had changed, that we had embarked on a new era in which military force applied in support of political ends would no longer operate without constraint.

Irrespective of arguments concerning sanctuaries, the conduct of the air war over North Korea differed greatly from that of the Second World War; it had restrictions more typical (though on a thankfully smaller scale) of those encountered in North Vietnam over a decade later. It might reasonably be said that air power could not effectively come to grips with the Communists in Korea, short of expanding the war or greatly changing its character. For example, had the Allies maintained constant ground pressure against the North Koreans and Chinese, and forced them to use more resources, the interdiction effort would have paid off handsomely. Likewise, had the Allies been free to strike at the sources of production and supply—namely, the bases and supply points in Manchuria—interdiction could have proven decisive. But that was impossible, given the desire to limit the fighting to Korea itself and create a stalemate. Thus, the supplies that got through were more than adequate to keep the Communists resisting Allied forces. The greatest sore spot concerned the MiG sanctuary in Manchuria. It is difficult to condone the political pressures that allowed hundreds of Allied airmen to be imperiled by MiGs with the freedom to engage across the Yalu at their leisure and threatened over their home ground only by the occasional frustrated Sabre pilot determined to teach them a lesson.

Comparative statistics on the Navy and Marine Corps' effort in Korea, together with that of the U.S. Air Force, offer an interesting perspective on the nature and intensity of the air war, as well as the heavy naval involvement: fully 41% of all combat sorties flown were the combined efforts of U.S. Navy and U.S. Marine Corps forces. The following three charts list total sorties by mission type, the percentage distribution of the air war between the efforts of the Navy-Marine Corps and the Air Force and, finally, the percentage distribution of effort within the Air Force and the Navy/Marine Corps. Clearly, Korea was a ground-attack air war and one in which the Navy and Marine Corps played a major role.

Korea's Air War: Contributions of Navy/Marine Corps and Air Force

USN/USMC and USAF Combat Sorties, 1950–1953

Mission Type	USN/USMC	USAF
Interdiction	126,874	192,581
Close Air Support	65,748	57,665
Counter-Air Sorties	44,607	79,928
Reconnaissance	26,757	60,971
Antisubmarine Patrol	11,856	–
Strategic Bomber Sorties	–	994
Total Sorties	275,842	392,139

Distribution of USN/USMC and USAF Combat Effort

Mission Type	USN/USMC		USAF	
Interdiction	40%	+	60%	= 100%
Close Air Support	53%	+	47%	= 100%
Counter-Air Sorties	36%	+	64%	= 100%
Reconnaissance	30%	+	70%	= 100%
Antisubmarine Patrol	100%	+	–	= 100%
Strategic Bomber Sorties	–	+	100%	= 100%
Total Effort	41%	+	59%	= 100%

Distribution of Combat Effort within USN/USMC and USAF

Mission Type	USN/USMC	USAF
Interdiction	46%	49%
Close Air Support	24%	15%
Counter-Air Sorties	16%	20%
Reconnaissance	10%	16%
Antisubmarine Patrol	4%	—
Strategic Bomber Sorties	—	0.2%

(Totals do not necessarily equal 100% because of rounding)

Debate after Korea predictably raged between those who denigrated air power as marginal and those who saw it as decisive. Both missed the point. Critics failed to pay heed to the importance of rules of engagement in determining the outcome of air power application: given the constraints of Korea, air power simply could not function the same way that it had in the Second World War. Air power enthusiasts — and one has the feeling that they believed they had a special mission to defend the legacy of Mitchell, Trenchard, Arnold, et al. against all critics, without regard to logic — generated reams of statistics "proving" that air power had "won" in Korea.

Sources: Futrell, *USAF in Korea* (1983 ed.), p. 690; USAF Historical Division Liaison Office, *USAF Tactical Operations: World War II and Korea* (May 1962), Table 106, p. 162; USN, *CANA* (April–July 1953), Table 15, p. 71.

In fact, what was too often omitted is the very nature of warfare itself: warfare is inevitably a *combined arms* exercise. As a part of the war-fighting triad, air power played a significant role in Korea. So, too, did sea power and land power. Air power on its own could not win the Korean War, any more than the other two. North Korea and China lost a total of 1.5 million men in the vain belief that ground forces fighting alone could swamp defenders and win wars. A balanced Allied response emphasizing the strength of each element of the triad generated enemy losses unequaled except in the bloody fighting of the First World War. As with FEAF, naval air power on its own was incapable of achieving victory. In a review of Robert W. Komer's *Maritime Strategy or Coalition Defense?*, Admiral Isaac Kidd wrote:

Trafalgar did not defeat Napoleon. Trafalgar helped, but Waterloo was decisive. And in the Pacific campaigns of World War II, Korea, and Vietnam, naval victory and control of the sea did not eliminate the need to confront the enemy on the ground. . . . More than forty [fleet] carriers had their hands full with the Axis. More than twenty certainly did not paralyze Hanoi.[16]

And, it might be added, more than 14 did not destroy North Korea's war aims on their own. But used in conjunction with ground forces, land-based air power, and other sea power elements, they certainly did, and in a fashion that confounded the expectations of critics who had dismissed them as useless less than five years before.

What final assessment, then, can be made concerning air power in Korea? On balance, the answer must be that it worked: not that it won in every situation, but that overall it worked. A strange episode occurred during negotiations at Kaesong in August 1951. The chief North Korean delegate, Lieutenant General Nam Il, stated in discussions with his Allied counterparts that "It is owing to your strategic air effort of indiscriminate bombing of our area, rather than to your tactical air effort of direct support to the front line, that your ground forces are able to maintain barely and temporarily their present positions."[17] Much has been made of this quote since the war. But a more relevant issue is why Nam Il said this. It is hard to imagine that he took pity on the wasted tonnage being dropped by tactical aircraft in "direct support to the front line." It is far likelier that this was clever disinformation that has become enshrined in the history books. An examination of the employment of tactical air power over Korea's battleground reveals at least five episodes where massive application of close air support (including both the "Air Force" and "Navy-Marine" versions) proved genuinely decisive: the defense of the Pusan perimeter, the Inch'on landing and breakout, the retreat from the Yalu (especially the Marine evacuation to Hungnam), the stabilization of the front and resumption of the drive north (until blunted by political pressures), and, finally, the intense air effort during the last weeks of war. Beyond question, battlefield application of tactical air power prevented North Korean and Chinese forces from overwhelming the South. To that degree, then, air power "won" in Korea.

Interdiction was clearly quite a different story. Given the lack of clearance to attack the enemy's sources of production and supply, and given the innate flexibility and "non-technology-dependent" nature of North Korea's logistical network, interdiction resulted in large numbers of aircraft lost for relatively meager gains. While it is an exaggeration to state that it failed, it clearly did not succeed. At best, interdiction complicated the Communists' efforts to supply their front. Had the Allies launched a major offensive forcing Chinese and North Korean troops to exhaust their supplies at the front, the results of the ongoing interdiction effort would have been palpable. As it was, the *Cherokee* strikes of the last months of the war that destroyed supply stockpiles that were not readily replaceable achieved results that could not be equaled by the heroic and ill-fated interdiction efforts further behind the bombline. Likewise FEAF's air pressure campaign, particularly the power plant strikes in 1952 and the dam bombings of the last few weeks threatened to have an impact upon North Korea's war effort that could not be offset. Had such efforts been made in 1951–1952, rather than 1952–1953, the war might have been shortened by at least a year. Admittedly, however, that would have required a very different political climate.

What was never in question was control of the skies. Virtually from the moment that the war broke out, the Allies had control of the air, outflying and outfighting the various Yaks, Ilyushins, Lavochkins, and MiGs that rose in opposition. As a result Allied ground forces were able to go about their work with little fear of enemy air strikes. It cannot be stressed too much that without control of the air, Korea would have had a different outcome. And it was fortunate that the MiG had its counter in the graceful Sabre, under whose protection the various Mustangs, F-80s, Panthers, Banshees, Skyraiders, and Corsairs could carry the air war to the enemy.

Though the nature of the Korean War was such that "big" air power—typified by the atomic bomber of the late 1940s—could not be brought to bear without irrevocably widening the war, there were ways in which the limited air power in this limited war could have been more effective, as the previous discussion indicates. It is wise to remember that one must never confuse the notion of a limited war with a stalemated one. Commenting in an interview on the 10th anniversary of the fall of Saigon, former Secretary of State Henry A. Kissinger noted that Vietnam offers an important lesson for the future:

> If we commit ourselves, we must prevail. You cannot fight a war for a stalemate; you can only fight a war for a victory and then you can be generous in the settlements. You may be able to make a compromise if you are on the way to victory. But if you proclaim stalemate as an objective, you're likely to lose or at any rate get into so protracted a conflict that the public will not sustain it.[18]

309

That was almost the case in Korea. It was the case in Vietnam.

Secretary Kissinger's remarks echo those of George Haering, head of the Strike Warfare Branch within the Chief of Naval Operations' Systems Analysis Division. In his provocative essay "How Tactical Air Works," Haering raises a number of points that reflect on Korean and Vietnamese naval aviation. He starts with an important caveat: "Overestimating our own power increases in proportion to the distance of the estimator from a cockpit."[19] Haering makes a point valid for Korea but especially so for Vietnam: do not attack critical target systems piecemeal, as such attacks alert the enemy to the potential dangers they face if such are destroyed and allow them the time to offset the danger with proper defensive planning. He leaves his readers with five generalizations, applicable to all wars in which tactical air power has confronted an enemy, from the First World War onwards:

The tactical offense is easier and more effective than the tactical defense.

The offense must attack an important target system and *pulverize* it.

The offensive planning should not rely heavily on new weapons as sources of revolutionary effectiveness to make the attack overwhelming.

Double and triple check your intelligence. Don't take *anything* for granted.

If you want an initial learning period, or have inadequate force, *don't* alert the enemy by

310

attacking a fragment of a decisive target system.[20]

It is disturbing how quickly the Korean War is sinking from the national consciousness. Replaced in most minds by the morass of Southeast Asia, the Korean War is rapidly becoming America's forgotten conflict. Yet it was a war of sacrifice, courage, and principle, a war not sought but thrust upon as, a war rich in images, none richer than those of the air war. The finger-fours of Sabres that whistled aloft from Kimpo, gleaming aluminum and yellow-banded, trailing sooty banners of burnt kerosene, as curvacious and deadly as the ancient sword whose name they bore; the dark blue Panthers and Banshees that rolled in on bridges and railroad lines set securely amidst North Korea's unforgiving blue-grey hills; the throaty cough of a Corsair or Skyraider, as it lifted off with a seemingly impossible load of ordnance, and tried to stem the onslaught of the Chinese Communist army; the darting Mosquito FACs, mindful of the fate that awaited them if shot down, but nevertheless willing to remain that little bit longer, to mark a target with "Willy Pete" for the merciless Shooting Stars and Thunderjets; of such stuff legends are made.

But it is men who make legends, and the airmen of Korea have no monument suitable to their accomplishments and sacrifices. They remember. And for those who have died, over Korea, or later, friends, relatives, and children have their own recollections. "I was three years old when my father died in Korea," one recently wrote,

311

Captain J. J. Bradway was a Marine Corps pilot whose airplane was shot down in September 1951. He was carried as 'missing in action' for several years until officially declared dead, never seeing my sister, born seven days after his airplane went down. My family has kept his memory alive since that time, as we loved him dearly and knew him as an honorable man who died doing his duty to a country he loved and died for.[21]

"Where do we get such men?" asked Admiral George Tarrant at the end of James Michener's *The Bridges of Toko-ri*. Well, they came from across America. Many, like Marine John Glenn, were seasoned veterans of the Central and South Pacific. Others, like Neil Armstrong, were cutting their teeth and would go on to bigger things. Some, like barrier-breaking Jesse Brown, did not—they died against the hard Korean earth or in its skies or frigid waters. More endured a hell as prisoners of war. When Bill Bettis, a future Martin P5M patrol plane skipper, first saw *The Bridges at Toko-ri* in the station theater at Pensacola, his fellow cadets whistled and cheered as "Admiral Tarrant" asked his question. It was a recognition—a recognition that Michener had hinted at the innermost truth of the naval air experience in Korea. *They* were the source. *They* were the continuum. They were there because they were Americans.

SPECIFICATIONS OF SELECTED NAVAL AIRCRAFT

FIGHTERS

Douglas F3D-2 Skyknight

Span: 50 ft; Length: 45 ft 5 in; Height: 16 ft 1 in; Wing area: 400 sq ft; Weight: 21,374 lbs; Engines: Two Westinghouse J34-WE-36 @ 3,400 lbs thrust each; Crew: two; Max speed: 493 mph; Range 1,145 miles.

Grumman F7F-3N Tigercat

Span 51 ft 6 in; Length: 45 ft 4 in; Height: 16 ft 7 in; Wing area: 455 sq ft; Weight: 21,476 lbs; Engines: Two Pratt & Whitney R-2800-34 W @ 1,850 hp each; Crew: two; Max speed: 423 mph; Range: 1,595 miles.

Grumman F9F-2B Panther

Span: 38; Length: 37 ft 3 in; Height: 11 ft 4 in;
Wing area: 250 sq ft; Weight: 14,235 lbs; Engine:
One Pratt & Whitney J42-P-8 @ 5,000 lbs thrust;
Crew: one; Max speed: 575 mph; Range: 1,353
miles.

Hawker Sea Fury F.B. Mk. 11

Span: 38 ft 4¾ in; Height: 15 ft 10 in; Wing area:
280 sq ft; Weight: 12,500 lbs; Engine: One Bristol
Centaurus 18 @ 2,4800 hp; Crew: one; Max speed:
460 mph; Range: 1,040 miles.

McDonnell F2H-2 Banshee

Span: 44 ft 10 in; Length: 40 ft 2 in; Height: 14 ft 6
in; Wing area: 294 sq ft; Weight: 15,640 lbs; Engines: Two Westinghouse J34-WE 34 @ 3,250 lbs
thrust each; Crew: one; Max speed: 582 mph;
Range: 1,475 miles.

Supermarine Seafire Mk. 47

Span: 36 ft 11 in; Length: 34 ft 4 in; Height: 12 ft 9
in; Wing area: 24 sq ft; Weight: 11,615 lbs; Engine:
One Rolls-Royce Griffon 87 @ 2,350 hp; Crew: one;
Max speed: 452 mph; Range: 940 miles.

Vought F4U-4B Corsair

Span: 41 ft; Length: 33 ft 8 in; Height: 14 ft 9 in;

Wing area: 314 sq ft; Weight: 12,420 lbs; Engine: One Pratt & Whitney R-2800-18W @ 1,850 hp; Crew: one; Max speed: 446 mph; Range: 1,005 miles.

ATTACK AIRCRAFT

Douglas AD-4 Skyraider

Span: 50 ft; Length: 39 ft 3 in; Height: 15 ft 8 in; Wing area: 400 sq ft; Weight: 21,483 lbs; Engine: One Wright R-3350-26WA @ 2,100 hp; Crew: one; Max speed: 349 mph; Range: 1,347 miles.

Fairey Firefly Mk. 4

Span: 41 ft 2 in; Length: 37 ft 11 in; Height: 14 ft 4 in; Wing area: 330 sq ft; Weight: 14,200 lbs; Engine: One Rolls-Royce Griffon 74 @ 2,245 hp; Crew: two; Max speed: 386 mph; Range: 1,300 miles.

Vought AU-1 Corsair

Span: 41 ft; Length: 34 ft 1 in; Height: 14 ft 10 in; Wing area: 314 sq ft; Weight: 18,979 lbs; Engine: One Pratt & Whitney R-2800-83W @ 2,300 hp; Crew: one; Max speed: 238 mph; Range: 484 miles.

PATROL AIRCRAFT

Convair PB4Y-2 (P4Y-2) Privateer

Span: 110 ft; Length: 74 ft 7 in; Height: 29 ft 2 in; Wing area: 1,048 sq ft; Weight: 64,000 lbs; Engines: Four Pratt & Whitney R-1830-94 @ 1,350 hp each; Crew: 11; Max speed: 247 mph; Range: 2,900 miles.

Lockheed P2V-4 Neptune

Span: 100 ft; Length: 77 ft 10 in; Height: 28 ft 1 in; Wing area: 1,000 sq ft; Weight: 67,500 lbs; Engines: Two Wright R-3350-30WA @ 2,650 hp each; Crew: nine; Max speed: 352 mph; Range: 4,200 miles.

Martin PBM-5 Mariner

Span: 118 ft; Length: 79 ft 10 in; Height: 27 ft 6 in; Wing area: 1,408 sq ft; Weight: 56,000 lbs; Engines: Two Pratt & Whitney R-2800-34 @ 1,700 hp each; Crew: seven; Max speed: 215 mph; Range: 2,700 miles.

HELICOPTERS

Sikorsky HO3S-1

Rotor diameter: 48 ft; Length: 41 ft 1¾ in; Height: 12 ft 11 in; Weight: 5,500 lbs; Engine: One Pratt &

Whitney R-985-AN-7 @ 450 hp; Crew: one + three passengers; Max speed; 85 mph; Range: 260 miles.

Sikorsky HO4S-1 (HRS-1)

Rotor diameter: 53 ft; Length: 42 ft 2 in; Height: 14 ft 8 in; Weight: 7,200 lbs; Engine: One Pratt & Whitney R-1340-57 @ 600 hp; Crew: two + six passengers; Max speed: 85 mph; Range: 405 miles.

NOTES

CHAPTER 1

1. Samuel Eliot Morison, *History of United States Naval Operations in World War II, XIV: Victory in the Pacific* (Boston: Little, Brown, & Co., 1960), pp. 361–367; Robert B. Carney, "Under the Cold Gaze of the Victorious," *U.S. Naval Institute Proceedings CIX*, 12 (Dec. 1983), pp. 41–50; Douglas MacArthur, *Reminiscences* (New York: Fawcett Crest, 1965), p. 315; William Manchester, *American Caesar* (New York: Dell Publishing Co., 1979), p. 350.

2. Adrain O. Van Wyen, Clarke Van Vleet, and Lee M. Pearson, *U.S. Naval Aviation, 1910–1970* (Washington, DC: Government Printing Office, 1970), pp. 297, 300, 365 (Hereafter cited as *USNA Chronology*).

3. Clark G. Reynolds, *The Fast Carriers: The Forging of an Air Navy* (New York: McGraw-Hill Book Co., 1968), p. 391; Reynolds' work is the finest study of the use of American carrier air power

in the Second World War.

4. Recollection of Grumman test pilot Corwin "Corky" Meyer in a conversation with the author, November 30, 1984.

5. Daniel Guggenheim Medal Board of Award, *Pioneering in Aeronautics: Recipients of the Daniel Guggenheim Medal, 1929–1952* (New York: Daniel Guggenheim Medal Board of Award, 1952), p. 117.

6. *USNA Chronology*, p. 160; Richard P. Hallion, *Test Pilots: The Frontiersmen of Flight* (Garden City, NY: Doubleday & Co., 1981), pp. 178–182.

7. *USNA Chronology*, pp. 161, 163–166; Rosario Rausa, *Skyraiders: The Douglas A-1 "Flying Dump Truck"* (Baltimore: Nautical & Aviation Publishing Co., 1982), p. 13; Richard P. Hallion, *Supersonic Flight: The Story of the Bell X-1 and Douglas D-558* (New York: Macmillan Publishing Co., 1972), pp. 129–131.

8. J. J. Clark with Clark G. Reynolds, *Carrier Admiral* (New York: David McKay Co., 1967), pp. 244–245; Chuck Hansen, "Nuclear Neptunes: Early Days of Composite Squadrons 5 & 6," *Journal of the American Aviation Historical Society*, XXIV, 4 (Winter 1979), p. 262.

9. Vannevar Bush, *Modern Arms and Free Men: A Discussion of the Role of Science in Preserving Democracy* (Cambridge: M.I.T. Press, 1968 ed.), pp. 45, 46.

10. Alexander P. de Seversky, *Victory Through Air Power* (New York: Simon & Schuster, 1942), pp. 153–183; Henry H. Arnold, *Global Mission* (New York: Harper & Brothers, 1949), p. 298.

11. Alexander P. de Seversky, *Air Power: Key to*

Survival (New York: Simon & Schuster, 1950), p. 102.

12. *Ibid*, p. 69.

13. Marshal Andrews, *Disaster Through Air Power* (New York: Rinehart & Co., 1950), pp. v–x, 54–69.

14. Allan R. Millett, *Semper Fidelis: The Story of the United States Marine Corps*, a volume in *The Macmillan Wars of the United States* series (New York: Macmillan Publishing Co., 1980), p. 461.

15. *Ibid*.; for Truman quote, see Robert Debs Heinl, Jr., *Victory at High Tide: The Inchon-Seoul Campaign*, a volume in the *Great Battles of History* series (Philadelphia: J. B. Lippincott, 1968), p. 5.

16. Millette, *Semper Fidelis*, pp. 460–464; Herman S. Wolk, *Planning and Organizing the Postwar Air Force, 1943–1947* (Washington, DC: Office of Air Force History, 1984), pp. 153–169.

17. Joseph Zikmund, "James P. Forrestal," and Paolo E. Coletta, "John Lawrence Sullivan," in Paolo E. Coletta (Ed.), *American Secretaries of the Navy, II: 1913–1972* (Annapolis: Naval Institute Press, 1980), pp. 736–742, 764, 771–772 (Hereafter cited as *SecNav*); Wolk, pp. 218–223; Leonard Mosley, *Marshall: Hero for Our Times* (New York: Hearst Books, 1982), pp. 448–449; Steven L. Rearden, *History of the Office of the Secretary of Defense, I: The Formative Years: 1947–1950* (Washington, DC: OSD, 1984), pp. 44–46.

18. *SecNav*, pp. 749–755; Paolo E. Coletta, "Louis Emil Denfield," in Robert William Love, Jr. (Ed.), *The Chiefs of Naval Operations* (Annapolis: Naval Institute Press, 1980), pp. 193–198 (Hereafter

cited as *CNO*). For a good survey of postwar Navy doctrinal debates and issues, see David Alan Rosenberg, "American Postwar Air Doctrine and Organization: The Navy Experience," in Alfred F. Hurley and Robert C. Ehrhart, *Air Power in Warfare: The Proceedings of the 8th Military History Symposium, USAF Academy, 18–20 October 1978* (Washington, DC: Office of Air Force History, 1979), pp. 245–278.

19. Wolk, p. 219; *SecNav*, p. 755; Thomas B. Cochran, William M. Arkin, and Milton M. Hoenig, *Nuclear Weapons Databook, I: U.S. Nuclear Forces and Capabilities* (Cambridge, MA: Ballinger Publishing Co., 1984), pp. 6–7, 10; Karl Schuon, *U.S. Navy Biographical Directory* (New York: Franklin Watts, Inc., 1964), pp. 111–112; *USNA Chronology*, p. 168; Hansen, p. 265; Rosenberg, pp. 253–255.

20. *SecNav*, p. 766; for details on the origins of the B-36, see Wesley Frank Craven and James Lee Cate, *The Army Air Forces in World War II, VI: Men and Planes* (Chicago: University of Chicago Press, 1955), pp. 243–246; E. T. Wooldridge, *Winged Wonders: The Story of the Flying Wings* (Washington, DC: Smithsonian Institution Press, 1983) is the most reliable and authoritative account of Northrop's ill-fated YB-49A; Roger E. Bilstein, *Flight in America, 1900–1983: From the Wrights to the Astronauts* (Baltimore: The Johns Hopkins University Press, 1984), p. 180; Rearden, p. 410; the Yeager anecdote is from Chuck Yeager and Leo Janos, *Yeager: An Autobiography* (New York: Bantam Books, 1985), p. 296, and from a conversation

with Brig. Gen. Charles E. "Chuck" Yeager at the Air Force Flight Test Center in 1985.

21. Walter Millis, *Arms and Men: A Study in American Military History* (New York: The New American Library, 1956), p. 290.

22. *SecNav*, pp. 773–774, 777; *CNO*, p. 199.

23. Heinl, p. 7; Rearden, pp. 412–413.

24. Coletta, "Francis P. Matthews," *SecNav*, pp. 791–792; Rearden, pp. 413–415; Clark, pp. 262–263.

25. Clark, p. 263.

26. *Ibid*.

27. *CNO*, p. 201.

28. U.S. Congress, House of Representatives, 81st Congress, 1st Session, *The National Defense Program: Unification and Strategy*, Hearings before the Committee on Armed Services, Oxt. 6–8, 10–13, and 17–21, 1949 (Washington, DC: Government Printing Office, 1949), pp. 5–30.

29. U.S. Congress, *The National Defense Program*, pp. 40–60, 257, 303, 349 *passim*; Rosenberg, pp. 261–263; Rearden, pp. 415–420.

30. *CNO*, p. 204.

31. Heinl, pp. 6–7.

32. Clark G. Reynolds, "Forrest P. Sherman," *CNO*, pp. 209–217; Richard G. Hewlett and Francis Duncan, *Nuclear Navy: 1946–1962* (Chicago: The University of Chicago Press, 1974), pp. 162–163, 196.

– CHAPTER 2

1. Millis, pp. 293–294.

2. David Rees, *Korea: The Limited War* (Balti-

more: Penguin Books, 1970 ed.), p. 10. Rees' book is the standard history of the war, and is remarkable for the thoroughness and balance of its discussion.

3. The quote is from a North Korean propaganda tract prepared by the Editing Committee of the Korean Revolution Museum (P'yongyang), entitled *The Korean Revolution, Vol. II* (Tokyo: Miraisha, 1975, and occurs repeatedly; see, for example, pp. 16, 21, and 40. A copy of this two-volume work is in the collections of the USMC Historical Center Library. See also Rees, p. 11; USAF, "North Korean Personalities," *Air Intelligence Digest, Vol. III*, 8 (Aug. 1950), p. 27, copy in the files of the Office of Air Force History (hereafter OAFH files).

4. J. Lawton Collins, *War in Peacetime: The History and Lessons of Korea* (Boston: Houghton Mifflin Co., 1969), pp. 86–87.

5. George F. Kennan, *Memoirs: 1925–1950* (Boston: Little, Brown & Co., 1967), pp. 354–367.

6. This memorandum is printed in full in Harry S. Truman's *Memoirs: II: Years of Trial and Hope* (New York: The New American Library, 1965 ed.), pp. 370–371.

7. Collins, p. 31; Malcolm W. Cagle and Frank A. Manson, *The Sea War in Korea* (Annapolis: Naval Institute Press, 1957), pp. 11–12.

8. Rees, pp. 18–19.

9. U.S. Department of State, *North Korea: A Case Study in the Techniques of Takeover* (Washington, DC: Government Printing Office, 1961), p. 3.

10. *Ibid*, pp. 3–4, 16–18, 100–101.

11. Robert F. Futrell, *The United States Air Force in Korea, 1950–1953* (Washington, DC: OAFH, 1983

ed.), pp. 18–19 is the definitive history of the USAF's Korean experience; USAF, "North Korean Personalities;" USAF, *Far East Air Forces Weekly Intelligence Roundup*, Oct. 29, 1950, p. 10 (hereafter *FEAF Intelligence Roundup*; copy in OAFH files).

12. Futrell, p. 17.

13. "USS *Boxer* Proves Herself a Champion," *Naval Aviation News* (August 1952), pp. 14–15 (hereafter *NAN*).

14. Collins, pp. 9–24; Glenn D. Paige's *The Korean Decision* (New York: The Free Press, 1968) is the single best analysis of events leading to U.S. intervention in the war; Futrell, pp. 12–13, 29–31.

15. James A. Field, *History of United States Naval Operations: Korea* (Washington, DC: USN, 1962), pp. 44–55, 60; Cagle and Manson, pp. 31–37; Walter Karig, Malcolm W. Cagle, and Frank A. Manson, *Battle Report, V: The War in Korea* (New York: Rinehart & Co., 1952), pp. 59–61.

16. USN, Deputy Chief of Naval Operations (Air), Aviation Statistics Section, Aviation Statistics Special Report (hereafter ASSR) 1–50, "Some Statistics of Naval Air Combat Operations During July 1950," (Sept. 20, 1950), p. 6, Naval Aviation History Office files (hereafter NAHO files); Field, p. 62; Cagle and Manson, pp. 37–38; Karig et al., pp. 75–85; Larry Davis, *MiG Alley: Air-to-Air Combat Over Korea* (Carrollton, TX: Squadron/Signal Publications, 1978), p. 5.

17. Field, p. 65; Karig et al., pp. 84–85.

18. *NAN* (Nov. 1950), p. 22.

19. *NAN* (Feb. 1952), p. 13.

20. Transcript of interview of Vice Admiral Gerald E. Miller, USN (ret.) by Dr. John T. Mason, U.S. Naval Institute (hereafter USNI) Oral History Program, p. 130.

21. USN, Commander-in-Chief Pacific Fleet, Interim Evaluation Report No. 1 (hereafter IER 1), III, pp. 312, 317, NAHO files.

22. Futrell, pp. 24–34, 84–103.

23. Quoted in Richard H. Kohn and Joseph P. Harahan, *Air Interdiction in World War II, Korea, and Vietnam*, a volume in the *USAF Warrier Studies* series (Washington, DC: OAFH, comment edition, 1984), p. 42; see also Futrell, pp. 59, 87.

24. Futrell, pp. 111–112; *USNA Chronology*, p. 183.

25. ASSR 1–50, p. 6; Futrell, pp. 114–115; Field, pp. 114–115; Cagle and Manson, pp. 47, 51–52.

26. IER 1, III, p. 223.

27. Richard P. Hallion, *Rise of the Fighter Aircraft, 1914–1918* (Baltimore: Nautical & Aviation Publishing Co., 1984), pp. 125–137, 146–148.

28. Peter B. Mersky, *U.S. Marine Corps Aviation: 1912 to the Present* (Baltimore: Nautical & Aviation Publishing Co., 1983), pp. 20–24; Futrell, pp. 80–81; Robert Sherrod, *History of Marine Corps Aviation in World War II* (Washington, DC: Combat Forces Press, 1952), pp. 408–411; IER 1, III, p. 223.

29. Futrell, pp. 78–83, 704–705; the governing manual for USAF air-to-ground operations was FM 31–35, *Air-Ground Operations* (Aug. 1946).

30. IER 1, III, p. 224; Sherrod, p. 411.

31. Dario Politella, *Operation Grasshopper* (Tyler, TX: The Robert R. Longo Company, Inc. 1958), pp.

15-17, 20-21. This is an excellent account of the role that U.S. Army aviation played in the Korean War.

32. Futrell, pp. 81-83, 106-107; Tim Cline, "Forward Air Control in the Korean War," *Journal of the American Aviation Historical Society*, XXI, 4 (Winter 1976), pp. 257-262.

33. Cagle and Manson, pp. 52-54; Field, pp. 118-119.

34. Kohn and Harahan, *Air Interdiction*, pp. 54-55; CAS scrub statistics from IER 1, III, p. 242.

35. *Valley Forge* Preliminary Action Report (Aug. 20, 1950), NAHO files.

36. *Philippine Sea* Preliminary Action Report (Aug. 16, 1950), NAHO files.

37. Transcript of interview of Admiral John S. Thach, USN (ret.) by Commander Etta-Belle Kitchen, USNI Oral History Program, p. 533.

38. *Ibid*, p. 536.

39. IER 1, III, p. 235; ASSR 1-50, p. 7; Warren Thompson, "Shooting Stars Over Korea," *Airpower*, XV, 2 (March 1985), p. 33.

40. O. P. Weyland, "Some Lessons of the Korean War and Conclusions and Recommendations Concerning USAF Tactical Air Responsibilities," (Oct. 10, 1950), p. 5, and attached ltr., Weyland to Vandenberg (Oct. 12, 1950), OAFH files; see also Field, p. 129.

41. Thach interview, pp. 537-540; Field, p. 129. For an appreciation of the seriousness of the ground situation, see Roy E. Appleman, *United States Army in the Korean War, I: South to the Naktong, North to the Yalu* (Washington, DC: USA, 1961), pp. 227-247.

42. IER, 1, II, p.16.

43. "Fire Bomb," *NAN* (May 1951), *passim*; Appleman, p. 379.

44. For machine gun versus cannon dispute, see the report of Maj. Joseph Reinburg, USMC, in National Archives and Records Service Record Group 127, 65A-4620, Box 89, folder "VMF(N)-513 Korean War Rept Major Reinburg, 18 Jan 1951," Federal Records Center, Suitland, MD; for jets versus props, see 5th AF HQ, Operations Analysis Office, "Incidence of Targets in Close Support and Interdiction Attacks," (May 23, 1951), OAFH files; U.S. Army, Army Air Support Center, "Air Support in Korean Campaign" (Dec. 1, 1950), OAFH files; see also Rausa, *Skyraider*, pp. 91–93.

45. IER 1, II, p. 55; USN DCNO (Air), ASSR 2-50, "Combat Activity of Navy Aircraft in Korean Theater, August 1950," (Oct. 25, 1950), pp. 4–6 and Table 5, NAHO files; *NAN* (Nov. 1950), p. 21.

46. *Valley Forge* Preliminary Action Report (Aug. 20, 1950); Thach interview, p. 541; *NAN* (Nov. 1950), p. 20; Andrew Geer, *The New Breed: The Story of the U.S. Marines in Korea* (New York: Harper & Brothers, 1952), pp. 38–39; Mersky, p. 132; there are other similar incidents described in Cagle and Manson, pp. 57–60, 63–65.

47. Ernest H. Giusti, "Marine Air Over the Pusan Perimeter," *Marine Corps Gazette* (Hereafter *MGG*) XXXVI, 5 (May 1952), pp. 18–27; the best study of Marine operations during the Pusan campaign is Lynn Montross and Nicholas A. Canzona, *U.S. Marine Operations in Korea, 1950–1953, I: The Pusan Perimeter* (Washington, DC: USMC, 1954).

48. Thach interview, p. 548.

49. Giusti, "Marine Air Over the Pusan Perimeter," *passim*; Field, pp. 152–153, 159–162; Cagle and Manson, pp. 64–65.

50. ASSR 1-50, p. 4; ASSR 2-50, p. 25; IER 1, II, pp. 55, 57; *NAN* (Dec. 1950), p. 8.

51. *NAN* (Nov. 1950), pp. 18–19; Cagle and Manson, p. 63–64; Gary W. Parker and Frank M. Tatha, Jr., *A History of Marine Observation Squadron Six* (Washington, DC: USMC History and Museums Division, 1982), pp. 15–18.

CHAPTER 3

1. Rees, p. 96; MacArthur, p. 398; Heinl, p. 42; Cagle and Manson, p. 76.

2. Niccolò Machiavelli, *The Prince and The Discourses* (New York: The Modern Library, 1950), p. 94.

3. ASSR 3-50, "Statistics of Naval Air Combat Operations During September 1950," (Dec. 18, 1950), p. 3, NAHO files.

4. *USNA Chronology*, p. 181; Heinl, p. 31; Karig et al., pp. 12–13; Field, pp. 167–168; Barrett Tillman, *Corsair: The F4U in World War II and Korea* (Annapolis: Naval Institute Press, 1979), pp. 161–162.

5. ASSR 3-50, p. 4–5; Heinl, pp. 59, 77–79.

6. MacArthur, p. 401.

7. Heinl, pp. 86–120; his book *Victory at High Tide* is the definitive history of the Inch'on-Seoul campaign, and is among the very finest of military

histories; Field, pp. 197–202.

8. ASSR 3-50, pp. 3–6; see also Ernest H. Giusti and Kenneth W. Condit, "Marine Air Over Inchon-Seoul," *MCG*, XXXVI, 7 (July 1952), pp. 18–25.

9. *Ibid*; Heinl, p. 123, 203, 222; Thach interview, p. 560; Field, pp. 215–215; Appleman, pp. 508–509.

10. VMF(N)-542 Historical Report, July–December 1950, in National Archives and Records Service Record Group 127, 65A-4620, Box 95, folder "VMF(N)-542 Hist Rept July–Dec. 1950," Federal Records Center, Suitland, MD; *NAN* (Dec. 1950), pp. 10–11.

11. USN, Commander-in-Chief Pacific Fleet, Interim Evaluation Report No. 3, (hereafter IER 3), Pamphlet 1, p. 18; emphasis in original text, NAHO files.

12. Marguerite Higgins, *War in Korea: The Report of a Woman Combat Correspondent* (Garden City, NY: Doubleday & Co., 1951), p. 153.

13. Heinl, pp. 248, 267.

14. USN, Chief of Naval Operations, *Combat Activity of Naval Aviation: October 1950* (Jan. 31, 1951), pp. 3–4 (hereafter referred to as *CANA*, followed by the appropriate months of coverage). NAHO files; Cagle and Manson, pp. 146–147.

15. Futrell, p. 213.

16. Quoted in Pat Meid and James M. Yingling, *U.S. Marine Operations in Korea, 1950*–1953, V: Operations in West Korea (Washington, DC: USMC, 1972), p. 493.

17. *Ibid*, p. 492.

18. *CANA*, October 1950, p. 8.

19. Field, pp. 233–235; Cagle and Manson, pp.

140–141.

20. IER 1, III, 285; *CANA*, November 1950, p. 3; see also Field, pp. 252–253.

21. MacArthur, pp. 419–420; Futrell, pp. 220–222.

22. The best English-language sources on the MiG-15 are Bill Gunston's encyclopedic *Aircraft of the Soviet Union* (London: Osprey Publishing Ltd., 1983), pp. 174–176, and Jean Alexander's *Russian Aircraft Since 1940* (London: Putnam & Company Ltd., 1975), pp. 214–215; the sale of the Nene to the USSR is detailed in Sir Stanley Hooker (assisted by Bill Gunston), *Not Much of an Engineer: An Autobiography* (Shrewsbury, England: Airlife Publishing Ltd., 1984), pp. 98–99.

23. *Naval Aviation Confidential Bulletin* 1–50 (January 1950), p. 7, NAHO files; "Soviet Air Shows: 1946–1950," *Air Intelligence Digest*, III, 7 (July 1950), pp. 4–5, OAFH files.

24. *CANA*, November 1950, p. 5; Field, pp. 257–259; Cagle and Manson, pp. 224–225; there are good discussions of this issue in Futrell, pp. 222–224, and in MacArthur, pp. 419–424.

25. Futrell, p. 223.

26. IER 1, III, pp. 310–311; *Valley Forge* Action Report, 5–19 Nov. 1950, pp. 2–3, NAHO files.

27. *CANA*, November 1950, p. 5; Karig et al., pp. 381–382.

28. *CANA*, November 1950, p. 6; "Tactics: MiG vs. USN," *Air Intelligence Digest*, IV, 3 (March 1951), pp. 4–5, OAFH files.

29. *Valley Forge* Action Report, 5–19 Nov. 1950, p. 3.

30. *Ibid*, attached COMCARDIV 3 endorsement, p. 2.

31. IER 1, II, p. 57.

32. IER 1, III, pp. 331–339.

33. *Ibid*, p. 311; *CANA*, November 1950, pp. 5–7; Field, p. 259; Appleman, p. 687, 750–751, 766–767.

34. Rees, pp. 155–161 is a good summary; *CANA*, November 1950, pp. 5–7; James F. Schnabel, *United States Army in the Korean War, III: Policy and Direction: The First Year* (Washington, DC: USA, 1972), pp. 233, 274–278; Anthony J. Campigno, *A Marine Division in Nightmare Alley* (New York: Comet Press Books, 1958), pp. 32–46 offers a good first-person account; S. L. A. Marshall's *The River and the Gauntlet: Defeat of the Eighth Army by the Chinese Communist Forces, November 1950, in the Battle of the Chongchon River, Korea* (New York: William Morrow & Co., 1953) is an excellent account from a succession of small-unit actions; Lynn Montross and Nicholas A. Canzona, *U.S. Marine Operations in Korea, 1950–1953, III: The Chosin Reservoir* (Washington, DC: USMC, 1957) is the official Marine history; Robert Leckie's *The March to Glory* (Cleveland: World Publishing Co., 1960) is a good popular account.

35. *CANA*, November 1950, pp. 5–7; *CANA*, December 1950, pp. 4–6; Field, pp. 267–268.

36. *CANA*, December 1950, *passim*.

37. These figures were computed by the author based on various source documents. Since there are slight disparities and some contradictions within the records themselves, an "absolute" total appears im-

possible to compute precisely. When doubt existed, the author relied upon *CANA*, November and December 1950 for final authority.

38. Thach interview, pp. 584–585; Campigno, p. 38; Higgins, p. 191; Field, pp. 278–284; Donald W. McMaster, "The Evolution of Tactical Airpower—With Particular Emphasis Upon Its Application by the U.S. Navy and U.S. Marine Corps in the Korean War, June 1950–July 1953; unpublished Master's Thesis, Department of History, University of Maryland, College Park, MD, April 9, 1959, pp. 148–153; Kenneth W. Condit and Ernest H. Giusti, "Marine Air at the Chosin Reservoir," *MCG*, XXXVI, 7 (July 1952), pp. 18–25; and Ernest H. Giusti and Kenneth W. Condit, "Marine Air Covers the Breakout," *MCG*, XXXVI, 8 (August 1952), pp. 20–27.

39. See, for example, Alexander L. George, *The Chinese Communist Army in Action: The Korean War and its Aftermath* (New York: Columbia University Press, 1967), pp. 165–166, 172.

40. IER 1, III, p. 236.

41. Montross and Canzona, *Inchon-Seoul Operation*, pp. 335–336; Montross and Canzona, *The Chosin Reservoir*, p. 403.

42. Anne Briscoe Pye and Nancy Shea, *The Navy Wife* (New York: Harper & Brothers, 1941), pp. 28–29.

43. Cagle and Manson, pp. 176–177; the best reference on Brown's life and ordeal is John E. Weems, "Black Wings of Gold," *USNI Proceedings*, CIX, 7 (July 1983), pp. 35–39.

44. Field, pp. 295–305; Cagle and Manson, pp. 189–190.

CHAPTER 4

1. *CANA*, Jan.–June issues, 1951.
2. *Ibid*.
3. *CANA* (April 1951), p. 11.
4. IER 3, Chapter 10 *Interdiction*, p. 10–16.
5. Futrell, p. 313.
6. *Ibid*, p. 314; Field, pp. 322–323; IER 3, p. 10–41; Cagle and Manson, pp. 229–230.
7. IER 3, p. 10–41.
8. IER 3, p. 10–17, Field, p. 333.
9. The survey document, with a preface by Rear Admiral G. R. Henderson, is titled *U.S. Naval Interdiction in Korea*, and consists of 15 high-quality captioned photographs of the bridge and surrounding terrain. Copy in NAHO files. See also Barrett Tillman and Joseph G. Handelman, "The Hwachon Dam and Carlson's Canyon: Air Group 19's *Princeton* Deployment of 1950–51," *The Hook*, XII, 1 (Spring 1984), p. 32.
10. James A. Van Fleet, *Rail Transport and the Winning of Wars* (Washington, DC: Association of American Railroads, 1956), p. 35.
11. James A. Michener, *The Bridges at Toko-ri* (New York: Random House, 1953), pp. 37–38.
12. *Ibid*, p. 147.
13. IER 2, *Major Lessons*, p. 13, NAHO files.
14. IER 3, p. 10–1.
15. IER 4, p. 1–5, NAHO files.
16. IER 5, *Major Lessons*, pp. 1, 3, NAHO files.
17. Van Fleet, p. 1.

18. Matthew B. Ridgway, *The Korean War: How We Met the Challenge; How All-Out Asian War Was Averted; Why MacArthur Was Dismissed; Why Today's War Objectives Must Be Limited* (Garden City, NY: Doubleday & Co., 1967), p. 186. For the perspective of a Marine pilot wounded on one such mission, see William H. Rankin's excellent memoir, *The Man Who Rode the Thunder* (New York: Pyramid Books, 1961), pp. 62–66.

19. Transcript of speech, Vice Admiral Ralph A. Ofstie to the Aircraft Industries Association, Williamsburg, VA, May 22, 1953, copy in the files of the Naval Air Systems Command History Office.

20. IER 3, p. 10–27.

21. *Ibid*, p. 10–45; IER 5, *Major Lessons*, p. 3; Futrell, pp. 324–325, 441–442, 451, 471–473; Field, pp. 327, 419.

22. IER 3, p. 10–36; Field, pp. 436–437; Ministry of National Defense, *The History of the United Nations Forces in the Korean War*, V (Seoul, Ministry of National Defense, 1976), p. 540.

23. IER 3, p. 10–66.

24. Cagle and Manson, pp. 253–254.

25. IER 3, p. 10–68.

26. *Ibid*., pp. 10-68–10-69.

27. "Korea: Flak," *Air Intelligence Digest*, III, 8 (Aug. 1950), p. 13; OAFH files.

28. *Ibid*., pp. 9–13.

29. For characteristics of Soviet and North Korean radars in this time period, see "Antiaircraft Fire Control Radar and Performance Characteristics," *Air Intelligence Digest*, III, 8 (Aug. 1950), pp. 37–38; "Soviet RUS-Type Radar Equipment," *AID*,

IV, 1 (Jan. 1951), pp. 15–17; "What We Learned," *AID*, VI, 9–10 (Sept.–Oct. 1953), p. 38; "Six Communist Fire-Control Radars," *AID*, VII, 1 (Jan. 1954), pp. 10–18; "Round-Up of Red Radars," *AID*, VII, 8 (Aug. 1954), pp. 20–27; Far East Air Forces, "FEAF History of Electronic Countermeasures During the Korean War Conflict," (FEAF, 1 Feb. 1954), pp. 3–6, and related annexes; all in OAFH files. See also Bruce M. Bailey, *"We See All:" A History of the 55th Strategic Reconnaissance Wing, 1947–1967* (Tucson, AZ: privately printed, 1982), pp. 21–24; copy in the collection of the Library of Congress, Washington, DC.

30. IER 4, p. 3–50.

31. *Ibid.*, p. 3–51; *Oriskany* Action Report, 28 Oct.–28 Nov. 1952, p. vi–4; *Princeton* Action Report, 8 Mar.–3 Apr. 1953, p. 19; *CANA* (Apr.–Jul. 1953), pp. 39, 43; all in NAHO files; FEAF ECM History, p. 6; *USNA Chronology*, p. 204.

32. Extracted and compiled from the *CANA* reports, July 1951–July 1953, NAHO files.

33. Rausa, *Skyraider*, pp. 31–36; *NAN* (April 1952), n.p.

34. *NAN*, (Dec. 1951), p. 11; Armstrong et al. with Gene Farmer and Dora Jane Hamblin, *First on the Moon: A Voyage with Neil Armstrong, Michael Collins, [and] Edwin E. Aldrin Jr.* (Boston: Little, Brown & Co.), p. 115.

35. *NAN* (Feb. 1953), p. 8.

36. *NAN* (Apr. 1951), p. 26.

37. *NAN* (June 1952), pp. 8–9; *NAN* (Sept. 1953), pp. 9–10.

38. *NAN* (Jan. 1952), p. 11.

39. *NAN* (Sept. 1953), p. 10–11.

40. William J. Sambito, *A History of Marine Fighter Attack Squadron 312* (Washington, DC: USMC History and Museums Divisions, 1978), pp. 12–13.

41. William J. Sambito. *A History of Marine Attack Squadron 311* (Washington DC: USMC History and Museums Division, 1978), pp. 21–25; John E. Kinney, "The Case for Jet Attack Aircraft in Korea," *Foundation* (the magazine of the Naval Aviation Museum Foundation), IV, 2 (Fall 1983), pp. 23–29, 61–64; M. Scott Carpenter, et al., *We Seven* (New York: Simon & Schuster, 1962), pp. 30–32; Frank Van Riper, *Glenn* (New York: Empire Books, 1983), p. 105; Mersky, *U.S. Marine Corp Aviation*, pp. 189–190.

42. *NAN* (Dec. 1950), p. 9; *NAN* (Oct. 1951), n.p.

43. IER 3, pp. 3–3, 3–10, 3–13; IER 3, pp. 5–18, 5–19.

44. *Boxer* Action Report, 1 Aug.–11 Aug. 1952, p. 3, NAHO files.

45. *Ibid.*, p. 3.

46. *Ibid.*, pp. 3–4, 12–13; *NAN* (Oct. 1952), p. 16.

CHAPTER 5

1. *Princeton* action report, 16 Apr.–22 May, 1951, p. 6, NAHO files; Tillman and Handelman, "Hwachon Dam and Carlson's Canyon," pp. 32–37; Field, p. 347.

2. CANA (May 1951), pp. 7, 8; IER 3, p. 3–1,

both in NAHO files; Field, p. 349.

3. For a comprehensive discussion of the Rashin problem, see Futrell, pp. 183–184, 187, 192–193, 295, and 434.

4. FEAF ECM History, Annex XV, "Aircraft Losses—FEAF Bomber Command," OAFH files; Futrell, pp. 297–300.

5. *Essex* action report, 18 Aug.–19 Sept. 1951, p. 16; CANA (July–Sept. 1951), pp. 15–16; CANA (Oct.–Dec. 1952), pp. 6–7; IER 3, p. 3–9; all in NAHO files. See also Field, p. 417; Cagle and Manson, pp. 246–247; Clark, *Carrier Admiral*, pp. 277–278; and James T. Stewart (Ed.), *Airpower: The Decisive Force in Korea* (Princeton, NJ: Van Nostrand Co., 1957), p. 89.

6. Clark, *Carrier Admiral*, p. 276; Clark, *From the Danube to the Yalu*, pp. 210–211.

7. Clark, *Carrier Admiral*, p. 277; *Essex* action report, 1–31, Oct. 1951, p. 16, NAHO files; Cagle and Manson, pp. 250–251; Rausa, *Skyraider*, p. 34; Rees, p. 369.

8. IER 3, p. 5–38, NAHO files.

9. NAN (Nov. 1950), p. 21.

10. Air Group 5 action report, 18 Aug–19 Sept. 1951, pp. 19–20; *Lake Champlain* action reports, 11–29, June 1952, p. 8, and 11–27, July 1953, p. 21; IER 3, p. 5–38; all in NAHO files. See also *NAN* (July 1951), p. 18.

11. IER 3, pp. 5–39 and 10–28, NAHO files.

12. IER 3, p. 5–39, NAHO files.

13. John F. Bolt, "Bridge Busting With Jets," *Naval Aviation Bulletin*, 4–53 (November 1953), pp. 2–6, NAHO files.

14. Kohn and Harahan, *Air Interdiction*, p. 57; see also Miller interview, p. 200; Futrell, pp. 477-485.

15. Stewart, pp. 121-130.

16. Clark, *Carrier Admiral*, pp. 285-286; CANA (April-June 1952), p. 17; Field, p. 437.

17. CANA (April-June 1952), pp. 17, 20-21; *Princeton* action report, 2-28 (June 1952), pp. 4-5; *Boxer* action report, 9 June-9 July, 1952, *passim; Philippine Sea* action report, 21 June-6 July 1952, p. 2; all in NAHO files. See also Clark, *Carrier Admiral*, p. 287; and Futrell, pp. 487-489.

18. *Princeton* action report, 4 July-6 Aug. 1952, p. 11; *Bon Homme Richard* action report, 2 July-4 August 1952, p. 3; CANA (July-Sept. 1952), pp. 6-8; all in NAHO files. Field, p. 439; Cagle and Manson, pp. 450-453, have good eyewitness accounts.

19. CANA (July-Sept. 1952), pp. 5-17; CANA (Oct.-Dec. 1952), pp. 5-7; both in NAHO files.

20. CANA (Oct.-Dec. 1952), pp. 5-7, NAHO files; Field, pp. 444-45; Cagle and Manson, pp. 391-397; Futrell, pp. 529-532.

21. Clark, *Carrier Admiral*, pp. 288-289. There is confusion about when Clark conceived the idea of the *Cherokee* strike; his autobiography says it was September 1952, but in an oral interview with authors Cagle and Manson on January 30, 1956, he said May 1952. Given his urgent discussions with Rear Admirals Perry and Hickey, it is most likely that he conceived the idea in May, when Perry (then COMCARDIV 1 as well) operated in the Sea of Japan aboard *Valley Forge*. See also Cagle and

Manson, pp. 460–461.

22. Compiled from various issues of *CANA*, 1951–1953, in NAHO files; see also Clark, *Carrier Admiral*, pp. 289–290; Cagle and Manson, pp. 462–469; Field, p. 443; Futrell, p. 539.

23. Field, p. 443.

24. See *CANA* (Oct.–Dec. 1952), pp. 5–4; *CANA* (Jan.–Mar. 1953), pp. 7–18; *CANA* (Apr.–July 1953), pp. 6–33; all in NAHO files; see also Cagle and Manson for Van Fleet quote, p. 469.

25. ATG 1 action report, 10 May–21 June 1953, pp. 3–7; corrections and annotations are based upon information gathered subsequently. NAHO files.

26. Field, p. 455.

27. Appendix D, Pt. 1, p. 1, "Typical Night MPQ Mission," in VMF(N)-513 Historical Diary, Nov. 1952, folder "VMF(N)-513 Hist Diary, Nov. 52–Dec. 52;" and VMF(N)-513 Historical Diary, May 1953, folder "VMF(N)-513 Comm Diary, May–June 1953"; both in National Archives and Records Group 127, 65A-4620, Box 93, Federal Records Center, Suitland, MD; IER 6, 1 Feb. 1953–27 July 1953, Chapter 10, "Fleet Marine Force—Air," pp. 10-103–10-104, NAHO files.

28. J. D. Tikalsky, "Radar Raiders," *NAN* (Nov. 1953), pp. 1–5.

29. Cagle and Manson have the best account, pp. 265–266; for the Uong Bi raid, see Malcolm W. Cagle, "Task Force 77 in Action Off Vietnam," *USNI Proceedings*, XCVIII, 831 (May 1972), p. 80.

30. "Kinsella's Fellas' as Night Hecklers," *NAN* (Jan. 1954), p. 5.

31. Clark, *Carrier Admiral*, p. 304.

32. For details of the last days (including the dam strikes) I have drawn upon *CANA* (April–July 1953), pp. 27–35; and IER 6, Chronology, pp. 2-27-2-30, both in NAHO files; Stewart, pp. 166–188; Clark, *Carrier Admiral*, pp. 305–306; Field, pp. 457–459; Cagle and Manson, pp. 480–489; and Pat Meid and James M. Yingling, *U.S. Marine Operations in Korea, 1950-1953, V: Operations in West Korea* (Washington, DC: USMC, 1972), pp. 374–375, 393–397.

CHAPTER 6

1. Walker M. Mahurin, *Honest John* (New York: G. P. Putnam's Sons, 1962), pp. 81–83.

2. *Ibid.*, pp. 86–87, 92–93; the "Who were those guys?" theme is explored in two interesting Korean war novels: James Salter's excellent *The Hunters* — a book worth reprinting — and Walt Sheldon's *Troubling of a Star*. See also Richard M. Bueschel, *Communist Chinese Air Power* (New York: Frederick A. Praeger, Publishers, 1968), p. 25.

3. "Operation MiG: An Untold Story of the Korean War," *Air Intelligence Digest*, VI, 9–10 (Sept.–Oct. 1953), pp. 47–48, OAFH files. USAF, Concepts Division, *Guerilla Warfare and Airpower in Korea, 1950–53* (Maxwell AFB, AL: Aerospace Studies Institute, January 1964), pp. 71, 117, and 135.

4. CANA (July–Sept. 1951), pp. 6–9; NAHO files; Field, p. 409; Alexander, *Russian Aircraft Since 1940*, p. 215.

5. "These Pilots Flew the MiG," *Air Intelligence Digest*, VI, 12 (Dec. 1953), pp. 9–11; Yeager, pp.

205–209.

6. *Bataan* action report, 8 Apr.–11 May 1951, pp. 1-1-1-1-1-I-4, II-3; "Yak vs. Corsair," *Naval Aviation Confidential Bulletin*, 2-51 (Aug. 1951), pp. 26–28, both in NAHO files.

7. Sambito, pp. 19–20.

8. *CANA* (Oct.–Dec. 1951), pp. 13, 15, NAHO files.

9. *CANA* (March 1952), p. 20, NAHO files; "Korea Photo Banshees Are Busy," *NAN* (Sept. 1952), p. 32.

10. Sambito, pp. 21–22.

11. *CANA* (July–Sept. 1952), p. 9, NAHO files; Cagle and Manson, p. 383.

12. *CANA* (July–Sept. 1952), p. 6, NAHO files; Robert Jackson, *Air War Over Korea* (New York: Charles Scribner's Sons, 1973), p. 145.

13. *CANA* (July–Sept. 1952), p. 11, NAHO files.

14. *CANA* (July–Sept. 1952), p. 17, NAHO files; Tillman, *Corsair*, pp. 171–174; "Prop Plane Bags a MiG-15," *NAN* (Nov. 1952), p. 10.

15. *CANA* (Oct.–Dec. 1951), pp. 6, 7, NAHO files.

16. *Oriskany* action report, 28 Oct.–22 Nov. 1952, p. VI-1, NAHO files; *CANA* (Oct.–Dec. 1952), p. 10, NAHO files; "Two *Oriskany* Pilots Bag a Pair of MiG's," *NAN* (Feb. 1953), pp. 18–19; Field, pp. 440–441.

17. *Ibid.*

18. *Oriskany* action report, 28 Oct.–22 Nov. 1952, pp. VI-1–VI-3, NAHO files.

19. *NAN* (Feb. 1953), p. 19.

20. Clark, *Carrier Admiral*, pp. 297–298; Mark

W. Clark, *From the Danube to the Yalu* (New York: Harper & Brothers, 1954), pp. 237–238.

21. Much of the discussion in this chapter is based upon historical diaries and reports from VMF(N)-513 and -542 contained in Record Group 127 (65A-4620), Boxes 89, 90, 92, 93, and 95, at the Federal Records Center, Suitland, Maryland. To avoid space-consuming repetitive footnoting, I will subsequently cite only the document and the box number. Researchers can expedite their use of these documents by contacting the Archives Section, Marine Corps Historical Center, Building 58, Washington Navy Yard, Washington, DC 20374. Information for this paragraph from "VMF(N)-513 Korean War Report of Major Reinburg," Box 89; and "VMF(N)-542 Historical Report, July–Dec. 1950." Box 95.

22. Transcript of interview of Vice Admiral Charles S. Minter, Jr., USN (ret.) by Dr. John T. Mason, USNI Oral History Program, p. 263 (I wish to acknowledge with deep appreciation the permission of Admiral Minter to reprint portions of his Naval Institute interview); see also IER 3, p. 3–4; Futrell, pp. 329–330.

23. Minter interview, p. 264. See also "Flares Light the Way for Fighters," *NAN* (Jan. 1953), pp. 14–15; Frank Smyth, "Night Support: A New Weapon," *MCG*, XXXV, 11 (Nov. 1951), pp. 16–21; and Norval E. Packwood, Jr., "Night Strike," *MCG*, XXVI, 5 (May 1952), pp. 18–27.

24. Summary of Night Fighter Kills by Marine All Weather Fighter Squadron-513 Marine Air Group-33 of the First Marine Air Wing as of 31 January 1953," pp. 1–2; in "F3D Skynight" folder, Douglas

Aircraft Company Historical Archives, McDonnell-Douglas Corporation, Long Beach, CA. See also "Night Hecklers in Korea," *Naval Aviation Confidential Bulletin* 1-52 (August 1952), pp. 24–26, NAHO files. An interesting overview can be found in Mike O'Connor's "Coping With Charlie," *Journal of the American Aviation Historical Society*, XXX, 1 (Spring 1985), pp. 2–11.

25. "VMF(N)-513 Hist Diary, June 1952," p. 13, Box 92.

26. Quote from FEAF ECM History, p. 19; see also pp. 6, 10–11; OAFH files. The "red ink-blue ink" anecdote is from an interview with Captain Gerald G. O'Rourke, USN (ret.) on Feb. 7, 1985, at Crystal City, VA. I am indebted to Captain O'Rourke for his assistance and many valuable insights into the night air war over North Korea. See also USAF Historical Division, *United States Air Force Operations in the Korean Conflict, 1 July 1952–27 July 1953*, USAF Historical Study No. 127 (Maxwell AFB, AL: Air University 1 July 1956), pp. 70–71; OAFH files.

27. FEAF ECM History, pp. 8–9, 12–18, OAFH files; for a good account of the intense ECM/ECCM war that characterized bomber operations over Northern Europe in 1942–1945, see Martin Middlebrook's excellent case study, *The Nuremberg Raid: 30–31 March 1944* (New York: William Morrow & Co., 1974).

28. "Enemy Night Fighter Capabilities," FEAF *Command Report* (Jan. 1953), Comment No. 2 (IN-EVAL to IN-REQ, 12 Jan. 1953), pp. 2–3, OAFH files.

29. *Ibid*; also *USAF Ops in Korean Conflict, 1 July 1952–July 1953*, p. 71.

30. Jiri Moravec, "Monographie MiG-17," USAF Foreign Technology Division translation FTD-ID(RS)I-1518-75 (Santa Barbara, CA: SCITRAN, 14 July 1975), p. 4; Gunston, *Aircraft of the Soviet Union*, pp. 174–176; Alexander, *Russian Aircraft Since 1940*, p. 214.

31. For details on F3D, see IER 5, p. 9–82, NAHO files, and Rene J. Fancillon, *McDonnell-Douglas Aircraft Since 1920* (London: Putnam & Co., Ltd., 1979), pp. 442–447.

32. "Combat Evaluation of the F3D-2," Appendix F, pp. 1–5, in "VMF(N)-513 Hist Diary, July 1952," Box 93. See also 1st MAW News Release 22,175 (May 1953), copy in the Douglas archives, "F3D Skyknight" folder.

33. 1st MAW News Release 22,175; "VMF(N)-513 Diary, Aug. 1952," pp. 16, 21, Box 93.

34. VMF(N)-513 Hist. Diary, Nov. 1952, Box. 93.

35. *Ibid*; "Summary of Night Fighter Kills. . .", pp. 3–4. Douglas archives.

36. "Aircrew Statements," Appendix D, Pt. 4, VMF(N)-513 Hist. Diary, Dec. 1952, pp. 1–4, Box 93.

37. VMF(N)-513 Hist. Diary, Jan. 1953, Box 93; *USAF Ops in Korean Conflict, 1 July 1952–1 July 1953*, pp. 71–72; FEAF ECM History, Annex XV, pp. 5–6; *History of the 319th Fighter Interceptor Squadron, 1 Jan. 1953–30 June 1953,* pp. 3–4; OAFH files.

38. Quote from VMF(N)-513 Hist. Diary, March 1953, p. 59; see also p. 58; VMF(N)-513 Hist. Diary,

May 1953, p. 56; both in Box 93; for overall USMC view of -513 at this time, see IER 6, Chapter 10, p. 99, NAHO files.

40. Quote from VMF(N)-513 Hist. Diary, March 1953, p. 59, Box 93.

41. *319th History*, p. 6; O'Rourke interview; conversation with Colonel Tighe Carvey, 340 AREFW/DO, Altus AFB, OK, April 17, 1985.

42. VC-44 Det 44N action report, 19 June–27 July 1953, pp. 1–5, NAHO files; O'Rourke interview, "Night Fighter Team Back Home," *NAN* (March 1954), p. 25.

43. *Ibid*; VMF(N)-513 Hist. Diary, July 1953, p. G-3, Box 93.

44. *NAN* (Oct. 1953), p. 6; Clark, *Carrier Admiral*, pp. 302–303; Cagle and Manson, pp. 475–478; *FEAF Intelligence Roundup and Operational Summary*, Issue no. 139 (June 1953), p. I-5, OAFH files.

45. *319th History*, July–Dec. 1953, pp. 6–7, OAFH files.

CHAPTER 7

1. There are a number of good articles in various professional journals concerning the experiences of aircrew taken prisoner in Korea. See "48 Navy, Marine Airmen Red POW's," *NAN* (Nov. 1953), pp. 9–11; "I Lived Two Months in my 'Poopy Suit,'" *NAN* (Dec. 1953), pp. 18–19; and "Religion Was His Refuge for 33 Months," *NAN* (Feb. 1954), p. 10. For a good summary account of the Korean POW situation in general and Burchett in particular, see Rees, pp. 328–346, 355–356, 360–362. It is disturbing how

Burchett continues, in some quarters, to have a reputation for "honesty"; for an example of this wishful thinking, see Alden Whitman's apologia, "Wilfred Burchett — the Other Side, but With Honesty," *Los Angeles Times*, 4 October 1983. A good counter to his view, spawned in part by Burchett's autobiography *At the Barricades*, are two letters to the editor (by Reed Irvine of Accuracy in Media, Inc., and William M. Creamer of the Association of Former Intelligence Officers) printed in "Wilfred Burchett: Behind the Red Line," *Washington Post Book World*, 19 July 1981, p. 15.

2. Statistics from Office of the CNO, *Korean Area Aircraft Losses: Month of July 1953 and Campaign to Date* (OCNO, 14 Sept. 1953), copy in NAHO files.

3. Transcript of interview of Vice Admiral Gerald E. Miller, USN (ret.) by Dr. John T. Mason, USNI Oral History Program, p. 212.

4. IER 5, Chapter 1 *Major Lessons*, p. 1, Naval Historical Center, Washington Navy Yard, Washington, DC.

5. See, for example, *Annual Report of the Chief of Naval Operations to the Secretary of the Navy* (Washington, DC: OCNO, FY 1954), pp. 10–11, copy in NAHO files.

6. D. S. Fahrney, "Guided Missiles — U.S. Navy the Pioneer," *Journal of the American Aviation Historical Society*, XXVII, 1 (Spring 1982), pp. 21–26; *USNA Chronology*, pp. 132, 134, 188–191, 217; Letter, David A. Anderton to author, 8 November 1984, *NAN* (November 1952), p. 14.

7. For a summary of relevant helicopter experi-

ence, see Meid and Yingling, *Operations in West Korea*, pp. 493–498; see also Gary W. Parker, *A History of Marine Medium Helicopter Squadron 161* (Washington, DC: USMC History and Museums Division, 1978), pp. 4–12.

8. For various Reserve accounts see "Reserves on (War) Wagon," *NAN* (March 1951), pp. 1–5; "Air Reserves Strike Enemy in Korea," *NAN* (November 1951), pp. 26–27; "Air Reserves Get Heroes' Welcome," *NAN* (May 1953), pp. 30–31. For a good account of one squadron's journey from peace to war, see W. H. Vernor, Jr., "Standby Squadron," *USNI Proceedings*, LXXVIII, 7 (July 1952), pp. 729–739.

9. *Essex* action report, 18 July–4 Sept. 1952, p. II-6, NAHO files; see also "F4U Shoots Korea Photos at 100 Feet," *NAN* (August 1951), p. 27; and "Jet F9F Photo Unit Maps North Korea," *NAN* (September 1951), p. 31; and IER 3, pp. 5-47–5-49, NAHO files.

10. Meid and Yingling, *Operations in West Korea*, pp. 490–491; "Korea Photo Banshees are Busy," *NAN* (September 1952), p. 32; "Relief Maps and Korea Bombing," *NAN* (May 1953), p. 16; and "All is Not Calm on a Photo Mission," *NAN* (August 1953), pp. 14–15.

11. IER 3, p. 5-47, NAHO files.

12. *Annual Report of the Chief of the Bureau of Aeronautics to the Secretary of the Navy, Fiscal Year 1952*, (submitted 16 Dec. 1952), pp. 1–2, copy in NAHO files. For carrier munition statistics and replenishment question, see IER 4, p. 3-34, copy in Naval Historical Center files.

13. Statistics from *USNA Chronology*, pp. 297, 300, 365.

14. Rees, pp. 418–420.

15. Robert McClintock, *The Meaning of Limited War* (Boston: Houghton Mifflin Co., 1967), p. 48.

16. Isaac Kidd, "On Thin Ice," *Air Force Magazine* (December 1984), p. 180.

17. Quoted in William W. Momyer, *Air Power in Three Wars* (Washington, DC: USAF, 1978), p. 117.

18. Henry A. Kissinger (interviewed by Jack Burby and Art Seidenbaum), "The Fall of Saigon: A Death of Consensus," *Los Angeles Times* (28 April 1985), p. 2. For an excellent interpretation of the subsequent Southeast Asian debacle, see Adm. U.S. Grant Sharp's thought-provoking *Strategy for Defeat: Vietnam in Retrospect* (San Rafael, CA: Presidio Press, 1978).

19. George Haering, "How Tactical Air Works," *USNI Proceedings*, CVIII, 11 (November 1982), p. 62.

20. *Ibid*., p. 65.

21. Donald J. Bradway, letter to the editor, *Los Angeles Times* (18 Dec. 1984).

SOURCES AND SELECTED BIBLIOGRAPHY

The research documentation utilized in this study was drawn from a variety of archives and depositories, as is indicated by the source note citations themselves. Of principal value were the holdings of a group of archives clustered within Washington, DC, and readily accessible for the researcher fortunate enough to be able to arrange a visit. The source notes offer publication data for various published printed materials both primary (by the history makers) and secondary (by historians, journalists, and others). Three dated works that nevertheless still have much to offer the reader seeking an introduction to the naval campaign in Korea are James A. Field's *History of United States Naval Operations: Korea* (Washington, DC: USN, 1962); Walter Karig, Malcolm W. Cagle, and Frank A. Manson's *Battle Report: The War in Korea* (New York: Rinehart & Co., 1952); and Malcolm W. Cagle and Frank A. Manson's *The Sea War in Korea* (Annapolis: Naval Institute Press, 1957). The latter two works in particular offer a number of quotations from decision makers down to combat aircrew that give the reader a flavor of what it was like to fight a limited conflict just a few years after the conclusion of the great Pacific war. Robert F. Futrell's classic, *The United States Air Force in Korea, 1950–1953* (Washington, DC: USAF, 1983 ed.), is the definitive history of Air Force operations in the war. The Army and Marines have each issued their own multivolume histories of Korean combat operations, and citations to relevant volumes appear in the notes.

It is the primary documents of the war, however, that yield the greatest opportunity to study the actions, hopes, frustrations, and accomplishments of those who went to war in Korea. Of particular value are the group of monthly combat activity reports (*Combat Activity of Naval Aviation,* abbreviated *CANA* in the notes) issued during the war, together with action reports from the various carriers and air groups, as well as the six multivolume Korean *Interim Evaluation Reports* (abbreviated *IER* in the notes). Researchers who desire to examine these can find them, together with a wealth of other material such as the *Naval Aviation Confidential Bulletin* and annual reports of the Bureau of Aeronautics, at the Naval Aviation History Office, Building 159E, Room 584, Washington Navy Yard Annex. The Naval Historical Center, Building 57, Washington Navy Yard, maintains the operational archives of the United States Navy, including a large amount of Korean materials (ranging from policy documents to strike reports) that is conveniently available. Marine Corps Korean aviation materials have been retired to the Federal Records Center, Suitland, Maryland, by the Marine Corps Historical Center, Building 58, Washington, DC. Researchers can arrange to study these records by visiting the Archives Section of the USMC Historical Center before journeying to the Suitland records center. A particularly rich oral history collection of interviews undertaken by the United States Naval Institute is maintained in the Special Collections Department, Nimitz Library, U.S. Naval Academy, Annapolis, Maryland. While some are under restriction, arrangements for duplication and permission to publish can be obtained from the Naval Institute itself, located on Academy grounds less than a block from the library. The Office of Air Force History, Bolling Air Force Base, Washington, DC, maintains microfilm records of Air Force involvement in the Korean War, as well as an extensive collection of documents and publications. Much of this relates to the naval air war, and has to be examined if the context of naval air operations over Korea is to be established. The History Office of Naval Air Systems Command, Jefferson Plaza Complex, Building JP-2, Room 278, Crystal City, Virginia (next to The Pentagon) maintains a small collection of documents about the technical development of naval aircraft during the Korean War. Finally, the manufacturers themselves, notably Grumman at Bethpage, New York, and Douglas at Long Beach, California, operate extensive and professionally maintained historical archives that contain very useful information on their own designs. The Audiovisual Department of the U.S. National Archives, Washington, DC, the United

States Naval Institute, and the National Air and Space Museum of the Smithsonian Institution maintain extensive photographic holdings of naval aircraft development and the Korean War.

The following is a selected listing of published sources and major documents that proved useful in the course of this study.

Abrams, R. (1981). *F4U Corsair at War*. New York: Charles Scribner's Sons.

Alexander, J. (1975). *Russian Aircraft Since 1940*. London: Putnam & Co. Ltd.

Anderton, D. A. (1975). *Strategic Air Command*. New York: Charles Scribner's Sons.

Andrews, M. (1950). *Disaster Through Air Power*. New York: Rinehart & Co.

Appleman, R. E. (1961). *United States Army in the Korean War. I: South to the Naktong, North to the Yalu*. Washington, DC: U.S. Army.

Armstrong, N. A., et. al., with Farmer, G & Hamblin, D. J. (1970). *First on the Moon: A Voyage with Neil Armstrong, Michael Collins [and] Edwin E. Aldrin, Jr.* Boston: Little, Brown & Co.

Arnold, H. (1949). *Global Mission*. New York: Harper & Brothers.

Aron, R. (1956, April). A Half-Century of Limited War? *Bulletin of the Atomic Scientists, XII*, 4.

Bailey, B. M. (1982). *We See All: A History of the 55th Strategic Reconnaissance Wing, 1947–1967*. Tucson, AZ: Privately printed.

Baldwin, H. W. (1956, April). The New Face of War. *Bulletin of the Atomic Scientists, XII,* 4.

Beaver, P. (1983). *Carrier Air Operations Since 1945.* London: Arms and Armour Press.

Bilstein, R. E. (1984). *Flight in America, 1900–1983: From the Wrights to the Astronauts.* Baltimore: Johns Hopkins University Press.

Bolt, J. F. (1953, November). Bridge Busting with Jets. *Naval Aviation Bulletin,* 4–53.

Bolt, J. F. (1957, August). Point Blank Bombing. *Marine Corps Gazette, XLI,* 8.

Brown, W. L. (1961). *The Endless Hours.* New York: Norton.

Bueschel, R. M. (1968). *Communist Chinese Air Power.* New York: Praeger Publishers.

Bush, V. (1968). *Modern Arms and Free Men: A Discussion of the Role of Science in Preserving Democracy.* Cambridge: M.I.T. Press.

Cagle, M. W. (1972, May). Task Force 77 in Action off Vietnam. *U.S. Naval Institute Proceedings, XCVIII,* 831.

Cagle, M. W., & Manson, F. A. (1957). *The Sea War in Korea.* Annapolis: Naval Institute Press.

Campigno, A. J. (1958). *A Marine Division in Nightmare Alley.* New York: Comet Press Books.

Carney, R. B. (1983, December). Under the Cold Gaze of the Victorious. *U.S. Naval Institute Proceedings, CIX,* 12.

Carpenter, M. S., et al. (1962). *We Seven.* New York: Simon & Schuster.

Clark, J. J., with Reynolds, C. G. (1967). *Carrier Admiral.* New York: David McKay Co.

Clark, M. W. (1954). *From the Danube to the*

Yalu. New York: Harper & Brothers.

Cline, T. (1976, Winter). Forward Air Control in the Korean War. *Journal of the American Aviation Historical Society, XXI*, 4.

Cochran, T. B., Arkin, W. M., & Hoening, M. M. (1984). *Nuclear Weapons Databook. I: U.S. Nuclear Forces and Capabilities*. Cambridge: Ballinger Publishing Co.

Coletta, P. E. (Ed.) (1980). *American Secretaries of the Navy. II: 1913–1972*. Annapolis: Naval Institute Press.

Collins, J. L. (1969). *War in Peacetime: The History and Lessons of Korea*. Boston: Houghton Mifflin Co.

Condit, K. W., & Giusti, E. H. (1952, August). Marine Air at the Chosin Reservoir. *Marine Corps Gazette, XXXVI*, 8.

Cornelius, G. (1957, October). The Reconnaissance Drone: Present Weapon with a Future. *U.S. Naval Institute Proceedings, LXXXIII*, 10.

Cram, J. R., & Banks, C. L. (1951, December). Win, Place, and Show for the Jets. *Marine Corps Gazette, XXXV*, 12.

Craven, W. F., & Cate, J. L. (1955). *The Army Air Forces in World War II. VI: Men and Planes*. Chicago: University of Chicago Press.

Daniel Guggenheim Medal Board of Award. (1952). *Pioneering in Aeronautics: Recipients of the Daniel Guggenheim Medal, 1929–1952*. New York: Author.

Davis, L. (1978). *MiG Alley: Air-to-Air Combat over Korea*. Carrollton, TX: Squadron/Signal Publications.

Davis, L. (1982). *Air War over Korea: A Pictorial Record*. Carrollton, TX: Squadron/Signal Publications.

Doll, T. E., et al (1985). *Navy Air Colors: II. 1945-1985*. Carrollton, TX: Squadron/Signal Publications.

Editing Committee of the Korean Revolution Museum (P'yongyang). (1975). *The Korean Revolution (II)*. Tokyo: Miraisha.

Fahrney, D. S. (1982, Spring). Guided Missiles — U.S. Navy the Pioneer. *Journal of the American Aviation Historical Society, XXVII*, 1.

Ferguson, J. (1954, Summer). The Role of Tactical Air Forces. *Air University Quarterly Review, VII*, 2.

Field, J. A. (1962). *History of United States Naval Operations; Korea*. Washington, DC: U.S. Navy.

Francillon, R. J. (1979). *McDonnell Douglas Aircraft Since 1920*. London: Putnam & Co. Ltd.

Futrell, R. F. (1983). *The United States Air Force in Korea, 1950-1953*. Washington, DC: Office of Air Force History.

Geer, A. (1952). *The New Breed: The Story of the U.S. Marines in Korea*. New York: Harper & Brothers.

George, A. L. (1967). *The Chinese Communist Army in Action: The Korean War and Its Aftermath*. New York: Columbia University Press.

Giusti, E. H. (1952, May). Marine Air over the Pusan Perimeter. *Marine Corps Gazette, XXXVI*, 5.

Giusti, E. H., & Condit, K. W. (1952, July). Marine Air over Inchon-Seoul. *Marine Corps Gazette, XXXVI*, 7.

Giusti, E. H., & Condit, K. W. (1952, August).

Marine Air Covers the Breakout. *Marine Corps Gazette, XXXVI,* 8.

Gonseth, J. E. (1955, July). Tactical Air Support for Army Forces. *Military Review, XXXV,* 4, pp. 3–16.

Gunston, B. (1983). *Aircraft of the Soviet Union.* London: Osprey Publishing Ltd.

Haering, G. (1982, November). How Tactical Air Works. *U.S. Naval Institute Proceedings, CVIII,* 11.

Hallion, R. P. (1972). *Supersonic Flight: The Story of the Bell X-1 and Douglas D-558.* New York: Macmillan Co. in association with the National Air and Space Museum.

Hallion, R. P. (1981). *Test Pilots. The Frontiersmen of Flight.* Garden City, NY: Doubleday & Co.

Hallion, R. P. (1984). *Rise of the Fighter Aircraft, 1914–1918.* Baltimore: Nautical & Aviation Publishing Co.

Hammel, E. M. (1981). *Chosin: Heroic Ordeal of the Korean War.* New York: Vanguard Press.

Hansen, C. (1979, Winter). Nuclear Neptunes: Early Days of Composite Squadrons 5 & 6. *Journal of the American Aviation Historical Society, XXIV,* 4.

Heinl, R. D., Jr. (1951, January). And Now the ANGLICO. *Marine Corps Gazette, XXXV,* 1.

Heinl, R. D., Jr. (1968). *Victory at High Tide: The Inchon-Seoul Campaign,* a volume in the *Great Battles of History* series. Philadelphia: J. B. Lippincott Co.

Hermes, W. G. (1966). *United States Army in the Korean War. II: Truce Tent and Fighting Front.* Washington, DC: U.S. Army.

Hewlett, R. G., & Duncan, F. (1974). *Nuclear Navy: 1946-1962*. Chicago: University of Chicago Press.

Higgins, M. (1951). *War in Korea: The Report of a Woman Combat Correspondent*. Garden City, NY: Doubleday & Co.

Hooker, S., with Gunston, B. (1984). *Not Much of an Engineer: An Autobiography*. Shrewsbury, England: Airlife Publishing Ltd.

Hurley, A. F., & Ehrhart, R. C. (1974). *Air Power in Warfare: The Proceedings of the 8th Military History Symposium, USAF Academy, 18-20 October 1978*. Washington, DC: Office of Air Force History.

Huston, J. A. (1950, Winter), Tactical Use of Air Power in World War II: The Army Experience. *Military Affairs, XIV*, 4.

Jackson, R. (1973). *Air War over Korea*. New York: Charles Scribner's Sons.

Karig, W., Cagle, M. W., & Manson, F. A. (1952). *Battle Report: V: The War in Korea*. New York: Rinehart & Co.

Kasulka, D. A. (1985). *USN Aircraft Carrier Air Units. I: 1946-1956*. Carrollton, TX: Squadron/Signal Publications.

Kennan, G. F. (1967). *Memoirs: 1925-1950*. Boston: Little, Brown & Co.

Kinney, J. E. (1983, Fall). The Case for Jet Attack Aircraft in Korea. *Foundation, IV*, 2.

Kinter, W. R. (1950, November). Who Should Command Tactical Air Force? *Combat Forces Journal, I*, 4.

Knox, D. (1985). *The Korean War: An Oral His-*

tory; From Pusan to Chosin. New York: Harcourt Brace Jovanovich.

Kohn, R. H., & Harahan, J. P. (Eds.) (1983). *Air Superiority in World War II and Korea*. Washington, DC: Office of Air Force History.

Kohn, R. H., & Harahan, J. P. (Eds.) (1985). *Air Interdiction in World War II, Korea, and Vietnam*. Washington, DC: Office of Air Force History.

Korean Ministry of National Defense. (1976). *The History of United Nations Forces in the Korean War: V.* Seoul: Ministry of National Defense.

Leckie, R. (1960). *The March to Glory*. Cleveland: World Publishing Co.

Love, R. W., Jr. (Ed.) (1980). *The Chiefs of Naval Operations*. Annapolis: Naval Institute Press.

MacArthur, D. (1965). *Reminiscences*. New York: Fawcett Crest.

Mahurin, W. M. (1962). *Honest John*. New York: G. P. Putnam's Sons.

Manchester, W. (1979). *American Caesar*. New York: Dell Publishing Co.

Marshall, S. L. A. (1953). *The River and the Gauntlet: Defeat of the Eighth Army by the Chinese Communist Forces, November 1950, in the Battle of the Chongchon River, Korea*. New York: William Morrow & Co.

McClintock, R. (1967). *The Meaning of Limited War*. Boston: Houghton Mifflin Co.

McLaren, D.R. (1985, Summer). Mustangs in Aerial Combat: The Korean War. *Journal of the American Aviation Historical Society, XXX,* 2.

McMaster, D. W. (1959, April). *The Evolution of Tactical Airpower—With Particular Emphasis upon*

Its Application by the U.S. Navy and U.S. Marine Corps in the Korean War, June 1950–July 1953. Unpublished master's thesis, Department of History, University of Maryland, College Park, MD.

Meid, P., & Yingling, J. M. (1972). *U.S. Marine Operations in Korea, 1950–1953. V: Operations in West Korea.* Washington, DC: U.S. Marine Corps.

Mersky, P. B. (1983). *U.S. Marine Corps Aviation: 1912 to the Present.* Baltimore: Nautical & Aviation Publishing Co.

Mersky, P. B., & Polmar, N. (1981). *The Naval Air War in Vietnam.* Baltimore: Nautical & Aviation Publishing Co.

Michener, J. A. (1953). *The Bridges at Toko-ri.* New York: Random House.

Middlebrook, M. (1974). *The Nuremberg Raid: 30–31 March 1944.* New York: William Morrow & Co.

Miller, J., Jr., Carroll, O. J., & Tackley, M. E. (1956). *Korea, 1951–1953.* Washington, DC: U.S. Army.

Millett, A. R. (1980). *Semper Fidelis: The Story of the United States Marine Corps,* a volume in *The Macmillan Wars of the United States* series. New York: Macmillan Publishing Co.

Millis, W. (1956). *Arms and Men: A Study in American Military History.* New York: New American Library.

Momyer, W. (1978). *Air Power in Three Wars.* Washington, DC: U.S. Air Force.

Montross, L. (1953, September). Flying Windmills in Korea. *Marine Corps Gazette, XXXVII,* 9.

Montross, L., & Canzona, N. A. (1954). *U.S.*

Marine Operations in Korea, 1950-1953. I: The Pusan Perimeter. Washington, DC: U.S. Marine Corps.

Montross, L., & Canzona, N. A. (1955). *U.S. Marine Operations in Korea, 1950-1953. II: The Inchon-Seoul Operation.* Washington, DC: U.S. Marine Corps.

Montross, L., & Canzona, N. A. (1957). *U.S. Marine Operations in Korea, 1950-1953. III: The Chosin Reservoir.* Washington, DC: U.S. Marine Corps.

Montross, L., Kukokka, H. D., & Hicks, N. W. (1962). *U.S. Marine Operations in Korea, 1950-1953. IV: The East-Central Front.* Washington, DC: U.S. Marine Corps.

Morison, S. E. (1960). *History of United States Naval Operations in World War II. XIV: Victory in the Pacific.* Boston: Little, Brown & Co.

Mosley, L. (1982). *Marshall: Hero for Our Times.* New York: Hearst Books.

Novak, F. (1953, January). Sonne Sees All. *Marine Corps Gazette, XXXVII,* 1.

O'Connor, M. (1985, Spring). Coping with Charlie. *Journal of the American Aviation Historical Society, XXX,* 1.

Owens, E. G., & Veadry, W. F. (1951, April). Control of Tactical Air Power in Korea. *Combat Forces Journal, I,* 9.

Packwood, N. E., Jr. (1952, May). Night Strike. *Marine Corps Gazette, XXVI,* 5.

Page, H. R. (1953, May). They Hold Their Own. *Marine Corps Gazette, XXXVII,* 5.

Paige, G. D. (1968). *The Korean Decision.* New

York: The Free Press.

Parker, G. W. (1978). *A History of Marine Medium Helicopter Squadron 161*. Washington, DC: U.S. Marine Corps History and Museums Division.

Parker, G. W., & Batha, F. M., Jr. (1982). *A History of Marine Observation Squadron Six*. Washington, DC: U.S. Marine Corps History and Museums Division.

Politella, D. (1958). *Operation Grasshopper.* Tyler, TX: Robert R. Longo Co.

Pye, A. B., & Shea, N. (1941). *The Navy Wife.* New York: Harper & Brothers.

Rankin, W. H. (1961). *The Man Who Rode the Thunder.* New York: Pyramid Books.

Rausa, R. (1980). *Gold Wings, Blue Sea: A Naval Aviator's Story.* Annapolis: Naval Institute Press.

Rausa, R. (1982). *Skyraider: The Douglas A-1 "Flying Dump Truck."* Baltimore: Nautical & Aviation Publishing Co.

Rawlins, E. W., & Sambito, W. J. (1976). *Marines and Helicopters, 1946–1962.* Washington, DC: U.S. Marine Corps History and Museums Division.

Rearden, S. L. (1984). *History of the Office of the Secretary of Defense. 1: The Formative Years: 1947–1950.* Washington, DC: Office of the Secretary of Defense.

Rees, D. (1970). *Korea: The Limited War.* Baltimore: Penguin Books.

Reid, W. M. (1956, Spring). Tactical Air in Limited War. *Air University Quarterly Review, VIII,* 2.

Reynolds, C. G. (1968). *The Fast Carriers: The Forging of an Air Navy.* New York: McGraw-Hill Book Co.

Ridgway, M. B. (1967). *The Korean War: How We Met the Challenge; How All-Out Asian War Was Averted; Why MacArthur Was Dismissed; Why Today's War Objectives Must Be Limited*. Garden City, NY: Doubleday & Co.

Ridgway, M. B., & Martin, H. H. (1956). *Soldier: The Memoirs of Matthew B. Ridgway*. New York: Harper & Brothers.

Robinson, B. (1953, September). First Mission. *Marine Corps Gazette, XXXVII,* 9.

Sambito, W. (1978). *A History of Marine Attack Squadron 311*. Washington, DC: U.S. Marine Corps History and Museums Division.

Sambito, W. (1978). *A History of Marine Fighter Attack Squadron 312*. Washington, DC: U.S. Marine Corps History and Museums Division.

Schnabel, J. F. (1972). *United States Army in the Korean War. III: Policy and Direction: The First Year*. Washington, DC: U.S. Army.

Schuon, K. (1964). *U.S. Navy Biographical Directory*. New York: Franklin Watts.

Scutts, J. (1982). *Air War Over Korea*. London: Arms and Armour Press.

de Seversky, A. P. (1942). *Victory Through Air Power*. New York: Simon & Schuster.

de Seversky, A. P. (1950). *Air Power: Key to Survival*. New York: Simon & Schuster.

Sharp, U. S. G. (1978). *Strategy for Defeat: Vietnam in Retrospect*. San Rafael, CA: Presidio Press.

Sherrod, R. (1952). *History of Marine Corps Aviation in World War II*. Washington, DC: Combat Forces Press.

Simpson, A. F. (1951, Summer). Tactical Air Doctrine: Tunisia and Korea. *Air University Quarterly Review, IV,* 4.

Simpson, W. F. (1951, February). Advice for the Replacement Pilot. *Marine Corps Gazette, XXXV,* 2.

Smyth, F. (1951, November). Night Support: A New Weapon. *Marine Corps Gazette, XXXV,* 11.

Stewart, J. T. (Ed.) (1957). *Airpower: The Decisive Force in Korea.* Princeton, NJ: D. VanNostrand Co.

Sullivan, J. (1982). *F9F Panther/Cougar in Action.* Carrollton, TX: Squadron/Signal Publications.

Sullivan, J. (no date). *Skyraider in Action.* Carrollton, TX: Squadron/Signal Publications.

Thompson, W. (1985, March). Shooting Stars over Korea. *Airpower, XV,* 2.

Tillman, B. (1979). *Corsair: The F4U in World War II and Korea.* Annapolis: Naval Institute Press.

Tillman, B., & Handelman, J. G. (1984, Spring). The Hwachon Dam and Carlson's Canyon: Air Group 19's *Princeton* Development of 1950–51. *The Hook, XII,* 1.

Truman, H. S. (1965). *Memoirs. II: Years of Trial and Hope.* New York: New American Library.

Turnbull, A. D., & Lord, C. L. (1949). *History of United States Naval Aviation.* New Haven: Yale University Press.

United States Air Force. (1950–1953). *Air Intelligence Digest.* In the files of the Office of Air Force History, Bolling AFB, Washington, DC.

United States Air Force, Far East Air Forces. (1950–1953). *Weekly Intelligence Roundup.* In the files of the Office of Air Force History, Bolling AFB, Washington, DC.

United States Air Force Concepts Division. (1964, January) *Guerrilla Warfare and Airpower in Korea, 1950–53.* Maxwell AFB, Alabama: Aerospace Studies Institute. In the files of the Library, Air Force Systems Command, Andrews AFB, MD.

United States Air Force, Far East Air Forces. (1953, June). *REAF Intelligence Roundup and Operational Summary.* Issue No. 139. In the files of the Office of Air Force History, Bolling, AFB, Washington, DC.

United States Air Force, Far East Air Forces. (1954). *FEAF History of Electronic Countermeasures During the Korean War Conflict.* Far East Air Forces, Feb. 1, 1954. In the files of the Office of Air Force History, Bolling, AFB, Washington, DC.

United States Air Force, Historical Division. (1956). *United States Air Force Operations in the Korean Conflict, 1 July 1952–27 July 1953.* USAF Historical Study No. 127. Maxwell AFB, Alabama: Air University, July 1, 1956. In the files of the Office of Air Force History, Bolling AFB, Washington, DC.

United States Air Force, Historical Division. (1962, May). *USAF Tactical Operations: World War II and Korean War.* Washington, DC: USAF. In the files of the History Office, Air Force Systems Command, Andrews AFB, MD.

United States Congress, House of Representatives, Committee on Armed Services. (1949). *The National Defense Program: Unification and Strategy.* 81st Congress, 1st Session, Washington, DC: Government Printing Office.

United States Department of State. (1961). *North Korea: A Case Study in the Techniques of Takeover.* Washington, DC: Government Printing Office.

United States Navy. (1949–1954). *Naval Aviation News.* In the files of the Naval Aviation History Office, Washington Navy Yard Annex, Washington, DC.

United States Navy. (1949–1954). *Naval Aviation Confidential Bulletin* (subsequently the *Naval Aviation Bulletin*). In the files of the Naval Aviation History Office, Washington Navy Yard Annex, Washington, DC.

United States Navy, Chief of Naval Operations. (1950, October–July). *Combat Activity of Naval Aviation.* In the files of the Naval Aviation History Office, Washington Navy Yard Annex, Washington, DC.

United States Navy, Chief of Naval Operations. (1953, September). *Korean Area Aircraft Losses: Month of July 1953 and Campaign to Date.* In the files of the Naval Aviation History Office, Washington Navy Yard Annex, Washington, DC.

United States Navy, Chief of Naval Operations. (1950–1954). *Annual Report of the Chief of Naval Operations to the Secretary of the Navy.* In the files of the Naval Historical Center, Washington Navy Yard, Washington, DC.

United States Navy, Chief of the Bureau of Aeronautics. (1950–1954). *Annual Report of the Chief of the Bureau of Aeronautics to the Secretary of the Navy.* In the files of the Naval History Office, Washington Navy Yard Annex, Washington DC.

United States Navy, Commander-in-Chief Pacific Fleet. (1950–1953). *Interim Evaluation Reports,* 1–6. In the Naval Historical Center, Washington Navy Yard, and the Naval Aviation History Office, Washington Navy Yard Annex, Washington, DC.

United States Navy, Deputy Chief of Naval Operations (Air), Aviation Statistics Section. (1950, September–December). *Aviation Statistics Special Reports 1-50 through 3-50.* In the files of the Naval Aviation History Office, Washington Navy Yard Annex, Washington DC.

United States Navy, (1951–1953). *War Diaries of the Commander, Naval Forces Far East (COM-NAVFE).* In the files of the Naval Aviation History Office, Washington Navy Yard Annex, Washington, DC.

United States Navy, (1951). *Action Reports of Commander, TF 77.* In the files of the Naval Aviation History Office, Washington Navy Yard Annex, Washington DC.

United States Navy, (1951–1953). *Action Reports of Commander, Carrier Division 1 (COMCARDIV 1); Commander, Carrier Division 3 (COMCARDIV 3); and Commander, Carrier Division 5 (COMCAR-DIV 5).* In the files of the Naval Aviation History Office, Washington Navy Yard Annex, Washington DC.

United States Navy, (1950–1953). *Action Reports* of the following aircraft carriers and associated carrier air groups. In the files of the Naval Aviation History Office, Washington Navy Yard Annex, Washington DC.

U.S.S. *Boxer:* October 11–25, 1950; March

17–April 21, 1951; April 30–June 4, 1951; June 15–July 17, 1951; July 26–August 24, 1951; March 10–May 2, 1952; May 12–28, 1952; June 9–July 8, 1952; August 1–11, 1952; August 23–September 6, 1952; May 10–June 21, 1952; July 1–27, 1953.

U.S.S. *Kearsarge:* September 14–October 20, 1952; October 20–December 6, 1952; December 6–January 8, 1953; January 8–February 28, 1953.

U.S.S. *Bon Homme Richard:* September 19–October 18, 1951; October 31–November 30, 1951; June 21–27, 1952; July 2–August 4, 1952; August 7–18, 1952; August 20–September 28, 1952; September 30–November 5, 1952; November 8–December 18, 1952.

U.S.S. *Princeton:* June 2–28, 1952; July 4–August 6, 1952; August 16–September 20, 1952; September 28–October 18, 1952; March 8–April 3, 1953; June 9–August 3, 1953; April 13–May 19, 1953.

U.S.S. *Essex:* August 18–September 21, 1951; October 1–31, 1951; November 1–December 13, 1951; December 14, 1951–February 3, 1952; February 4–March 7, 1952; July 18–September 4, 1952; September 5–November 1, 1952; November 1–November 24, 1952; November 25, 1952–January 13, 1953.

U.S.S. *Oriskany:* October 28–November 22, 1952; December 8–December 27, 1952; March 1–29, 1953; April 8–22, 1953.

U.S.S. *Valley Forge*: November 5–19, 1950; January 31–March 26, 1951; December 7, 1951–January 19, 1952; January 30–February 22, 1952; March 3–April 4, 1952; April 14–May 16, 1952; May 24–June 13, 1952; December 30, 1952–January 25, 1953; February 8–March 19, 1953; March 26–April

13, 1953; April 20–May 17, 1953; May 25–June 9, 1953; Summary Report, December 31, 1952–June 9, 1953.

U.S.S. *Philippine Sea*: September 22–October 4, 1950; January 1–February 1, 1951; February 1–March 15, 1951; March 15–May 30, 1951; January 25–February 22, 1952; March 17–April 19, 1952; May 12–June 6, 1952; June 21–July 6, 1952; July 12–July 24, 1952; January 28–March 7, 1953; March 17–April 20, 1953; May 12–May 29, 1953; June 2–July 6, 1953; July 15–July 30, 1953.

U.S.S. *Bataan*: December 4, 1950–January 2, 1951; January 2–15, 1951; April 8–May 11, 1951; May 12–June 13, 1951.

U.S.S. *Lake Champlain*: June 11–29, 1953; July 11–27, 1953.

U.S.S. *Leyte*: January 7–19, 1952.

U.S.S. *Antietam*: October 15–November 16, 1951; November 26–December 31, 1951; January 16–February 9, 1952; February 18–March 22, 1952.

Van Fleet, J. A. (1956). *Rail Transport and the Winning of Wars*. Washington, D.C.: Association of American Railroads.

Van Riper, F. (1983). *Glenn*. New York: Empire Books.

Van Wyen, A. O., Van Vleet, C., & Pearson, L. M. (1970). *U.S. Naval Aviation, 1910–1970*. Washington, DC: Government Printing Office.

Vernor, W. H., Jr. (1952, July). Standby Squadron. *U.S. Naval Institute Proceedings, LXXVIII*, 7.

Ward, O. (1952). *Korea: 1950*. Washington, DC: U.S. Army.

Weems, J. E. (1983, July). Black Wings of Gold.

U.S. Naval Institute Proceedings, CIX, 7.

Wetke, W. G. (1951, January). Marine Aviation in Support of Amphibious Troops. *Marine Corps Gazette, XXXV*, 1.

Wolk, H. S. (1984). *Planning and Organizing the Postwar Air Force, 1943–1947*. Washington, DC: Office of Air Force History.

Wooldridge, E. T. (1983). *Winged Wonders: The Story of the Flying Wings*. Washington, DC: Smithsonian Institution Press.

Yeager, C., & Janos, L. (1985). *Yeager: An Autobiography*. New York: Bantam Books.

INDEX

372

375

378

**TOP-FLIGHT AERIAL ADVENTURE
FROM ZEBRA BOOKS!**

WINGMAN   (2015, $3.95)
by Mack Maloney
From the radioactive ruins of a nuclear-devastated U.S. emerges a
hero for the ages. A brilliant ace fighter pilot, he takes to the skies
to help free his once-great homeland from the brutal heel of the evil
Soviet warlords. He is the last hope of a ravaged land. He is Hawk
Hunter . . . Wingman!

WINGMAN #2: THE CIRCLE WAR   (2120, $3.95)
by Mack Maloney
A second explosive showdown with the Russian overlords and their
armies of destruction is in the wind. Only the deadly aerial ace
Hawk Hunter can rally the forces of freedom and strike one last
blow for a forgotten dream called "America"!

WINGMAN #3: THE LUCIFER CRUSADE (2232, $3.95)
by Mack Maloney
Viktor, the depraved international terrorist who orchestrated the
bloody war for America's West, has escaped. Ace pilot Hawk
Hunter takes off for a deadly confrontation in the skies above the
Middle East, determined to bring the maniac to justice or die in
the attempt!

GHOST PILOT   (2207, $3.95)
by Anton Emmerton
Flyer Ian Lamont is driven by bizarre unseen forces to relive the
last days in the life of his late father, an RAF pilot killed during
World War II. But history is about to repeat itself as a sinister secret from beyond the grave transforms Lamont's worst nightmares
of fiery aerial death into terrifying reality!

ROLLING THUNDER   (2235, $3.95)
by John Smith
Was the mysterious crash of NATO's awesome computerized attack
aircraft BLACKHAWK ONE the result of pilot error or Soviet
treachery? The deadly search for the truth traps RAF flight lieutenant Erica Macken in a sinister international power-play that will
be determined in the merciless skies — where only the most skilled
can survive!

*Available wherever paperbacks are sold, or order direct from the
Publisher. Send cover price plus 50¢ per copy for mailing and
handling to Zebra Books, Dept. 2267, 475 Park Avenue South,
New York, N.Y. 10016. Residents of New York, New Jersey and
Pennsylvania must include sales tax. DO NOT SEND CASH.*